THE ROSE TATTOO
CAMINO REAL
ORPHEUS DESCENDING

Tennessee Williams was born in 1911 in Columbus, Mississippi, where his grandfather was the episcopal clergyman. When his father, a travelling salesman, moved with his family to St Louis some years later, both he and his sister found it impossible to settle down to city life. He entered college during the Depression and left after a couple of years to take a clerical job in a shoe company. He stayed there for two years, spending the evenings writing. He entered the University of Iowa in 1938 and completed his course, at the same time holding a large number of part-time jobs of great diversity. He received a Rockefeller Fellowship in 1940 for his play *Battle of Angels*, and he won the Pulitzer prize in 1948 and 1955. Among his many plays Penguin have published *The Glass Menagerie* (1944), *A Streetcar Named Desire* (1947), *Summer and Smoke* (1948), *The Rose Tattoo* (1951), *Camino Real* (1953), *Cat on a Hot Tin Roof* (1955), *Baby Doll* (1957), *Orpheus Descending* (1957), *Something Unspoken* (1958), *Suddenly Last Summer* (1958), *Sweet Bird of Youth* (1959), *Period of Adjustment* (1960), *The Night of the Iguana* (1961), *The Milk Train Doesn't Stop Here Anymore* (1963; revised 1964) and *Small Craft Warnings* (1972). Tennessee Williams died in 1983.

Peter Shaffer has written of Tennessee Williams: 'He was a born dramatist as few are ever born. Whatever he put on paper, superb or superfluous, glorious or gaudy, could not fail to be electrifyingly actable. He could not write a dull scene . . . Tennessee Williams will live as long as drama itself.'

Tennessee Williams

THE ROSE TATTOO
CAMINO REAL
ORPHEUS DESCENDING

PENGUIN BOOKS

in association with Martin Secker & Warburg

PENGUIN BOOKS

Published by the Penguin Group
Penguin Books Ltd, 27 Wrights Lane, London W8 5TZ, England
Penguin Books USA Inc., 375 Hudson Street, New York, New York 10014, USA
Penguin Books Australia Ltd, Ringwood, Victoria, Australia
Penguin Books Canada Ltd, 10 Alcorn Avenue, Toronto, Ontario, Canada M4V 3B2
Penguin Books (NZ) Ltd, 182–190 Wairau Road, Auckland 10, New Zealand

Penguin Books Ltd, Registered Offices: Harmondsworth, Middlesex, England

The Rose Tattoo first published in Great Britain by Martin Secker & Warburg 1954
Copyright 1950 by Tennessee Williams
Revised and published version copyright 1951 by Tennessee Williams
The quotation from St John Perse is from the T. S. Eliot translation of his *Anabasis*
Copyright 1938, 1949 by Harcourt, Brace & Co., Inc.
Published in Penguin Books with *Camino Real* 1958
Reprinted 1968

Camino Real first published in Great Britain by Martin Secker & Warburg 1956
Copyright 1948 by Tennessee Williams
Revised and published version copyright 1953 by Tennessee Williams
Published in Penguin Books with *The Rose Tattoo* 1958
Reprinted 1968

Orpheus Descending first published 1955
First published in Great Britain by Martin Secker & Warburg 1958
Copyright © Tennessee Williams, 1955, 1958
Published in Penguin Books with *Something Unspoken* and *Suddenly Last Summer* 1961

This collection published in Penguin Books 1976
7 9 10 8 6

Printed in England by Clays Ltd, St Ives plc
Set in Monotype Bembo

CONTENTS

INTRODUCTION

MR WILLIAMS is a theatrical portent of the present time, as G.B.S. was (so very differently) of the earlier part of this century. Of all the dramatists now writing in English, Mr Williams is the one who gives the most complete theatrical experiences to his audience. One may like a play of his, or dislike it, even intensely, but one can't escape it: it exercises to the full the magic that is exclusive to the theatre.

Mr Williams is a poetic realist, or rather perhaps a realistic poet. His exposure of his characters is as complete as an autopsy. But with a difference: the person who is dissected is not a dead body but a living soul, and the dramatist who reveals its plight is also moved by it. Not only so: these lives have another dimension besides that exhibited in their material, and often sordid, individual circumstances. The poet, who conceives them in compassion, sees them luminous. He cannot help it: he is a poet, and reality is translucent to him.

I have said that he 'sees' his characters, whereas a poet, who is concerned primarily with words, might be expected rather to 'hear' them. But Mr Williams is a visual writer: this is one of the gifts which make him particularly of our time, for the theatre has been brought, by the effect of films and television on its audiences, to need the visual more than it used to. His imagination of the settings of his plays works strictly in terms of the theatre – but of a theatre far more flexible than that of the naturalistic writers. By conceiving such living stage-pictures as the apartment house of *The Glass Menagerie* with its fire escape, or the semi-transparent building of *Streetcar*, he has extended our theatre's visual range.

The same is true of aural rhythms, for he shows a musical composer's gift for orchestration in his use of the human voice and the noises of a city in counterpoint. This is perhaps more apparent in *Camino Real*, the least realistic of the plays, but it is no less present in the others which are limited to a single time-sequence and a single group of related characters.

'Truth, life or reality is an organic thing which the poetic imagination can represent or suggest, in essence, only through transformation, through changing into other forms than those which were merely present in appearance.' This, from the preface of *The Glass Menagerie*, is Mr Williams' expression of what the theatre means to him as an artist. His plays are the proof of its validity.

London, 1958   E. MARTIN BROWNE

THE ROSE TATTOO

*O slinger! crack the nut of my eye! my heart twit-
tered with joy under the splendour of the quicklime,
the bird sings O Senectus! . . . the streams are in
their beds like the cries of women and this world has
more beauty than a ram's skin painted red!*

St John Perse: *Anabasis*
T. S. Eliot translation

TO FRANK
in return for Sicily

THE TIMELESS WORLD OF A PLAY

CARSON MCCULLERS concludes one of her lyric poems with the line: 'Time, the endless idiot, runs screaming round the world.' It is this continual rush of time, so violent that it appears to be screaming, that deprives our actual lives of so much dignity and meaning, and it is, perhaps more than anything else, the *arrest of time* which has taken place in a completed work of art that gives to certain plays their feeling of depth and significance. In the London notices of *Death of a Salesman* a certain notoriously sceptical critic made the remark that Willy Loman was the sort of man that almost any member of the audience would have kicked out of an office had he applied for a job or detained one for conversation about his troubles. The remark itself possibly holds some truth. But the implication that Willy Loman is consequently a character with whom we have no reason to concern ourselves in drama, reveals a strikingly false conception of what plays are. Contemplation is something that exists outside of time, and so is the tragic sense. Even in the actual world of commerce, there exists in some persons a sensibility to the unfortunate situations of others, a capacity for concern and compassion, surviving from a more tender period of life outside the present whirling wire-cage of business activity. Facing Willy Loman across an office desk, meeting his nervous glance and hearing his querulous voice, we would be very likely to glance at our wrist watch and our schedule of other appointments. We would not kick him out of the office, no, but we would certainly *ease* him out with more expedition than Willy had feebly hoped for. But suppose there had been no wrist watch or office clock and suppose there had *not* been the schedule of pressing appointments, and suppose that we were not actually facing Willy across a desk – and facing a person is *not* the best way to *see* him! – suppose, in other words, that the meeting with Willy Loman had somehow occurred in a world *outside* of time. Then I think we would receive him with concern and kindness and even with respect. If the world of a play did not offer us this occasion to view its characters under that special condition of a *world without time*, then, indeed, the characters and occurrences of drama would become equally pointless, equally trivial, as corresponding meetings and happenings in life.

The classic tragedies of Greece had tremendous nobility. The actors wore great masks, movements were formal, dance-like, and the speeches had an epic quality and doubtless were as removed from the normal conversation of their contemporary society as they seem to-day. Yet they did not seem false to the Greek audiences: the magnitude of the events and the passions aroused by them did not seem ridiculously out of proportion to common experience. And I wonder if this was not because the Greek audiences knew, instinctively or by training, that the created world of a play is removed from that element which makes people *little* and their emotions fairly inconsequential.

Great sculpture often follows the lines of the human body: yet the repose of great sculpture suddenly transmutes those human lines to something that has an absoluteness, a purity, a beauty, which would not be possible in a living mobile form.

A play may be violent, full of motion: yet it has that special kind of repose which allows contemplation and produces the climate in which tragic importance is a possible thing, provided that certain modern conditions are met.

In actual existence the moments of love are succeeded by the moments of satiety and sleep. The sincere remark is followed by a cynical distrust. Truth is fragmentary, at best: we love and betray each other not in quite the same breath but in two breaths that occur in fairly close sequence. But the fact that passion occurred in *passing*, that it then declined into a more familiar sense of indifference, should not be regarded as proof of its inconsequence. And this is the very truth that drama wishes to bring us . . .

Whether or not we admit it to ourselves, we are all haunted by a truly awful sense of impermanence. I have always had a particularly keen sense of this at New York cocktail parties, and perhaps that is why I drink the martinis almost as fast as I can snatch them from the tray. This sense is the febrile thing that hangs in the air. Horror of insincerity, of *not meaning*, overhangs these affairs like the cloud of cigarette smoke and the hectic chatter. This horror is the only thing, almost, that is left unsaid at such functions. All social functions involving a group of people not intimately known to each other are always under this shadow. They are almost always (in an unconscious way) like that last dinner of the condemned: where steak or turkey, whatever the doomed man wants, is served in his cell as a mockingly cruel reminder of what the great-big-little-transitory world had to offer.

In a play, time is arrested in the sense of being confined. By a sort of legerdemain, events are made to remain *events*, rather than being reduced so quickly to mere *occurrences*. The audience can sit back in a comforting dusk to watch a world which is flooded with light and in which emotion and action have a dimension and dignity that they would likewise have in real existence, if only the shattering intrusion of time could be locked out.

About their lives people ought to remember that when they are finished, everything in them will be contained in a marvellous state of repose which is the same as that which they unconsciously admired in drama. The rush is temporary. The great and only possible dignity of man lies in his power deliberately to choose certain moral values by which to live as steadfastly as if he, too, like a character in a play, were immured against the corrupting rush of time. Snatching the eternal out of the desperately fleeting is the great magic trick of human existence. As far as we know, as far as there exists any kind of empiric evidence, there is no way to beat the game of *being* against *non-being*, in which non-being is the predestined victor on realistic levels.

Yet plays in the tragic tradition offer us a view of certain moral values in violent juxtaposition. Because we do not participate, except as spectators, we can view them clearly, within the limits of our emotional equipment. These people on the stage do not return our looks. We do not have to answer their questions nor make any sign of being in company with them, nor do we have to compete with their virtues nor resist their offences. All at once, for this reason, we are able to *see* them! Our hearts are wrung by recognition and pity, so that the dusky shell of the auditorium where we are gathered anonymously together is flooded with an almost liquid warmth of unchecked human sympathies, relieved of self-consciousness, allowed to function . . .

Men pity and love each other more deeply than they permit themselves to know. The moment after the phone has been hung up, the hand reaches for a scratch pad and scrawls a notation: 'Funeral Tuesday at five, Church of the Holy Redeemer, don't forget flowers.' And the same hand is only a little shakier than usual as it reaches, some minutes later, for a highball glass that will pour a stupefaction over the kindled nerves. Fear and evasion are the two little beasts that chase each other's tails in the revolving wirecage of our nervous world. They distract us from feeling too much about things. Time rushes toward us with its hospital tray of infinitely varied narcotics, even while it is preparing us for its inevitably fatal operation . . .

So successfully have we disguised from ourselves the intensity of our own feelings, the sensibility of our own hearts, that plays in the tragic tradition have begun to seem untrue. For a couple of hours we may surrender ourselves to a world of fiercely illuminated values in conflict, but when the stage is covered and the auditorium lighted, almost immediately there is a recoil of disbelief. 'Well, well!' we say as we shuffle back up the aisle, while the play dwindles behind us with the sudden perspective of an early Chirico painting. By the time we have arrived at Sardi's, if not as soon as we pass beneath the marquee, we have convinced ourselves once more that life has as little resemblance to the curiously stirring and meaningful occurrences on the stage as a jingle has to an elegy of Rilke.

This modern condition of his theatre audience is something that an author must know in advance. The diminishing influence of life's destroyer, time, must be somehow worked into the context of his play. Perhaps it is a certain foolery, a certain distortion toward the grotesque, which will solve the problem for him. Perhaps it is only restraint, putting a mute on the string that would like to break all bounds. But almost surely, unless he contrives in some way to relate the dimensions of his tragedy to the dimensions of a world in which time is *included* – he will be left among his magnificent debris on a dark stage, muttering to himself: 'Those fools . . .'

And if they could hear him above the clatter of tongues, glasses, chinaware, and silver, they would give him this answer: 'But you have shown us a world not ravaged by time. We admire your innocence. But we have seen our photographs, past and present. Yesterday evening we passed our first wife on the street. We smiled as we spoke but we didn't really see her! It's too bad, but we know what is true and not true, and at 3 A.M. your disgrace will be in print!'

TENNESSEE WILLIAMS

THE ROSE TATTOO

The Rose Tattoo was first produced by Cheryl Crawford at the Erlanger Theatre in Chicago on 29 December 1950. It had its Broadway opening on 3 February 1951, at the Martin Beck Theatre in New York City, with Daniel Mann as director, setting by Boris Aronson and music by David Diamond. Production Associate: Bea Lawrence. Assistant to Producer: Paul Bigelow.

Cast of the New York Production

SALVATORE	Salvatore Mineo
VIVI	Judy Ratner
BRUNO	Salvatore Taormina
ASSUNTA	Ludmilla Toretzka
ROSA DELLE ROSE	Phyllis Love
SERAFINA DELLE ROSE	Maureen Stapleton
ESTELLE HOHENGARTEN	Sonia Sorel
THE STREGA	Daisy Belmore
GIUSEPPINA	Rossana San Marco
PEPPINA	Augusta Merighi
VIOLETTA	Vivian Nathan
MARIELLA	Penny Santon
TERESA	Nancy Franklin
FATHER DE LEO	Robert Carricart
A DOCTOR	Andrew Duggan
MISS YORKE	Dorrit Kelton
FLORA	Jane Hoffman
BESSIE	Florence Sundstrom
JACK HUNTER	Don Murray
THE SALESMAN	Eddie Hyans
ALVARO MANGIACAVALLO	Eli Wallach
A MAN	David Stewart
ANOTHER MAN	Martin Balsam

ACT ONE

ACT TWO

ACT THREE

AUTHOR'S PRODUCTION NOTES

The locale of the play is a village populated mostly by Sicilians somewhere along the Gulf Coast between New Orleans and Mobile. The time is the present.

As the curtain rises we hear a Sicilian folk-singer with a guitar. He is singing. At each major division of the play this song is resumed and it is completed at the final curtain.

The first lighting is extremely romantic. We see a frame cottage, in a rather poor state of repair, with a palm tree leaning dreamily over one end of it and a flimsy little entrance porch, with spindling pillars, sagging steps and broken rails, at the other end. The setting seems almost tropical, for, in addition to the palm trees, there are tall canes with feathery fronds and a fairly thick growth of pampas grass. These are growing on the slope of an embankment along which runs a highway, which is not visible, but the cars passing on it can occasionally be heard. The house has a rear door which cannot be seen. The facing wall of the cottage is either a transparency that lifts for the interior scenes, or is cut away to reveal the interior.

The romantic first lighting is that of late dusk, the sky a delicate blue with an opalescent shimmer more like water than air. Delicate points of light appear and disappear like lights reflected in a twilight harbour. The curtain rises well above the low tin roof of the cottage.

We see an interior that is as colourful as a booth at a carnival. There are many religious articles and pictures of ruby and gilt, the brass cage of a gaudy parrot, a large bowl of goldfish, cut-glass decanters and vases, rose-patterned wallpaper and a rose-coloured carpet; everything is exclamatory in its brightness like the projection of a woman's heart passionately in love. There is a small shrine against the wall between the rooms, consisting of a prie-dieu and a little statue of the Madonna in a starry blue robe and gold crown. Before this burns always a vigil light in its ruby glass cup. Our purpose is to show these gaudy, childlike mysteries with sentiment and humour in equal measure, without ridicule and with respect for the religious yearnings they symbolize.

An outdoor sign indicates that Serafina, whose home the cottage is, does 'SEWING'. The interior furnishings give evidence of this

17

vocation. The most salient feature is a collection of dressmaker's dummies. There are at least seven of these life-size mannequins, in various shapes and attitudes. (They will have to be made especially for the play as their purpose is not realistic. They have pliable joints so that their positions can be changed. Their arms terminate at the wrist. In all their attitudes there is an air of drama, somewhat like the poses of declamatory actresses of the old school.) Principal among them are a widow and a bride who face each other in violent attitudes, as though having a shrill argument, in the parlour. The widow's costume is complete from black-veiled hat to black slippers. The bride's featureless head wears a chaplet of orange blossoms from which is depended a flowing veil of white marquisette, and her net gown is trimmed in white satin – lustrous, immaculate.

Most of the dummies and sewing equipment are confined to the dining-room which is also Serafina's work room. In that room there is a tall cupboard on top of which are several dusty bottles of imported Sicilian Spumanti.

ACT ONE

SCENE I

It is the hour that the Italians call 'prima sera', the beginning of dusk. Between the house and the palm tree burns the female star with an almost emerald lustre.

The mothers of the neighbourhood are beginning to call their children home to supper, in voices near and distant, urgent and tender, like the variable notes of wind and water. There are three children: Bruno, Salvatore, and Vivi, ranged in front of the house, one with a red paper kite, one with a hoop, and the little girl with a doll dressed as a clown. They are in attitudes of momentary repose, all looking up at something – a bird or a plane passing over – as the mothers' voices call them.

BRUNO: The white flags are flying at the Coast Guard station.
SALVATORE: That means fair weather.
VIVI: I love fair weather.
GIUSEPPINA: Vivi! Vieni mangiare!
PEPPINA: Salvatore! Come home!
VIOLETTA: Bruno! Come home to supper!

[*The calls are repeated tenderly, musically.*

The interior of the house begins to be visible. Serafina delle Rose is seen on the parlour sofa, waiting for her husband Rosario's return. Between the curtains is a table set lovingly for supper; there is wine in a silver ice-bucket and a great bowl of roses.

Serafina looks like a plump little Italian opera singer in the role of Madame Butterfly. Her black hair is done in a high pompadour that glitters like wet coal. A rose is held in place by glittering jet hairpins. Her voluptuous figure is sheathed in pale rose silk. On her feet are dainty slippers with glittering buckles and French heels. It is apparent from the way she sits, with such plump dignity, that she is wearing a tight girdle. She sits very erect, in an attitude of forced composure, her ankles daintily crossed and her plump little hands holding a yellow paper fan on which is painted a rose. Jewels gleam on her fingers, her wrists and her ears and about her throat. Expectancy shines in her eyes. For a few moments she seems to be posing for a picture.

Rosa delle Rose appears at the side of the house, near the palm tree. Rosa, the daughter of the house, is a young girl of twelve. She is pretty and vivacious, and has about her a particular intensity in every gesture.]

SERAFINA: Rosa, where are you?
ROSA: Here, Mama.
SERAFINA: What are you doing, cara?
ROSA: I've caught twelve lightning bugs.

[The cracked voice of Assunta is heard, approaching.]

SERAFINA: I hear Assunta! Assunta!

[Assunta appears and goes into the house, Rosa following her in. Assunta is an old woman in a grey shawl, bearing a basket of herbs, for she is a fattuchiere, a woman who practises a simple sort of medicine. As she enters the children scatter.]

ASSUNTA: Vengo, vengo. Buona sera. Buona sera. There is something wild in the air, no wind but everything's moving.
SERAFINA: I don't see nothing moving and neither do you.
ASSUNTA: Nothing is moving so you can see it moving, but everything is moving, and I can hear the star-noises. Hear them? Hear the star-noises?
SERAFINA: Naw, them ain't the star-noises. They're termites, eating the house up. What are you peddling, old woman, in those little white bags?

20

ASSUNTA: Powder, wonderful powder. You drop a pinch of it in your husband's coffee.

SERAFINA: What is it good for?

ASSUNTA: What is a husband good for! I make it out of the dry blood of a goat.

SERAFINA: Davvero!

ASSUNTA: Wonderful stuff! But be sure you put it in his coffee at supper, not in his breakfast coffee.

SERAFINA: My husband don't need no powder!

ASSUNTA: Excuse me, Baronessa. Maybe he needs the opposite kind of a powder, I got that, too.

SERAFINA: Naw, naw, *no* kind of powder at all, old woman. [*She lifts her head with a proud smile.*]

[*Outside the sound of a truck approaching up on the highway.*]

ROSA [*joyfully*]: Papa's truck!

[*They stand listening for a moment, but the truck goes by without stopping.*]

SERAFINA [*to Assunta*]: That wasn't him. It wasn't no 10-ton truck. It didn't rattle the shutters! Assunta, Assunta, undo a couple of hooks, the dress is tight on me!

ASSUNTA: Is it true what I told you?

SERAFINA: Yes, it is true, but nobody needed to tell me. Assunta, I'll tell you something which maybe you won't believe.

ASSUNTA: It is impossible to tell me anything that I don't believe.

SERAFINA: Va bene! Senti, Assunta! – I knew that I had conceived on the very night of conception! [*There is a phrase of music as she says this.*]

ASSUNTA: Ahhhh?

SERAFINA: Senti! That night I woke up with a burning pain on me, here, on my left breast! A pain like a needle, quick,

21

quick, hot little stitches. I turned on the light, I uncovered my breast! – On it I saw the rose tattoo of my husband!

ASSUNTA: Rosario's tattoo?

SERAFINA: On me, on my breast, his tattoo! And when I saw it I knew that I had conceived . . .

[*Serafina throws her head back, smiling proudly, and opens her paper fan. Assunta stares at her gravely, then rises and hands her basket to Serafina.*]

ASSUNTA: Ecco! *You* sell the powders! [*She starts toward the door.*]

SERAFINA: You don't believe that I saw it?

ASSUNTA [*stopping*]: Did Rosario see it?

SERAFINA: I screamed. But when he woke up, it was gone. It only lasted a moment. But I *did* see it, and I *did* know, when I seen it, that I had conceived, that in my body another rose was growing!

ASSUNTA: Did he believe that you saw it?

SERAFINA: No. He laughed. – He laughed and I cried . . .

ASSUNTA: And he took you into his arms, and you stopped crying!

SERAFINA: Si!

ASSUNTA: Serafina, for you everything has got to be different. A sign, a miracle, a wonder of some kind. You speak to Our Lady. You say that She answers your questions. She nods or shakes Her head at you. Look, Serafina, underneath Our Lady you have a candle. The wind through the shutters makes the candle flicker. The shadows move. Our Lady seems to be nodding!

SERAFINA: She gives me signs.

ASSUNTA: Only to you? Because you are more important? The wife of a barone? Serafina! In Sicily they called his uncle a baron, but in Sicily everybody's a baron that owns a piece of the land and a separate house for the goats!

SERAFINA: They said to his uncle 'Voscenza!' and they kissed their hands to him! [*She kisses the back of her hand repeatedly, with vehemence.*]

ASSUNTA: His uncle in Sicily! – Si – But *here* what's he do? Drives a truck of bananas?

SERAFINA [*blurting out*]: No! *Not* bananas!

ASSUNTA: Not bananas?

SERAFINA: Stai zitta! [*She makes a warning gesture.*] – No – Vien-qui, Assunta! [*She beckons her mysteriously. Assunta approaches.*]

ASSUNTA: Cosa dici?

SERAFINA: On top of the truck is bananas! But underneath – something else!

ASSUNTA: Che altre cose?

SERAFINA: Whatever it is that the Brothers Romano want hauled out of the state, he hauls it for them, underneath the bananas! [*She nods her head importantly.*] And money, he gets so much it spills from his pockets! Soon I don't have to make dresses!

ASSUNTA [*turning away*]: Soon I think you will have to make a black veil!

SERAFINA: To-night is the last time he does it! To-morrow he quits hauling stuff for the Brothers Romano! He pays for the 10-ton truck and works for himself. We live with dignity in America, then! Own truck! Own house! And in the house will be everything electric! Stove – deep-freeze – *tutto!* – But to-night, stay with me . . . I can't swallow my heart! – Not till I hear the truck stop in front of the house and his key in the lock of the door! – When I call him, and him shouting back, '*Sì, sono qui!*' In his hair, Assunta, he has – oil of roses. And when I wake up at night – the air, the dark room's – full of – roses . . . Each time is the first time with him. Time doesn't pass . . .

[*Assunta picks up a small clock on the cupboard and holds it to her ear.*]

ASSUNTA: Tick, tick, tick, tick. – You say the clock is a liar.

SERAFINA: No, the clock is a fool. I don't listen to it. My clock is my heart and my heart don't say tick-tick, it says love-love! And now I have two hearts in me, both of them saying love-love!

[*A truck is heard approaching, then passes. Serafina drops her fan. Assunta opens a bottle of spumanti with a loud pop. Serafina cries out.*]

ASSUNTA: Stai tranquilla! Calmati! [*She pours her a glass of wine.*] Drink this wine and before the glass is empty he'll be in your arms!

SERAFINA: I can't – swallow my heart!

ASSUNTA: A woman must not have a heart that is too big to swallow! [*She crosses to the door.*]

SERAFINA: Stay with me!

ASSUNTA: I have to visit a woman who drank rat poison because of a heart too big for her to swallow.

[*Assunta leaves. Serafina returns indolently to the sofa. She lifts her hands to her swelling breasts and murmurs aloud:*]

SERAFINA: Oh, it's so wonderful, having *two* lives in the body not *one* but two! [*Her hands slide down to her belly, luxuriously.*] I am heavy with life, I am big, big, big with life! [*She picks up a bowl of roses and goes into the back room.*]

[*Estelle Hohengarten appears in front of the house. She is a thin blonde woman in a dress of Egyptian design, and her blonde hair has an unnatural gloss in the clear, greenish dusk. Rosa appears from behind the house, calling out:*]

ROSA: Twenty lightning bugs, Mama!

ESTELLE: Little girl? Little girl?

ROSA [*resentfully*]: Are you talking to me? [*There is a pause.*]

ESTELLE: Come here. [*She looks Rosa over curiously.*] You're a twig off the old rose-bush. – Is the lady that does the sewing in the house?

ROSA: Mama's at home.

ESTELLE: I'd like to see her.

ROSA: Mama?

SERAFINA: Dimi?

ROSA: There's a lady to see you.

SERAFINA: Oh. Tell her to wait in the parlour. [*Estelle enters and stares curiously about. She picks up a small framed picture on the cupboard. She is looking at it as Serafina enters with a bowl of roses. Serafina speaks sharply.*] That is my husband's picture.

ESTELLE: Oh! – I thought it was Valentino. – With a moustache.

SERAFINA [*putting the bowl down on the table*]: You want something?

ESTELLE: Yes. I heard you do sewing.

SERAFINA: Yes, I do sewing.

ESTELLE: How fast can you make a shirt for me?

SERAFINA: That all depends. [*She takes the picture from Estelle and puts it back on the cupboard.*]

ESTELLE: I got the piece of silk with me. I want it made into a shirt for a man I'm in love with. To-morrow's the anniversary of the day we met . . . [*She unwraps a piece of rose-coloured silk which she holds up like a banner.*]

SERAFINA [*involuntarily*]: Che bella stoffa! – Oh, that would be wonderful stuff for a lady's blouse or for a pair of pyjamas!

ESTELLE: I want a man's shirt made with it.

SERAFINA: Silk this colour for a shirt for a *man*?

ESTELLE: This man is wild like a Gipsy.

SERAFINA: A woman should not encourage a man to be wild.

ESTELLE: A man that's wild is hard for a woman to hold, huh? But if he was tame – would the woman want to hold him? Huh?

SERAFINA: I am a married woman in business. I don't know

nothing about wild men and wild women and I don't have much time – so . . .

ESTELLE: I'll pay you twice what you ask me.

[*Outside there is the sound of the goat bleating and the jingle of its harness; then the crash of wood splintering.*]

ROSA [*suddenly appearing at the door*]: Mama, the black goat is loose! [*She runs down the steps and stands watching the goat. Serafina crosses to the door.*]

THE STREGA [*in the distance*]: Hyeh, Billy, hyeh, hyeh, Billy!

ESTELLE: I'll pay you three times the price that you ask me for it.

SERAFINA [*shouting*]: Watch the goat! Don't let him get in our yard! [*to Estelle*] – If I ask you five dollars?

ESTELLE: I will pay you fifteen. Make it twenty; money is not the object. But it's got to be ready to-morrow.

SERAFINA: To-morrow?

ESTELLE: Twenty-five dollars! [*Serafina nods slowly with a stunned look. Estelle smiles.*] I've got the measurements with me.

SERAFINA: Pin the measurements and your name on the silk and the shirt will be ready to-morrow.

ESTELLE: My name is Estelle Hohengarten.

[*A little boy races excitedly into the yard.*]

THE BOY: Rosa, Rosa, the black goat's in your yard!

ROSA [*calling*]: Mama, the goat's in the yard!

SERAFINA [*furiously, forgetting her visitor*]: Il becco della strega! – Scusi! [*She runs out onto the porch.*] Catch him, catch him before he gets at the vines!

[*Rosa dances gleefully. The Strega runs into the yard. She has a mop of wild grey hair and is holding her black skirts up from her bare hairy legs. The sound of the goat's bleating and the jingling of his harness is heard in the windy blue dusk.*]

26

Serafina descends the porch steps. The high-heeled slippers, the tight silk skirt and the dignity of a baronessa make the descent a little gingerly. Arrived in the yard, she directs the goat-chase imperiously with her yellow paper fan, pointing this way and that, exclaiming in Italian.

She fans herself rapidly and crosses back of the house. The goat evidently makes a sudden charge. Screaming, Serafina rushes back to the front of the house, all out of breath, the glittering pompadour beginning to tumble down over her forehead.]

SERAFINA: Rosa! You go in the house! Don't look at the Strega!

[Alone in the parlour, Estelle takes the picture of Rosario. Impetuously, she thrusts it in her purse and runs from the house, just as Serafina returns to the front yard.]

ROSA *[refusing to move]*: Why do you call her a witch?

[Serafina seizes her daughter's arm and propels her into the house.]

SERAFINA: She has a white eye and every finger is crooked. *[She pulls Rosa's arm.]*

ROSA: She has a cataract, Mama, and her fingers are crooked because she has rheumatism!

SERAFINA: Malocchio – the evil eye – *that's* what she's got! And her fingers are crooked because she shook hands with the devil. Go in the house and wash your face with salt water and throw the salt water away! *Go in! Quick!* She's coming!

[The boy utters a cry of triumph.

Serafina crosses abruptly to the porch. At the same moment the boy runs triumphantly around the house leading the captured goat by its bell harness. It is a middle-sized black goat with great yellow eyes. The Strega runs behind with the broken rope. As the grotesque little procession runs before her – the Strega, the

27

*goat, and the children — Serafina cries out shrilly. She crouches
over and covers her face. The Strega looks back at her with a
derisive cackle.*]

SERAFINA: Malocchio! Malocchio!

[*Shielding her face with one hand, Serafina makes the sign of the
horns with the other to ward off the evil eye. And the scene
dims out.*]

SCENE 2

*It is just before dawn the next day. Father De Leo, a priest, and several
black-shawled women, including Assunta, are standing outside the
house. The interior of the house is very dim.*

GIUSEPPINA: There is a light in the house.

PEPPINA: I hear the sewing machine!

VIOLETTA: There's Serafina! She's working. She's holding up
a piece of rose-coloured silk.

ASSUNTA: She hears our voices.

VIOLETTA: She's dropped the silk to the floor and she's . . .

GIUSEPPINA: Holding her throat! I think she . . .

PEPPINA: Who's going to tell her?

VIOLETTA: Father De Leo will tell her.

FATHER DE LEO: I think a woman should tell her. I think
Assunta must tell her that Rosario is dead.

ASSUNTA: It will not be necessary to tell her. She will know
when she sees us.

[*It grows lighter inside the house. Serafina is standing in a
frozen attitude with her hand clutching her throat and her eyes
staring fearfully toward the sound of voices.*]

28

ASSUNTA: I think she already knows what we have come to tell her!

FATHER DE LEO: Andiamo, Signore! We must go to the door.

[*They climb the porch steps. Assunta opens the door.*]

SERAFINA [*gasping*]: Don't speak!
[*She retreats from the group, stumbling blindly backwards among the dressmaker's dummies. With a gasp she turns and runs out the back door. In a few moments we see her staggering about outside near the palm tree. She comes down in front of the house, and stares blindly off into the distance.*]

SERAFINA [*wildly*]: Don't speak!

[*The voices of the women begin keening in the house. Assunta comes out and approaches Serafina with her arms extended. Serafina slumps to her knees, whispering hoarsely: 'Don't speak!' Assunta envelopes her in the grey shawl of pity as the scene dims out.*]

SCENE 3

It is noon of the same day. Assunta is removing a funeral wreath on the door of the house. A doctor and Father De Leo are on the porch.

THE DOCTOR: She's lost the baby. [*Assunta utters a low moan of pity and crosses herself.*] Serafina's a very strong woman and that won't kill her. But she is trying not to breathe. She's got to be watched and not allowed out of the bed. [*He removes a hypodermic and a small package from his bag and hands them to Assunta.*] – This is morphia. In the arm with the needle if she screams or struggles to get up again.

ASSUNTA: Capisco!

FATHER DE LEO: One thing I want to make plain. The body of Rosario must not be burned.

THE DOCTOR: Have you seen the 'body of Rosario'?

FATHER DE LEO: Yes, I have seen his body.

THE DOCTOR: Wouldn't you say it was burned?

FATHER DE LEO: Of course the body was burned. When he was shot at the wheel of the truck, it crashed and caught fire. But deliberate cremation is not the same thing. It's an abomination in the sight of God.

THE DOCTOR: Abominations are something I don't know about.

FATHER DE LEO: The Church has set down certain laws.

THE DOCTOR: But the instructions of a widow have to be carried out.

FATHER DE LEO: Don't you know why she wants the body cremated? So she can keep the ashes here in the house.

THE DOCTOR: Well, why not, if that's any comfort to her?

FATHER DE LEO: Pagan idolatry is what I call it!

THE DOCTOR: Father De Leo, you love your people but you don't understand them. They find God in each other. And when they lose each other, they lose God and they're lost. And it's hard to help them. – Who is that woman?

[*Estelle Hohengarten has appeared before the house. She is black-veiled, and bearing a bouquet of roses.*]

ESTELLE: I am Estelle Hohengarten.

[*Instantly there is a great hubbub in the house. The women mourners flock out to the porch, whispering and gesticulating excitedly.*]

FATHER DE LEO: What have you come here for?

ESTELLE: To say good-bye to the body.

FATHER DE LEO: The casket is closed; the body cannot be seen.

And you must never come here. The widow knows nothing about you. Nothing at all.

GIUSEPPINA: *We* know about you!

PEPPINA: Va via! Sporcacciona!

VIOLETTA: Puttana!

MARIELLA: Assassina!

TERESA: You sent him to the Romanos.

FATHER DE LEO: Shhh!

[*Suddenly the women swarm down the steps like a cloud of attacking birds, all crying out in Sicilian. Estelle crouches and bows her head defensively before their savage assault. The bouquet of roses is snatched from her black-gloved hands and she is flailed with them about the head and shoulders. The thorns catch her veil and tear it away from her head. She covers her white sobbing face with her hands.*]

FATHER DE LEO: Ferme! Ferme! Signore, fermate vi nel nome di Dio! – Have a little respect!

[*The women fall back from Estelle, who huddles weeping on the walk.*]

ESTELLE: See him, see him, just see him . . .

FATHER DE LEO: The body is crushed and burned. Nobody can see it. Now go away and don't ever come here again, Estelle Hohengarten!

THE WOMEN [*in both languages, wildly*]: Va via, va via, go away.

[*Rosa comes around the house. Estelle turns and retreats. One of the mourners spits and kicks at the tangled veil and roses. Father De Leo leaves. The others return inside, except Rosa.*

After a few moments the child goes over to the roses. She picks them up and carefully untangles the veil from the thorns.

She sits on the sagging steps and puts the black veil over her head. Then for the first time she begins to weep, wildly, histrionically. The little boy appears and gazes at her, momentarily impressed by her performance. Then he picks up a rubber ball and begins to bounce it.

Rosa is outraged. She jumps up, tears off the veil and runs to the little boy, giving him a sound smack and snatching the ball away from him.]

ROSA: Go home! My papa is dead!

[*The scene dims out, as the music is heard again.*]

SCENE 4

A June day, three years later. It is morning and the light is bright. A group of local mothers are storming Serafina's house, indignant over her delay in delivering the graduation dresses for their daughters. Most of the women are chattering continually in Sicilian, racing about the house and banging the doors and shutters. The scene moves swiftly and violently until the moment when Rosa finally comes out in her graduation dress.

GIUSEPPINA: Serafina! Serafina delle Rose!

PEPPINA: Maybe if you call her 'Baronessa' she will answer the door. [*with a mocking laugh*] Call her 'Baronessa' and kiss your hand to her when she opens the door.

GIUSEPPINA [*tauntingly*]: Baronessa! [*She kisses her hand toward the door.*]

VIOLETTA: When did she promise your dress?

PEPPINA: All week she say, 'Domani – domani – domani.' But yestiddy I told her . . .

VIOLETTA: Yeah?

PEPPINA: Oh yeah. I says to her, 'Serafina, domani's the high school graduation. I got to try the dress on my daughter to–day.' 'Domani,' she says, 'Sicuro! sicuro! sicuro!' So I

start to go away. Then I hear a voice call, 'Signora! Signora!'
So I turn round and I see Serafina's daughter at the window

VIOLETTA: Rosa?

PEPPINA: Yeah, Rosa. An' you know how?

VIOLETTA: How?

PEPPINA: *Naked!* Nuda, nuda! [*She crosses herself and repeats a prayer.*] In nominis padri et figlio et spiritus sancti. Aaahh!

VIOLETTA: What did she do?

PEPPINA: Do? She say, 'Signora! Please, you call this numero and ask for Jack and tell Jack my clothes are lock up so I can't get out from the house.' Then Serafina come and she grab-a the girl by the hair and she pull her way from the window and she slam the shutters right in my face!

GIUSEPPINA: Whatsa the matter the daughter?

VIOLETTA: Who is this boy? Where did she meet him?

PEPPINA: Boy! What boy? He's a sailor. [*At the word 'sailor' the women say 'Ahhh!'*] She met him at the high school dance and somebody tell Serafina. That's why she lock up the girl's clothes so she can't leave the house. She can't even go to the high school to take the examinations. Imagine!

VIOLETTA: Peppina, this time *you* go to the door, yeah?

PEPPINA: Oh yeah, I go. Now I'm getting nervous. [*The women all crowd to the door.*] Sera-feee-na!

VIOLETTA: Louder, louder!

PEPPINA: Apri la porta! Come on, come on!

THE WOMEN [*together*]: Yeah, apri la porta! . . . Come on, hurry up! . . . Open up!

GIUSEPPINA: I go get-a police.

VIOLETTA: Whatsa matta? You want more trouble?

GIUSEPPINA: Listen, I pay in advance five dollars and get no dress. Now what she wear, my daughter, to graduate in? A couple of towels and a rose in the hair? [*There is a noise inside: a shout and running footsteps.*]

THE WOMEN: Something is going on in the house! I hear someone! Don't I? Don't you?

33

[*A scream and running footsteps are heard. The front door opens and Serafina staggers out onto the porch. She is wearing a soiled pink slip and her hair is wild.*]

SERAFINA: Aiuto! Aiuto! [*She plunges back into the house.*]

[*Miss Yorke, a spinsterish high school teacher, walks quickly up to the house. The Sicilian women, now all chattering at once like a cloud of birds, sweep about her as she approaches.*]

MISS YORKE: You ladies know I don't understand Italian! So, please . . .

[*She goes directly into the house. There are more outcries inside. The Strega comes and stands at the edge of the yard, cackling derisively.*]

THE STREGA [*calling back to someone*]: The Wops are at it again! – She got the daughter lock up naked in there all week. Ho, ho, ho! She lock up all week – naked – shouting out the window tell people to call a number and give a message to Jack. Ho, ho, ho! I guess she's in trouble already, and only fifteen! – They ain't civilized, these Sicilians. In the old country they live in caves in the hills and the country's run by bandits. Ho, ho, ho! More of them coming over on the boats all the time. [*The door is thrown open again and Serafina reappears on the porch. She is acting wildly, as if demented.*]

SERAFINA [*gasping in a hoarse whisper*]: She cut her wrist, my daughter, she cut her wrist! [*She runs out into the yard.*] Aiiii-eeee! Aiutatemi, aiutatemi! Call the dottore! [*Assunta rushes up to Serafina and supports her as she is about to fall to her knees in the yard.*] Get the knife away from her! Get the knife, please! Get the knife away from – she cut her wrist with – Madonna! Madonna mia . . .

ASSUNTA: Smettila, smettila, Serafina.

MISS YORKE [*coming out of the back room*]: Mrs Delle Rose, your

34

daughter has not cut her wrist. Now come back into the house.

SERAFINA [*panting*]: Che dice, che dice? Che cosa? Che cosa dice?

MISS YORKE: Your daughter's all right. Come back into the house. And you ladies please go away!

ASSUNTA: Vieni, Serafina. Andiamo a casa. [*She supports the heavy, sagging bulk of Serafina to the steps. As they climb the steps one of the Sicilian mothers advances from the whispering group.*]

GIUSEPPINA [*boldly*]: Serafina, we don't go away until we get our dresses.

PEPPINA: The graduation begins and the girls ain't dressed.

[*Serafina's reply to this ill-timed request is a long, animal howl of misery as she is supported into the house. Miss Yorke follows and firmly closes the door upon the women, who then go around back of the house. The interior of the house is lighted up.*]

MISS YORKE [*to Serafina*]: No, no, no, she's not bleeding. Rosa? Rosa, come here and show your mother that you are not bleeding to death.

[*Rosa appears silently and sullenly between the curtains that separate the two rooms. She has a small white handkerchief tied around one wrist. Serafina points at the wrist and cries out: 'Aiieee!'*]

MISS YORKE [*severely*]: Now stop that, Mrs Delle Rose!

[*Serafina rushes to Rosa, who thrusts her roughly away.*]

ROSA: Lasciami stare, Mama! – I'm so ashamed I could die. This is the way she goes around all the time. She hasn't put on clothes since my father was killed. For three years she sits at the sewing machine and never puts a dress on or goes out of the house, and now she has locked my clothes up so *I* can't go out. She wants me to be like her, a freak of the neighbourhood, the way she is! Next time, next time, I won't cut my wrist but my throat! I don't want to live locked up with a bottle of ashes! [*She points to the shrine.*]

ASSUNTA: Figlia, figlia, figlia, non devi parlare cosí!

MISS YORKE: Mrs Delle Rose, please give me the key to the closet so that your daughter can dress for the graduation!

SERAFINA [*surrendering the key*]: Ecco la – chiave ... [*Rosa snatches the key and runs back through the curtains.*]

MISS YORKE: Now why did you lock her clothes up, Mrs Delle Rose?

SERAFINA: The wrist is still bleeding!

MISS YORKE: No, the wrist is not bleeding. It's just a skin cut, a scratch. But the child is exhausted from all this excitement and hasn't eaten a thing in two or three days.

ROSA [*running into the dining room*]: Four days! I only asked her one favour. Not to let me go out but to let Jack come to the house so she could meet him! – Then she locked my clothes up!

MISS YORKE: Your daughter missed her final examinations at the high school, but her grades have been so good that she will be allowed to graduate with her class and take the examinations later. – You understand me, Mrs Delle Rose!

[*Rosa goes into the back of the house.*]

SERAFINA [*standing at the curtains*]: See the way she looks at me? I've got a wild thing in the house, and her wrist is still bleeding!

MISS YORKE: Let's not have any more outbursts of emotion!

SERAFINA: Outbursts of – you make me sick! Sick! Sick at my stomach you make me! Your school, you make all this trouble! You give-a this dance where she gets mixed up with a sailor.

MISS YORKE: You are talking about the Hunter girl's brother, a sailor named Jack, who attended the dance with his sister?

SERAFINA: 'Attended with sister!' – Attended with *sister!* – My daughter, she's nobody's sister!

[*Rosa comes out of the back room. She is radiantly beautiful in her graduation gown.*]

ROSA: Don't listen to her, don't pay any attention to her, Miss Yorke. – I'm ready to go to the high school.

SERAFINA [*stunned by her daughter's beauty, and speaking with a wheedling tone and gestures, as she crouches a little*]: O tesoro, tesoro! Vieni qua, Rosa, cara! – Come here and kiss Mama one minute! – Don't go like that, now!

ROSA: Lasciami stare!

[*She rushes out on the porch. Serafina gazes after her with arms slowly drooping from their imploring gesture and jaw dropping open in a look of almost comic desolation.*]

SERAFINA: Ho solo te, solo te – in questo mondo!

MISS YORKE: Now, now, Mrs Delle Rose, no more excitement, please!

SERAFINA [*suddenly plunging after them in a burst of fury*]: Senti, senti, per favore!

ROSA: Don't you dare come out on the street like that! – *Mama!*

[*She crouches and covers her face in shame, as Serafina heedlessly plunges out into the front yard in her shocking déshabillé, making wild gestures.*]

SERAFINA: You give this dance where she gets mixed up with a sailor. What do you think you want to do at this high school? [*In weeping despair, Rosa runs to the porch.*] How high is this high school? Listen, how high is this high school? Look, look, look, I will show you! It's high as that horse's dirt out there in the street! [*Serafina points violently out in front of the house.*] Si! 'Sta fetentissima scuola! Scuola maledetta!

[*Rosa cries out and rushes over to the palm tree, leaning against it, with tears of mortification.*]

MISS YORKE: Mrs Delle Rose, you are talking and behaving extremely badly. I don't understand how a woman that acts like you could have such a sweet and refined young girl for a daughter! – You don't deserve it! – Really . . . [*She crosses to the palm tree.*]

SERAFINA: Oh, you want me to talk refined to you, do you? Then do me one thing! Stop ruining the girls at the high school! [*As Serafina paces about, she swings her hips in the exaggeratedly belligerent style of a parading matador.*]

ASSUNTA: Piantala, Serafina! Andiamo a casa!

SERAFINA: No, no, I ain't through talking to this here teacher!

ASSUNTA: Serafina, look at yourself, you're not dressed!

SERAFINA: I'm dressed okay; I'm not naked! [*She glares savagely at the teacher by the palm tree. The Sicilian mothers return to the front yard.*]

ASSUNTA: Serafina, cara? Andiamo a casa, adesso! – Basta! Basta!

SERAFINA: Aspetta!

ROSA: I'm so ashamed I could die, I'm so ashamed. Oh, you don't know, Miss Yorke, the way that we live. She never puts on a dress; she stays all the time in that dirty old pink slip! – And talks to my father's ashes like he was living.

SERAFINA: Teacher! Teacher, senti! What do you think you want to do at this high school? Sentite! per favore! You give this-a dance! What kind of a spring dance is it? Answer this question, please, for me! What kind of a spring dance is it? She meet this boy there who don't even go to no high school. What kind of a boy? Guardate! *A sailor that wears a gold earring!* That kind of a boy is the kind of boy she meets there! – That's why I lock her clothes up so she can't go back to the high school! [*suddenly to Assunta*] She cut her wrist!

It's still bleeding! [*She strokes her forehead three times with her fist.*]

ROSA: Mama, you look disgusting! [*She rushes away.*]

[*Miss Yorke rushes after her. Serafina shades her eyes with one hand to watch them departing down the street in the brilliant spring light.*]

SERAFINA: Did you hear what my daughter said to me? – 'You look – disgusting.' – She calls me . . .

ASSUNTA: Now, Serafina, we must go in the house. [*She leads her gently to the porch of the little house.*]

SERAFINA [*proudly*]: How pretty she look, my daughter, in the white dress, like a bride! [*to all*] Excuse me! Excuse me, please! Go away! Get out of my yard!

GIUSEPPINA [*taking the bull by the horns*]: No, we ain't going to go without the dresses!

ASSUNTA: Give the ladies the dresses so the girls can get dressed for the graduation.

SERAFINA: That one there, she only paid for the goods. I charge for the work.

GIUSEPPINA: Ecco! I got the money!

THE WOMEN: We *got* the money!

SERAFINA: The names are pinned on the dresses. Go in and get them. [*She turns to Assunta.*] Did you hear what my daughter called me? She called me 'disgusting'!

[*Serafina enters the house, slamming the door. After a moment the mothers come out, cradling the white voile dresses tenderly in their arms, murmuring 'carino!' and 'bellissimo!'*

As they disappear the inside light is brought up and we see Serafina standing before a glazed mirror, looking at herself and repeating the daughter's word.]

SERAFINA: Disgusting!

[*The music is briefly resumed to mark a division.*]

SCENE 5

Immediately following. Serafina's movements gather momentum. She snatches a long-neglected girdle out of a bureau drawer and holds 't experimentally about her waist. She shakes her head doubtfully, drops the girdle and suddenly snatches the $8.98 hat off the millinery dummy and plants it on her head. She turns around distractedly, not remembering where the mirror is. She gasps with astonishment when she catches sight of herself, snatches the hat off and hastily restores it to the blank head of the dummy. She makes another confused revolution or two, then gasps with fresh inspiration and snatches a girlish frock off a dummy – an Alice blue gown with daisies crocheted on it. The dress sticks on the dummy. Serafina mutters savagely in Sicilian. She finally overcomes this difficulty but in her exasperation she knocks the dummy over. She throws off the robe and steps hopefully into the gown. But she discovers it won't fit over her hips. She seizes the girdle again; then hurls it angrily away. The parrot calls to her; she yells angrily back at the parrot: 'Zitto!'

In the distance the high school band starts playing. Serafina gets panicky that she will miss the graduation ceremonies, and hammers her forehead with her fist, sobbing a little. She wriggles despairingly out of the blue dress and runs out back in her rayon slip just as Flora and Bessie appear outside the house. Flora and Bessie are two female clowns of middle years and juvenile temperament. Flora is tall and angular; Bessie is rather stubby. They are dressed for a gala. Flora runs up the steps and bangs at the cottage door.

BESSIE: I fail to understand why it's so important to pick up a polka-dot blouse when it's likely to make us miss the twelve o'clock train.

FLORA: Serafina! Serafina!

BESSIE: We only got fifteen minutes to get to the depot and I'll get faint on the train if I don't have m' coffee . . .

FLORA: Git a coke on th' train, Bessie.

40

BESSIE: Git nothing on the train if we don't git the train!

[*Serafina runs back out of the bedroom, quite breathless, in a purple silk dress. As she passes the millinery dummy she snatches the hat off again and plants it back on her head.*]

SERAFINA: Wrist-watch! Wrist-watch! Where'd I put th' wrist-watch? [*She hears Flora shouting and banging and rushes to the door.*]

BESSIE: Try the door if it ain't open.

FLORA [*pushing in*]: Just tell me, is it ready or not?

SERAFINA: Oh! You. Don't bother me. I'm late for the graduation of my daughter and now I can't find her graduation present.

FLORA: You got plenty of time.

SERAFINA: Don't you hear the band playing?

FLORA: They're just warming up. Now, Serafina, where is my blouse?

SERAFINA: Blouse? Not ready! I had to make fourteen graduation dresses!

FLORA: A promise is a promise and an excuse is just an excuse!

SERAFINA: I got to get to the high school!

FLORA: I got to get to the depot in that blouse!

BESSIE: We're going to the American Legion parade in New Orleans.

FLORA: There, there, there, there it is! [*She grabs the blouse from the machine.*] Get started, woman, stitch them bandanas together! If you don't do it, I'm a-gonna report you to the Chamber of Commerce and get your licence revoked!

SERAFINA [*anxiously*]: What licence you talking about? I got no licence!

FLORA: You hear that, Bessie? *She hasn't got no licence!*

BESSIE: *She ain't even got a licence?*

SERAFINA [*crossing quickly to the machine*]: I – I'll stitch them together! But if you make me late to my daughter's graduation, I'll make you sorry some way . . .

[*She works with furious rapidity. A train whistle is heard.*]

BESSIE [*wildly and striking at Flora with her purse*]: Train's pullin' out! Oh, God, you made us miss it!

FLORA: Bessie, you know there's another at 12.45!

BESSIE: It's the selfish – principle of it that makes me sick! [*She walks rapidly up and down.*]

FLORA: Set down, Bessie. Don't wear out your feet before we git to th' city . . .

BESSIE: Molly tole me the town was full of excitement. They're dropping paper sacks full of water out of hotel windows.

FLORA: Which hotel are they dropping paper sacks out of?

BESSIE: What a fool question! The Monteleone Hotel.

FLORA: That's an old-fashioned hotel.

BESSIE: It might be old-fashioned but you'd be surprised at some of the modern, up-to-date things that go on there.

FLORA: I heard, I heard that the Legionnaires caught a girl on Canal Street! They tore the clothes off her and sent her home in a taxi!

BESSIE: I double dog dare anybody to try that on me!

FLORA: You?! Huh! You never need any assistance gittin' undressed!

SERAFINA [*ominously*]: You two ladies watch how you talk in there. This here is a Catholic house. You are sitting in the same room with Our Lady and with the blessed ashes of my husband!

FLORA [*acidly*]: Well, ex-cuse *me!* [*She whispers maliciously to Bessie.*] It sure is a pleasant surprise to see you wearing a dress, Serafina, but the surprise would be twice as pleasant if it was more the right size. [*to Bessie, loudly*] She used to have a sweet figure, a little bit plump but attractive, but setting there at that sewing machine for three years in a kimona and not stepping out of the house has naturally given her hips!

SERAFINA: If I didn't have hips I would be a very uncomfortable woman when I set down.

[*The parrot squawks. Serafina imitates its squawk.*]

FLORA: Polly want a cracker?

SERAFINA: No. He don't want a cracker! What is she doing over there at that window?

BESSIE: Some Legionnaires are on the highway!

FLORA: A Legionnaire? No kidding?

[*She springs up and joins her girl friend at the window. They both laugh fatuously, bobbing their heads out the window.*]

BESSIE: He's looking this way; yell something!

FLORA [*leaning out the window*]: Mademoiselle from Armentieres, parley-voo!

BESSIE [*chiming in rapturously*]: Mademoiselle from Armentieres, parley-voo!

A VOICE OUTSIDE [*gallantly returning the salute*]: Mademoiselle from Armentieres, hadn't been kissed for forty years!

BOTH GIRLS [*together; very gaily*]: Hinky-dinky parley-voooo!

[*They laugh and applaud at the window. The Legionnaires are heard laughing. A car horn is heard as the Legionnaires drive away. Serafina springs up and rushes over to the window, jerks them away from it and slams the shutters in their faces.*]

SERAFINA [*furiously*]: I told you wimmen that you was not in a honky-tonk! Now take your blouse and git out! Get out on the streets where you kind a wimmen belong. – This is the house of Rosario delle Rose and those are his ashes in that marble urn and I won't have – unproper things going on here or dirty talk, neither!

FLORA: Who's talking dirty?

BESSIE: What a helluva nerve.

FLORA: I want you to listen!

SERAFINA: You are, you are, dirty talk, all the time men, men, men! You men-crazy things, you!

FLORA: Sour grapes – sour grapes is your trouble! You're wild with envy!

BESSIE: Isn't she green with jealousy? Huh!

SERAFINA [*suddenly and religiously*]: When I think of men I think about my husband. My husband was a Sicilian. We had love together every night of the week, we never skipped one, from the night we was married till the night he was killed in his fruit truck on that road there! [*She catches her breath in a sob.*] And maybe that is the reason I'm not man-crazy and don't like hearing the talk of women that are. But I am interested, now, in the happiness of my daughter who's graduating this morning out of high school. And now I'm going to be late, the band is playing! And I have lost her wrist watch! – her graduation present! [*She whirls about distractedly.*]

BESSIE: Flora, let's go! – The hell with that goddam blouse!

FLORA: Oh, no, just wait a minute! I don't accept insults from no one!

SERAFINA: Go on, go on to New Orleans, you two man-crazy things, you! And pick up a man on Canal Street but not in my house, at my window, in front of my dead husband's ashes! [*The high school band is playing a martial air in the distance. Serafina's chest is heaving violently; she touches her heart and momentarily seems to forget that she must go.*] I am not at all interested, I am not interested in men getting fat and bald in soldier-boy play suits, tearing the clothes off girls on Canal Street and dropping paper sacks out of hotel windows. I'm just not interested in that sort of man-crazy business. I remember my husband with a body like a young boy and hair on his head as thick and black as mine is and skin on him smooth and sweet as a yellow rose petal.

FLORA: Oh, a *rose*, was he?

SERAFINA: Yes, yes, a rose, a rose!

FLORA: Yes, a rose of a Wop! – of a gangster! – shot smuggling dope under a load of bananas!

BESSIE: Flora, Flora, let's go!

SERAFINA: My folks was peasants, contadini, but he – he come from *land*-owners! *Signorile*, my husband! – At night I sit here and I'm satisfied to remember, because I had the best. – Not the third best and not the second best, but the *first* best, the *only* best! – So now I stay here and am satisfied now to remember . . .

BESSIE: Come on, come out! To the depot!

FLORA: Just wait, I wanta hear this, it's too good to miss!

SERAFINA: I count up the nights I held him all night in my arms, and I can tell you how many. Each night for twelve years. Four thousand – three hundred – and eighty. The number of nights I held him all night in my arms. Sometimes I didn't sleep, just held him all night in my arms. And I am satisfied with it. I grieve for him. Yes, my pillow at night's never dry – but I'm satisfied to remember. And I would feel cheap and degraded and not fit to live with my daughter or under the roof with the urn of his blessed ashes, those – ashes of a rose – if after that memory, after knowing that man, I went to some other, some middle-aged man, not young, not full of young passion, but getting a pot belly on him and losing his hair and smelling of sweat and liquor – and trying to fool myself that *that* was love-making! I *know* what love-making was. And I'm satisfied just to remember . . . [*She is panting as though she had run upstairs.*] Go on, you do it, you go on the streets and let them drop their sacks of dirty water on you! – I'm satisfied to remember the love of a man that was mine – *only mine!* Never touched by the hand *to nobody! Nobody* but *me*! – Just me! [*She gasps and runs out of the porch. The sun floods her figure. It seems to astonish her. She finds herself sobbing. She digs in her purse for her handkerchief.*]

FLORA [*crossing to the open door*]: Never touched by nobody?

SERAFINA [*with fierce pride*]: Never nobody but me!

FLORA: *I* know somebody that could a tale unfold! And not so far from here neither. Not no further than the Square Roof is, that place on Esplanade!

BESSIE: Estelle Hohengarten!

FLORA: Estelle Hohengarten! – the blackjack dealer from Texas!

BESSIE: Get into your blouse and let's go!

FLORA: Everybody's known it but Serafina. I'm just telling the facts that come out at the inquest while she was in bed with her eyes shut tight and the sheet pulled over her head like a female ostrich! Tie this damn thing on me! It was a romance, not just a fly-by-night thing, but a steady affair that went on for more than a year.

[*Serafina has been standing on the porch with the door open behind her. She is in the full glare of the sun. She appears to have been struck senseless by the words shouted inside. She turns slowly about. We see that her dress is unfastened down the back, the pink slip showing. She reaches out gropingly with one hand and finds the porch column which she clings to while the terrible words strike constantly deeper. The high school band continues as a merciless counterpoint.*]

BESSIE: Leave her in ignorance. Ignorance is bliss.

FLORA: He had a rose tattoo on his chest, the stuck-up thing, and Estelle was so gone on him she went down to Bourbon Street and had one put on her. [*Serafina comes onto the porch and Flora turns to her, viciously.*] Yeah, a rose tattoo on her chest same as the Wop's!

SERAFINA [*very softly*]: Liar ... [*She comes inside; the word seems to give her strength.*]

BESSIE [*nervously*]: Flora, let's go, let's go!

SERAFINA [*in a terrible voice*]: Liar! – Lie-arrrrr!

[*She slams the wooden door shut with a violence that shakes the walls.*]

BESSIE [*shocked into terror*]: Let's get outa here, Flora!

FLORA: Let her howl her head off. I don't care.

[*Serafina has snatched up a broom.*]

BESSIE: What's she up to?

FLORA: I don't care what she's up to!

BESSIE: I'm a-scared of these Wops.

FLORA: I'm not afraid of nobody!

BESSIE: She's gonna hit you.

FLORA: She'd better not hit me!

[*But both of the clowns are in retreat to the door. Serafina suddenly rushes at them with the broom. She flails Flora about the hips and shoulders. Bessie gets out. But Flora is trapped in a corner. A table is turned over. Bessie, outside, screams for the police and cries: 'Murder! Murder!' The high school band is playing* The Stars and Stripes Forever. *Flora breaks wildly past the flailing broom and escapes out of the house. She also takes up the cry for help. Serafina follows them out. She is flailing the brilliant noon air with the broom. The two women run off, screaming.*]

FLORA [*calling back*]: I'm going to have her arrested! Police, police! I'm going to have you arrested!

SERAFINA: *Have* me arrested, *have* me, you dirt, you devil, you *liar!* Li-i-arrrr!

[*She comes back inside the house and leans on the work table for a moment, panting heavily. Then she rushes back to the door, slams it and bolts it. Then she rushes to the windows, slams the shutters and fastens them. The house is now dark except for the vigil light in the ruby glass cup before the Madonna, and the delicate beams admitted through the shutter slats.*]

SERAFINA [*in a crazed manner*]: Have me – have me – arrested – dirty slut – bitch – liar! [*She moves about helplessly, not knowing what to do with her big, stricken body. Panting for breath, she*] *repeats the word 'liar' monotonously and helplessly as she thrashes about. It is necessary for her, vitally necessary for her, to believe that the woman's story is a malicious invention. But the words of it stick in her mind and she mumbles them aloud as she thrashes crazily around the small confines of the parlour.*] Woman – Estelle – [*The sound of band music is heard.*] Band, band, already – started. – Going to miss – graduation. Oh! [*She retreats toward the Madonna.*] Estelle, Estelle Hohengarten? – 'A shirt for a man I'm in love with! This man – is – wild like a gipsy.' – Oh, oh, Lady – The – rose-coloured – silk. [*She starts toward the dining room, then draws back in terror.*] No, no, no, no, no! I don't remember! It wasn't that name, I don't remember the name! [*The band music grows louder.*] High school – graduation – late! I'll be – late for it. – Oh, Lady, give me a – sign! [*She cocks her head toward the statue in a fearful listening attitude.*] Che? Che dice, Signora? *Oh, Lady! Give me a sign!*

[*The scene dims out.*]

SCENE 6

It is two hours later. The interior of the house is in complete darkness except for the vigil light. With the shutters closed, the interior is so dark that we do not know Serafina is present. All that we see clearly is the starry blue robe of Our Lady above the flickering candle of the ruby glass cup. After a few moments we hear Serafina's voice, very softly, in the weak, breathless tone of a person near death.

SERAFINA [*very softly*]: Oh, Lady, give me a sign . . .

[*Gay, laughing voices are heard outside the house. Rosa and Jack appear, bearing roses and gifts. They are shouting back to others in a car.*]

JACK: Where do we go for the picnic?

A GIRL'S VOICE [*from the highway*]: We're going in three sail-boats to Diamond Key.

A MAN'S VOICE: Be at Municipal Pier in half an hour.

ROSA: Pick us up here! [*She races up the steps.*] Oh, the door's locked! Mama's gone *out*! There's a key in that bird bath.

[*Jack opens the door. The parlour lights up faintly as they enter.*]

JACK: It's dark in here.

ROSA: Yes, Mama's gone out!

JACK: How do you know she's out?

ROSA: The door was locked and all the shutters are closed! Put down the roses.

JACK: Where shall I . . .

ROSA: Somewhere, anywhere! – Come here! [*He approaches her rather diffidently.*] I want to teach you a little Dago word. The word is 'bacio'.

JACK: What does this word mean?

ROSA: This and this and this! [*She rains kisses upon him till he forcibly removes her face from his.*] Just think. A week ago Friday – I didn't know boys existed! – Did you know girls existed before the dance?

JACK: Yes, I knew they existed . . .

ROSA [*holding him*]: Do you remember what you said to me on the dance floor? 'Honey, you're dancing too close?'

JACK: Well, it was – hot in the Gym and the – floor was crowded.

ROSA: When my girl friend was teaching me how to dance, I asked her, 'How do you know which way the boy's going to move?' And she said, 'You've got to feel how he's going to move with your body!' I said, 'How do you feel with your body?' And she said, 'By pressing up close!' – That's why I pressed up close! I didn't realize that I was – Ha, ha! Now you're blushing! Don't go *away!* – And a few minutes later you said to me, 'Gee, you're beautiful!' I said, 'Excuse me,' and ran to the ladies' room. Do you know why? To look at myself in the mirror! And I saw that I was! For the first time in my life I was beautiful! You'd made me beautiful when you *said* that I was!

JACK [*humbly*]: You *are* beautiful, Rosa! So much, I . . .

ROSA: *You've* changed, *too*. You've stopped laughing and joking. Why have you gotten so old and serious, Jack?

JACK: Well, honey, you're sort of . . .

ROSA: What am I 'sort of'?

JACK [*finding the exact word*]: *Wild!* [*She laughs. He seizes the bandaged wrist.*] I didn't know nothing like this was going to happen.

ROSA: Oh, that, that's nothing! I'll take the handkerchief off and you can forget it.

JACK: How could you do a thing like that over me? I'm – nothing!

ROSA: Everybody is nothing until you love them!

JACK: Give me that handkerchief. I want to show it to my shipmates. I'll say, 'This is the blood of a beautiful girl who cut her wrist with a knife because she loved me!'

ROSA: Don't be so pleased with yourself. It's mostly Mercurochrome!

SERAFINA [*violently, from the dark room adjoining*]: *Stai zitta!* – *Cretina!*

[*Rosa and Jack draw abruptly apart.*]

JACK [*fearfully*]: I knew somebody was here!

ROSA [*sweetly and delicately*]: Mama? Are you in there, Mama?

SERAFINA: No, no, no, I'm not, I'm dead and buried!

ROSA: Yes, Mama's in there!

JACK: Well, I – better go and – wait outside for a – while . . .

ROSA: You stay right here! – Mama? – Jack is with me. – Are you dressed up nicely? [*There is no response.*] Why's it so dark in here? – Jack, open the shutters! – I want to introduce you to my mother . . .

JACK: Hadn't I better go and . . .

ROSA: No. Open the shutters!

[*The shutters are opened and Rosa draws apart the curtains between the two rooms. Sunlight floods the scene. Serafina is revealed slumped in a chair at her work table in the dining-room near the Singer sewing machine. She is grotesquely surrounded by the dummies, as though she had been holding a silent conference with them. Her appearance, in slovenly déshabillé, is both comic and shocking.*]

ROSA [*terribly embarrassed*]: Mama, Mama, you said you were dressed up pretty! Jack, stay out for a minute! What's happened, Mama?

[*Jack remains in the parlour. Rosa pulls the curtains, snatches a robe and flings it over Serafina. She brushes Serafina's hair back from her sweat-gleaming face, rubs her face with a handkerchief and dusts it with powder. Serafina submits to this cosmetic enterprise with a dazed look.*]

ROSA [*gesturing vertically*]: Su, su, su, su, su, su, su, su, su!

[*Serafina sits up slightly in her chair, but she is still looking stupefied. Rosa returns to the parlour and opens the curtains again.*]

ROSA: Come in, Jack! Mama is ready to meet you!

[*Rosa trembles with eagerness as Jack advances nervously from the parlour. But before he enters Serafina collapses again into her slumped position, with a low moan.*]

ROSA [*violently*]: Mama, Mama, su, Mama! [*Serafina sits half erect.*] She didn't sleep good last night. – Mama, this is Jack Hunter!

JACK: Hello, Mrs Delle Rose. It sure is a pleasure to meet you.

[*There is a pause. Serafina stares indifferently at the boy.*]

ROSA: Mama, Mama, say something!

JACK: Maybe your Mama wants me to . . . [*He makes an awkward gesture toward the door.*]

ROSA: No, no, Mama's just tired. Mama makes dresses; she made a whole lot of dresses for the graduation! How many, Mama, how many graduation dresses did you have to make?

SERAFINA [*dully*]: Fa niente . . .

JACK: I was hoping to see you at the graduation, Mrs Delle Rose.

ROSA: I guess that Mama was too worn out to go.

SERAFINA: Rosa, shut the front door, shut it and lock it. There was a – policeman . . . [*There is a pause.*] What? – What?

JACK: My sister was graduating. My mother was there and my aunt was there – a whole bunch of cousins – I was hoping that you could – all – get together . . .

ROSA: Jack brought you some flowers.

JACK: I hope you are partial to roses as much as I am. [*He hands her the bouquet. She takes them absently.*]

ROSA: Mama, say something, say something simple like 'Thanks'.

SERAFINA: Thanks.

ROSA: Jack, tell Mama about the graduation; describe it to her.

JACK: My mother said it was just like fairyland.

ROSA: Tell her what the boys wore!

JACK: What did – what did they wear?

ROSA: Oh, you know what they wore. They wore blue coats and white pants and each one had a carnation! And there were three couples that did an old-fashioned dance, a minuet, Mother, to Mendelssohn's *Spring Song*! Wasn't it lovely, Jack? But one girl slipped; she wasn't used to long dresses! She slipped and fell on her – ho, ho! Wasn't it funny, Jack, wasn't it, wasn't it, Jack?

JACK [*worriedly*]: I think that your Mama . . .

ROSA: Oh, my prize, my prize, I have forgotten my prize!

JACK: Where is it?

ROSA: You set them down by the sewing sign when you looked for the key.

JACK: Aw, excuse me, I'll get them. [*He goes out through the parlour. Rosa turns to her mother and kneels by her chair.*]

ROSA [*in a terrified whisper*]: Mama, something has happened! What has happened, Mama? Can't you tell me, Mama? Is it because of this morning? Look. I took the bandage off, it was only a scratch! So, Mama, forget it! Think it was just a bad dream that never happened! Oh, Mama! [*She gives her several quick kisses on the forehead. Jack returns with two big books tied in white satin ribbon.*]

JACK: Here they are.

ROSA: Look what I got, Mama.

SERAFINA [*dully*]: What?

ROSA: The Digest of Knowledge!

JACK: Everything's in them, from Abracadabra to Zoo! My sister was jealous. She just got a diploma!

SERAFINA [*rousing a bit*]: Diploma, where is it? Didn't you get no diploma?

ROSA: Si, si, Mama! Eccolo! Guarda, guarda! [*She holds up the diploma tied in ribbon.*]

SERAFINA: Va bene. – Put it in the drawer with your father's clothes.

JACK: Mrs Delle Rose, you should be very, very proud of your daughter. She stood in front of the crowd and recited a poem.

ROSA: Yes, I did. Oh, I was so excited!

JACK: And Mrs Delle Rose, your daughter, Rosa, was so pretty when she walked on the stage – that people went 'Ooooooo-ooo!' – like that! Y'know what I mean? They all went – 'Oooooooooo!' Like a – like a – *wind* had – blown over! Because your daughter, Rosa, was so – *lovely* looking! [*He has crouched over to Serafina to deliver this description close to her face. Now he straightens up and smiles proudly at Rosa.*] How does it feel to be the mother of the prettiest girl in the world?

ROSA [*suddenly bursting into pure delight*]: Ha, ha, ha, ha, ha, ha!
[*She throws her head back in rapture.*]

SERAFINA [*rousing*]: Hush!

ROSA: Ha, ha, ha, ha, ha, ha, ha, ha, ha, ha! [*She cannot control her ecstatic laughter. She presses her hand to her mouth but the laughter still bubbles out.*]

SERAFINA [*suddenly rising in anger*]: Pazza, pazza, pazza! Finiscila! Basta, via! [*Rosa whirls around to hide her convulsions of joy. To Jack:*] Put the prize books in the parlour, and shut the front door; there was a policeman come here because of – some trouble . . . [*Jack takes the books.*]

ROSA: Mama, I've never seen you like this! What will Jack think, Mama?

SERAFINA: Why do I care what Jack thinks? – You wild, wild crazy thing, you – with the eyes of your – father . . .

JACK [*returning*]: Yes, ma'am, Mrs Delle Rose, you certainly got a right to be very proud of your daughter.

SERAFINA [*after a pause*]: I am proud of the – memory of her – father. – He was a baron . . . [*Rosa takes Jack's arm.*] And who are *you*? What are you? – per piacere!

ROSA: Mama, I just introduced him; his name is Jack Hunter.

SERAFINA: Hunt-er?

JACK: Yes, ma'am, Hunter. Jack Hunter.

SERAFINA: What are you hunting? – Jack?

ROSA: Mama!

SERAFINA: What all of 'em are hunting? To have a good time, and the Devil cares who pays for it? I'm sick of men, I'm almost as sick of men as I am of wimmen. – Rosa, get out while I talk to this boy!

ROSA: I didn't bring Jack here to be insulted!

JACK: Go on, honey, and let your Mama talk to me. I think your Mama has just got a slight wrong – impression . . .

SERAFINA [*ominously*]: Yes, I got an impression!

ROSA: I'll get dressed! Oh, Mama, don't spoil it for me! – the happiest day of my life! [*She goes into the back of the house.*]

JACK [*after an awkward pause*]: Mrs Delle Rose . . .

SERAFINA [*correcting his pronunciation*]: Delle Rose!

JACK: Mrs Delle Rose, I'm sorry about all this. Believe me, Mrs Delle Rose, the last thing I had in mind was getting mixed up in a family situation. I come home after three months to sea, I docked at New Orleans, and come here to see my folks. My sister was going to a high school dance. She took me with her, and there I met your daughter.

SERAFINA: What did you do?

JACK: At the high school dance? We danced! My sister had told me that Rosa had a very strict mother and wasn't allowed to go on dates with boys so when it was over, I said, 'I'm sorry you're not allowed to go out.' And she said, 'Oh! What gave you the idea I *wasn't*!' So then I thought my sister had made a mistake and I made a date with her for the next night.

SERAFINA: What did you do the next night?

JACK: The next night we went to the movies.

SERAFINA: And what did you do – that night?

JACK: At the movies? We ate a bag of popcorn and watched the movie!

SERAFINA: She came home at midnight and said she had been with a girl-friend studying 'civics.'

JACK: Whatever story she told you, it ain't my fault!

SERAFINA: And the night after that?

JACK: Last Tuesday? We went roller skating!

SERAFINA: And afterwards?

JACK: After the skating? We went to a drug store and had an ice cream soda!

SERAFINA: Alone?

JACK: At the drug store? No. It was crowded. And the skating rink was full of people skating!

SERAFINA: You mean that you haven't been alone with my Rosa?

JACK: Alone or not alone, what's the point of that question? I still don't see the point of it.

SERAFINA: We are Sicilians. We don't leave the girls with the boys they're not engaged to!

JACK: Mrs Delle Rose, this is the United States.

SERAFINA: But we are Sicilians, and we are not cold-blooded. – My girl is a *virgin*! She *is* – or she *was* – I would like to know – *which*!

JACK: Mrs Delle Rose! I got to tell you something. You might not believe it. It is a hard thing to say. But I am – *also* a – *virgin* . . .

SERAFINA: *What? No.* I do not believe it.

JACK: Well, it's true, though. This is the first time – I . . .

SERAFINA: First time you *what*?

JACK: The first time I really wanted to . . .

SERAFINA: Wanted to what?

JACK: Make – love . . .

SERAFINA: You? A sailor?

JACK [*sighing deeply*]: Yes, ma'am. I had opportunities to! – But I – always thought of my mother . . . I always asked myself, would she or would she not – think – this or that person was – decent!

SERAFINA: But with my daughter, my Rosa, your mother tells you *okay*? – go ahead, son!

JACK: Mrs Delle Rose! [*with embarrassment*] – Mrs Delle Rose, I . . .

SERAFINA: Two weeks ago I was slapping her hands for scratching mosquito bites. She rode a bicycle to school. Now all at once – I've got a wild thing in the house. She says she's in love. And you? Do you say *you're* in love?

JACK [*solemnly*]: Yes, ma'am, I do, I'm in love! – very much . . .

SERAFINA: Bambini, tutti due, bambini!

[*Rosa comes out, dressed for the picnic.*]

ROSA: I'm ready for Diamond Key!

SERAFINA: Go out on the porch. Diamond Key!

ROSA [with a sarcastic curtsy]: Yes, Mama!

SERAFINA: What are you? Catholic?

JACK: Me? Yes, ma'am, Catholic.

SERAFINA: You don't look Catholic to me!

ROSA [shouting, from the door]: Oh, God, Mama, how do Catholics look? How do they look different from anyone else?

SERAFINA: Stay out till I call you! [Rosa crosses to the bird bath and prays. Serafina turns to Jack.] Turn around, will you?

JACK: Do what, ma'am?

SERAFINA: I said, turn around! [Jack awkwardly turns around.] Why do they make them Navy pants so tight?

ROSA [listening in the yard]: Oh, my God . . .

JACK [flushing]: That's a question you'll have to ask the Navy, Mrs Delle Rose.

SERAFINA: And that gold earring, what's the gold earring for?

ROSA [yelling from the door]: For crossing the equator, Mama; he crossed it three times. He was initiated into the court of Neptune and gets to wear a gold earring! He's a shellback!

[Serafina springs up and crosses to slam the porch door. Rosa runs despairingly around the side of the house and leans, exhausted with closed eyes, against the trunk of a palm tree. The Strega creeps into the yard, listening.]

SERAFINA: You see what I got. A wild thing in the house!

JACK: Mrs Delle Rose, I guess that Sicilians are very emotional people . . .

SERAFINA: I want nobody to take advantage of that!

JACK: You got the wrong idea about me, Mrs Delle Rose.

SERAFINA: I know what men want – not to eat popcorn with girls or to slide on ice! And boys are the same, only younger. – Come here. Come here!

[Rosa hears her mother's passionate voice. She rushes from the palm tree to the back door and pounds on it with both fists.]

ROSA: Mama! Mama! Let me in the door, Jack!

JACK: Mrs Delle Rose, your daughter is calling you.

SERAFINA: Let her call! – Come here. [*She crosses to the shrine of Our Lady.*] *Come here!*

[*Despairing of the back door, Rosa rushes around to the front. A few moments later she pushes open the shutters of the window in the wall and climbs half in. Jack crosses apprehensively to Serafina before the Madonna.*]

SERAFINA: You said you're Catholic, ain't you?

JACK: Yes, ma'am.

SERAFINA: Then kneel down in front of Our Lady!

JACK: Do – do what, did you say?

SERAFINA: I said to get down on your knees in front of Our Lady!

[*Rosa groans despairingly in the window. Jack kneels awkwardly upon the hassock.*]

ROSA: Mama, Mama, *now* what?!

[*Serafina rushes to the window, pushes Rosa out and slams the shutters.*]

SERAFINA [*returning to Jack*]: Now say after me what I say!

JACK: Yes, ma'am.

[*Rosa pushes the shutters open again.*]

SERAFINA: I promise the Holy Mother that I will respect the innocence of the daughter of . . .

ROSA [*in anguish*]: Ma-maaa!

SERAFINA: Get back out of that window! – Well? Are you gonna say it?

JACK: Yes, ma'am. What was it, again?

SERAFINA: I promise the Holy Mother . . .

JACK: I promise the Holy Mother . . .

SERAFINA: As I hope to be saved by the Blessed Blood of
Jesus . . .

JACK: As I hope to be saved by the . . .

SERAFINA: Blessed Blood of . . .

JACK: Jesus . . .

SERAFINA: That I will respect the innocence of the daughter,
Rosa, of Rosario delle Rose.

JACK: That I will respect the innocence – of – Rosa . . .

SERAFINA: Cross yourself! [*He crosses himself.*] Now get up
get up, get up! I am satisfied now . . .

[*Rosa jumps through the window and rushes to Serafina with
arms outflung and wild cries of joy.*]

SERAFINA: Let me go, let me breathe! [*Outside the Strega
cackles derisively.*]

ROSA: Oh, wonderful Mama, don't breathe! Oh, Jack! *Kiss*
Mama! *Kiss Mama!* Mama, please kiss Jack!

SERAFINA: Kiss? Me? No, no, no, no! – Kiss my *hand* . . .

[*She offers her hand, shyly, and Jack kisses it with a loud smack.
Rosa seizes the wine bottle.*]

ROSA: Mama, get some wine glasses!

[*Serafina goes for the glasses, and Rosa suddenly turns to Jack.
Out of her mother's sight, she passionately grabs hold of his
hand and presses it, first to her throat, then to her lips and finally
to her breast. Jack snatches his hand away as Serafina returns
with the glasses. Voices are heard calling from the highway.*]

VOICES OUTSIDE: Ro-osa! – Ro-osa! – Ro-osa!

[*A car horn is heard blowing.*]

SERAFINA: Oh, I forgot the graduation present.

[*She crouches down before the bureau and removes a fancily
wrapped package from its bottom drawer. The car horn is
honking, and the voices are calling.*]

ROSA: They're calling for us! *Coming!* Jack! [*She flies out the door, calling back to her mother.*] G'bye, Mama!

JACK [*following Rosa*]: Good-bye, Mrs Delle Rose!

SERAFINA [*vaguely*]: It's a Bulova wrist watch with seventeen jewels in it . . . [*She realizes that she is alone.*] Rosa! [*She goes to the door, still holding out the present. Outside the car motor roars, and the voices shout as the car goes off. Serafina stumbles outside, shielding her eyes with one hand, extending the gift with the other.*] Rosa, Rosa, your present! Regalo, regalo – tesoro!

[*But the car has started off, with a medley of voices shouting farewells, which fade quickly out of hearing. Serafina turns about vaguely in the confusing sunlight and gropes for the door. There is a derisive cackle from the witch next door. Serafina absently opens the package and removes the little gold watch. She winds it and then holds it against her ear. She shakes it and holds it again to her ear. Then she holds it away from her and glares at it fiercely.*]

SERAFINA [*pounding her chest three times*]: Tick – tick – tick! [*She goes to the Madonna and faces it.*] Speak to me, Lady! Oh, Lady, give me a sign!

[*The scene dims out.*]

ACT TWO

SCENE I

It is two hours later the same day.

Serafina comes out onto the porch, barefooted, wearing a rayon slip. Great shadows have appeared beneath her eyes; her face and throat gleam with sweat. There are dark stains of wine on the rayon slip. It is difficult for her to stand, yet she cannot sit still. She makes a sick moaning sound in her throat almost continually.

A hot wind rattles the cane-brake. Vivi, the little girl, comes up to the porch to stare at Serafina as at a strange beast in a cage. Vivi is chewing a liquorice stick which stains her mouth and her fingers. She stands chewing and staring. Serafina evades her stare. She wearily drags a broken grey wicker chair down off the porch, all the way out in front of the house, and sags heavily into it. It sits awry on a broken leg.

Vivi sneaks toward her. Serafina lurches about to face her angrily. The child giggles and scampers back to the porch.

SERAFINA [*sinking back into the chair*]: Oh, Lady, Lady, Lady, give me a – sign . . . [*She looks up at the white glare of the sky.*]

[*Father De Leo approaches the house. Serafina crouches low in the chair to escape his attention. He knocks at the door. Receiving no answer, he looks out into the yard, sees her, and approaches her chair. He comes close to address her with a gentle severity.*]

FATHER DE LEO: Buon giorno, Serafina.
SERAFINA [*faintly, with a sort of disgust*]: Giorno . . .
FATHER DE LEO: I'm surprised to see you sitting outdoors like this. What is that thing you're wearing? – I think it's an

61

undergarment! – It's hanging off one shoulder, and your head, Serafina, looks as if you had stuck it in a bucket of oil. Oh, I see now why the other ladies of the neighbourhood aren't taking their afternoon naps! They find it more entertaining to sit on the porches and watch the spectacle you are putting on for them! – Are you listening to me? – I must tell you that the change in your appearance and behaviour since Rosario's death is shocking – shocking! A woman can be dignified in her grief but when it's carried too far it becomes a sort of self-indulgence. Oh, I knew this was going to happen when you broke the Church law and had your husband cremated! [*Serafina lurches up from the chair and shuffles back to the porch. Father De Leo follows her.*] – Set up a little idolatrous shrine in your house and give worship to a bottle of ashes. [*She sinks down upon the steps.*] – Are you listening to me?

[*Two women have appeared on the embankment and descend toward the house. Serafina lurches heavily up to meet them, like a weary bull turning to face another attack.*]

SERAFINA: You ladies, what you want? I don't do sewing! Look, I quit doing sewing. [*She pulls down the 'SEWING' sign and hurls it away.*] Now you got places to go, you ladies, go places! Don't hang around front of my house!

FATHER DE LEO: The ladies want to be friendly.

SERAFINA: Naw, they don't come to be friendly. They think they know something that Serafina don't know; they think I got *these* on my head! [*She holds her fingers like horns at either side of her forehead.*] Well, I ain't got them! [*She goes padding back out in front of the house. Father De Leo follows.*]

FATHER DE LEO: You called me this morning in distress over something.

SERAFINA: I called you this morning but now it is afternoon.

FATHER DE LEO: I had to christen the grandson of the Mayor.

SERAFINA: The Mayor's important people, not Serafina!

FATHER DE LEO: You don't come to confession.

SERAFINA [*starting back toward the porch*]: No, I don't come, I don't go, I – Ohhh! [*She pulls up one foot and hops on the other.*]

FATHER DE LEO: You stepped on something?

SERAFINA [*dropping down on the steps*]: No, no, no, no, no, I don't step on – noth'n . . .

FATHER DE LEO: Come in the house. We'll wash it with antiseptic. [*She lurches up and limps back toward the house.*] Walking barefooted you will get it infected.

SERAFINA: Fa niente . . .

[*At the top of the embankment a little boy runs out with a red kite and flourishes it in the air with rigid gestures, as though he were giving a distant signal. Serafina shades her eyes with a palm to watch the kite, and then, as though its motions conveyed a shocking message, she utters a startled soft cry and staggers back to the porch. She leans against a pillar, running her hand rapidly and repeatedly through her hair. Father De Leo approaches her again, somewhat timidly.*]

FATHER DE LEO: Serafina?

SERAFINA: Che, che, che cosa vuole?

FATHER DE LEO: I am thirsty. Will you go in the house and get me some water?

SERAFINA: Go in. Get you some water. The faucet is working. – I can't go in the house.

FATHER DE LEO: Why can't you go in the house?

SERAFINA: The house has a tin roof on it. I got to breathe.

FATHER DE LEO: You can breathe in the house.

SERAFINA: No, I can't breathe in the house. The house has a tin roof on it and I . . .

[*The Strega has been creeping through the cane-brake pretending to search for a chicken.*]

THE STREGA: Chick, chick, chick, chick, chick? [*She crouches to peer under the house.*]

SERAFINA: What's that? Is that the . . . ? Yes, the Strega! [*She picks up a flower pot containing a dead plant and crosses the yard.*] Strega! Strega! [*The Strega looks up, retreating a little.*] Yes, you, I mean you! You ain't look for no chick! Getta hell out of my yard! [*The Strega retreats, viciously muttering, back into the cane-brake. Serafina makes the protective sign of the horns with her fingers. The goat bleats.*]

FATHER DE LEO: You have no friends, Serafina.

SERAFINA: I don't want friends.

FATHER DE LEO: You are still a young woman. Eligible for – loving and – bearing again! I remember you dressed in pale blue silk at Mass one Easter morning, yes, like a lady wearing a – piece of the – weather! Oh, how proudly you walked, *too* proudly! – But now you crouch and shuffle about bare-footed; you live like a convict, dressed in the rags of a convict. You have no companions; women you don't mix with. You . . .

SERAFINA: No, I don't mix with them women. [*glaring at the women on the embankment*] The dummies I got in my house, I mix with them better because they don't make up no lies! – What kind of women are them? [*mimicking fiercely*] 'Eee, Papa, eeee, baby, eee, me, me, me!' At thirty years old they got no more use for the letto matrimoniale, no. The big bed goes to the basement! They got little beds from Sears Roe-buck and sleep on their bellies!

FATHER DE LEO: Attenzione!

SERAFINA: They make the life without glory. Instead of the heart they got the deep-freeze in the house. The men, they don't feel no glory, not in the house with them women; they go to the bars, fight in them, get drunk, get fat, put horns on the women because the women don't give them the love which is glory. – I did, I give him the glory. To me the big bed was beautiful like a religion. Now I lie on it with dreams, with memories only! But it is still beautiful to me and I don't believe that the man in my heart gave me horns! [*The women whisper.*] What, what are they saying? Does ev'ry-body know something that I don't know? – No, all I want is a sign, a sign from Our Lady, to tell me the lie is a lie! And then I . . . [*The women laugh on the embankment. Serafina starts fiercely toward them. They scatter.*] Squeak, squeak, squawk, squawk! Hens – like water thrown on them! [*There is the sound of mocking laughter.*]

FATHER DE LEO: People are laughing at you on all the porches.

SERAFINA: I'm laughing, too. Listen to me, I'm laughing! [*She breaks into loud, false laughter, first from the porch, then from the foot of the embankment, then crossing in front of the house.*] Ha, ha, ha, ha, ha, ha, ha! Now everybody is laughing. Ha, ha, ha, ha, ha, ha!

FATHER DE LEO: Zitta ora! – Think of your daughter.

SERAFINA [*understanding the word 'daughter'*]: You, you think of my daughter! To-day you give out the diplomas, to-day at the high school you give out the prizes, diplomas! You give to my daughter a set of books call the Digest of Know-ledge! What does she know? How to be cheap already? – Oh, yes, that is what to learn, how to be cheap and to cheat! – You know what they do at this high school? They ruin the girls there! They give the spring dance because the girls are man-crazy. And there at that dance my daughter goes with a sailor that has in his ear a gold ring! And pants so tight that a woman ought not to look at him! This morning, this morning she cuts with a knife her wrist if I don't let her go!– Now all of them gone to some island, they call it a picnic, all of them, gone in a – boat!

FATHER DE LEO: There *was* a school picnic, chaperoned by the teachers.

SERAFINA: Oh, lo so, lo so! The man-crazy old-maid teachers! – They all run wild on the island!

FATHER DE LEO: Serafina delle Rose! [*He picks up the chair by the back and hauls it to the porch when she starts to resume her seat.*] – I *command* you to go in the house.

SERAFINA: Go in the house? I will. I will go in the house if you will answer one question. – Will you answer one question?

FATHER DE LEO: I will if I know the answer.

SERAFINA: Aw, you know the answer! – You used to hear the confessions of my husband. [*She turns to face the priest.*]

FATHER DE LEO: Yes, I heard his confessions . . .

SERAFINA [*with difficulty*]: Did he ever speak to you of a woman?

> [*A child cries out and races across in front of the house. Father De Leo picks up his panama hat. Serafina paces slowly toward him. He starts away from the house.*]

SERAFINA [*rushing after him*]: Aspettate! Aspettate un momento!

FATHER DE LEO [*fearfully, not looking at her*]: Che volete?

SERAFINA: Rispondetemi! [*She strikes her breast.*] Did he speak of a woman to you?

FATHER DE LEO: You know better than to ask me such a question. I don't break the Church laws. The secrets of the confessional are sacred to me. [*He walks away.*]

SERAFINA [*pursuing and clutching his arm*]: I got to know. You could tell me.

FATHER DE LEO: Let go of me, Serafina!

SERAFINA: Not till you tell me, Father. Father, you tell me, please tell me! Or I will go mad! [*in a fierce whisper*] I will go back in the house and smash the urn with the ashes – if you don't tell me! I will go mad with the doubt in my heart and I will smash the urn and scatter the ashes – of my husband's body!

FATHER DE LEO: What could I tell you? If you would not believe the known facts about him . . .

SERAFINA: Known facts, who knows the known facts?

> [*The neighbour women have heard the argument and begin to crowd around, muttering in shocked whispers at Serafina's lack of respect.*]

FATHER DE LEO [*frightened*]: Lasciatemi, lasciatemi stare!– Oh, Serafina, I am too old for this – please! – Everybody is . . .

SERAFINA [*in a fierce, hissing whisper*]: Nobody knew my rose of the world but me and now they can lie because the rose ain't living. They want the marble urn broken; they want me to smash it. They want the rose ashes scattered because I had too much glory. They don't want glory like *that* in nobody's heart. They want – mouse-squeaking! – known facts. – Who knows the known facts? You – padres – wear black because of the fact that the facts are known by nobody!

FATHER DE LEO: Oh, Serafina! There are people watching!

SERAFINA: Let them watch something. That will be a change for them. – It's been a long time I wanted to break out like this and now I . . .

FATHER DE LEO: I am too old a man; I am not strong enough. I am sixty-seven years old! Must I call for help, now?

SERAFINA: Yes, call! Call for help, but I won't let you go till you tell me!

FATHER DE LEO: You're not a respectable woman.

SERAFINA: No, I'm not a respectable; I'm a woman.

FATHER DE LEO: No, you are not a woman. You are an animal!

SERAFINA: Sì, sì, animale! Sono animale! Animale. Tell them all, shout it all to them, up and down the whole block! The widow Delle Rose is not respectable, she is not even a woman she is an animal! She is attacking the priest! She will tear the black suit off him unless he tells her the whores in this town are lying to her!

[*The neighbour women have been drawing closer as the argument progresses, and now they come to Father De Leo's rescue and assist him to get away from Serafina, who is on the point of attacking him bodily. He cries out, 'Officer! Officer!' but the women drag Serafina from him and lead him away with comforting murmurs.*]

SERAFINA [*striking her wrists together*]: Yes, it's me, it's me! !

67

Lock me up, lock me, lock me up! Or I will – *smash!* – the marble . . . [*She throws her head far back and presses her fists to her eyes. Then she rushes crazily to the steps and falls across them.*]

ASSUNTA: Serafina! Figlia! Figlia! Andiamo a casa!

SERAFINA: Leave me alone, old woman.

[*She returns slowly to the porch steps and sinks down on them, sitting like a tired man, her knees spread apart and her head cupped in her hands. The children steal back around the house. A little boy shoots a bean-shooter at her. She starts up with a cry. The children scatter, shrieking. She sinks back down on the steps, then leans back, staring up at the sky, her body rocking.*]

SERAFINA: Oh, Lady, Lady, Lady, give me a sign!

[*As if in mocking answer, a novelty salesman appears and approaches the porch. He is a fat man in a seersucker suit and a straw hat with a yellow, red, and purple band. His face is beet-red and great moons of sweat have soaked through the armpits of his jacket. His shirt is lavender, and his tie, pale blue with great yellow polka dots, is a butterfly bow. His entrance is accompanied by a brief, satiric strain of music.*]

THE SALESMAN: Good afternoon, lady. [*She looks up slowly. The salesman talks sweetly, as if reciting a prayer.*] I got a little novelty here which I am offering to just a few lucky people at what we call an introductory price. Know what I mean? Not a regular price but a price which is less than what it costs to manufacture the article, a price we are making for the sake of introducing the product in the Gulf Coast territory. Lady, this thing here that I'm droppin' right in youah lap is bigger than television; it's going to revolutionize the domestic life of America. – Now I don't do house to house canvassing. I sell directly to merchants but when I stopped over there to have my car serviced, I seen you taking the air on the steps and I thought I would just drop over and . . .

[*There is the sound of a big truck stopping on the highway, and a man's voice, Alvaro's, is heard, shouting.*]

ALVARO: Hey! Hey, you road hog!

THE SALESMAN [*taking a sample out of his bag*]: Now, lady, this little article has a deceptive appearance. First of all, I want you to notice how *compact* it is. It takes up no more space than . . .

[*Alvaro comes down from the embankment. He is about twenty-five years old, dark and very good looking. He is one of those Mediterranean types that resemble glossy young bulls. He is short in stature, has a massively sculptural torso and bluish-black curls. His face and manner are clownish; he has a charming awkwardness. There is a startling, improvised air about him; he frequently seems surprised at his own speeches and actions, as though he had not at all anticipated them. At the moment when we first hear his voice the sound of a timpani begins, at first very pianissimo, but building up as he approaches, till it reaches a vibrant climax with his appearance to Serafina beside the house.*]

ALVARO: Hey.

THE SALESMAN [*without glancing at him*]: Hay is for horses! – Now, madam, you see what happens when I press this button?

[*The article explodes in Serafina's face. She slaps it away with an angry cry. At the same time Alvaro advances, trembling with rage, to the porch steps. He is sweating and stammering with pent-up fury at a world of frustrations which are temporarily localized in the gross figure of this salesman.*]

ALVARO: Hey, you! Come here! What the hell's the idea, back there at that curve? You make me drive off the highway!

THE SALESMAN [*to Serafina*]: Excuse me for just one minute. [*He wheels menacingly about to face Alvaro.*] Is something giving you gas pains, Maccaroni?

ALVARO: My name is not Maccaroni.

THE SALESMAN: All right. Spaghetti.

ALVARO [*almost sobbing with passion*]: I am not maccaroni. I am not spaghetti. I am a human being that drives a truck of bananas. I drive a truck of bananas for the Southern Fruit Company for a living, not to play cowboys and Indians on no highway with no rotten road hog. You got a 4-lane highway between Pass Christian and here. I give you the sign to pass me. You tail me and give me the horn. You yell 'Wop' at me and 'Dago'. 'Move over, Wop, move over, Dago.' Then at the goddam curve, you go pass me and make me drive off the highway and yell back 'Son of a bitch of a Dago!' I don't like that, no, no! And I am glad you stop here. Take the cigar from your mouth, take out the cigar!

THE SALESMAN: Take it out for me, greaseball.

ALVARO: If I take it out I will push it down your throat. I got three dependants! If I fight, I get fired, but I will fight and get fired. Take out the cigar!

[*Spectators begin to gather at the edge of the scene. Serafina stares at the truck driver, her eyes like a somnambule's. All at once she utters a low cry and seems about to fall.*]

ALVARO: Take out the cigar, take out, take out the cigar!

[*He snatches the cigar from the salesman's mouth and the salesman brings his knee up violently into Alvaro's groin. Bending double and retching with pain, Alvaro staggers over to the porch.*]

THE SALESMAN [*shouting, as he goes off*]: I got your licence number, Maccaroni! I know your boss!

ALVARO [*howling*]: Drop dead! [*He suddenly staggers up the steps.*] Lady, lady, I got to go in the house!

[*As soon as he enters, he bursts into rending sobs, leaning against a wall and shaking convulsively. The spectators outside laugh*] *as they scatter. Serafina slowly enters the house. The screen door rasps loudly on its rusty springs as she lets it swing gradually shut behind her, her eyes remaining fixed with a look of stupefied wonder upon the sobbing figure of the truck driver. We must understand her profound unconscious response to this sudden contact with distress as acute as her own. There is a long pause as the screen door makes its whining, catlike noise swinging shut by degrees.]*

SERAFINA: Somebody's – in my house? [*finally, in a hoarse, tremulous whisper*] What are you – doing in here? Why have you – come in my house?

ALVARO: Oh, lady – leave me alone! – Please – now!

SERAFINA: You – got no business – in here . . .

ALVARO: I got to cry after a fight. I'm sorry, lady. I . . .

[*The sobs still shake him. He leans on a dummy.*]

SERAFINA: Don't lean on my dummy. Sit down if you can't stand up. – What is the matter with you?

ALVARO: I always cry after a fight. But I don't want people to see me. It's not like a man. [*There is a long pause; Serafina's attitude seems to warm toward the man.*]

SERAFINA: A man is not no different from no one else . . . [*All at once her face puckers up, and for the first time in the play Serafina begins to weep, at first soundlessly, then audibly. Soon she is sobbing as loudly as Alvaro. She speaks between sobs.*] – I always cry – when somebody else is crying . . .

ALVARO: No, no, lady, *don't* cry! Why should *you* cry? I will stop. I will stop in a minute. This is not like a man. I am ashamed of myself. I will stop now; please, lady . . .

[*Still crouching a little with pain, a hand clasped to his abdomen, Alvaro turns away from the wall. He blows his nose between two fingers. Serafina picks up a scrap of white voile and gives it to him to wipe his fingers.*]

SERAFINA: Your jacket is torn.

ALVARO [*sobbing*]: My company jacket is torn?

SERAFINA: Yes . . .

ALVARO: Where is it torn?

SERAFINA [sobbing]: Down the – back.

ALVARO: Oh, Dio!

SERAFINA: Take it off. I will sew it up for you. I do – sewing.

ALVARO: Oh, Dio! [sobbing] I got three dependants! [He holds up three fingers and shakes them violently at Serafina.]

SERAFINA: Give me – give me your jacket.

ALVARO: He took down my licence number!

SERAFINA: People are always taking down licence numbers and telephone numbers and numbers that don't mean nothing – all them numbers . . .

ALVARO: Three, three dependants! Not citizens, even! No relief checks, no nothing! [Serafina sobs.] He is going to complain to the boss.

SERAFINA: I wanted to cry all day.

ALVARO: He said he would fire me if I don't stop fighting!

SERAFINA: Stop crying so I can stop crying.

ALVARO: I am a sissy. Excuse me. I am ashame.

SERAFINA: Don't be ashame of nothing, the world is too crazy for people to be ashame in it. I'm not ashame and I had two fights on the street and my daughter called me 'disgusting'. I got to sew this by hand; the machine is broke in a fight with two women.

ALVARO: That's what – they call a cat fight . . . [He blows his nose.]

SERAFINA: Open the shutters, please, for me. I can't see to work. [She has crossed to her work table. He goes over to the window. As he opens the shutters, the light falls across his fine torso, the undershirt clinging wetly to his dark olive skin. Serafina is struck and murmurs: 'Ohhh . . .' There is the sound of music.]

ALVARO: What, lady?

SERAFINA [in a strange voice]: The light on the body was like a man that lived here . . .

ALVARO: Che dice?

72

SERAFINA: Niente. – Ma com'è strano! – Lei è Napoletano? [*She is threading a needle.*]

ALVARO: Io sono Siciliano! [*Serafina sticks her finger with her needle and cries out.*] Che fa?

SERAFINA: I – stuck myself with the – needle! – You had – better wash up . . .

ALVARO: Dov'è il gabinetto?

SERAFINA [*almost inaudibly*]: Dietro. [*She points vaguely back.*]

ALVARO: Con permesso! [*He moves past her. As he does so, she picks up a pair of broken spectacles on the work table. Holding them up by the single remaining side piece, like a lorgnette, she inspects his passing figure with an air of stupefaction. As he goes out, he says:*] A kick like that can have serious consequences! [*He goes into the back of the house.*]

SERAFINA [*after a pause*]: Madonna Santa! – My husband's body, with the head of a *clown*! [*She crosses to the Madonna.*] O Lady, O Lady! [*She makes an imploring gesture.*] Speak to me! – What are you saying? – Please, Lady, I can't hear you! Is it a sign? Is it a sign of something? What does it mean? Oh, *speak to me*, Lady! – Everything is too strange!

[*She gives up the useless entreaty to the impassive statue. Then she rushes to the cupboard, clambers up on a chair and seizes a bottle of wine from the top shelf. But she finds it impossible to descend from the chair. Clasping the dusty bottle to her breast, she crouches there, helplessly whimpering like a child, as Alvaro comes back in.*]

ALVARO: Ciao!

SERAFINA: I can't get up.

ALVARO: You mean you can't get down?

SERAFINA: I mean I – can't get down . . .

ALVARO: Con permesso, Signora! [*He lifts her down from the chair.*]

SERAFINA: Grazie.

ALVARO: I am ashame of what happen. Crying is not like a man. Did anyone see me?

SERAFINA: Nobody saw you but me. To me it don't matter.

ALVARO: You are simpatica, molto! – It was not just the fight that makes me break down. I was like this all to-day! [*He shakes his clenched fists in the air.*]

SERAFINA: You and – me, too! – What was the trouble to-day?

ALVARO: My name is Mangiacavallo which means 'Eat-a-horse'. It's a comical name, I know. Maybe two thousand and seventy years ago one of my grandfathers got so hungry that he ate up a horse! That ain't my fault. Well, to-day at the Southern Fruit Company I find on the pay envelope not 'Mangiacavallo' but 'EAT A HORSE' in big print! Ha, ha, ha, very funny! – I open the pay envelope! In it I find a notice. – The wages have been *garnishee*! You know what garnishee is? [*Serafina nods gravely.*] Garnishee! – Eat a horse! – Road hog! – All in one day is too much! I go crazy, I boil, I cry and I am ashame but I am not able to help it! – Even a Wop truck driver's a human being! And human beings must cry . . .

SERAFINA: Yes, they must cry. I couldn't cry all day but now I have cried and I am feeling much better. – I will sew up the jacket . . .

ALVARO [*licking his lips*]: What is that in your hand? A bottle of vino?

SERAFINA: This is Spumanti. It comes from the house of the family of my husband. The Delle Rose! A very great family. I was a peasant, but I married a baron! – No, I still don't believe it! I married a baron when I didn't have shoes!

ALVARO: Excuse me for asking – but where is the Baron, now? [*Serafina points gravely to the marble urn.*] Where did you say?

SERAFINA: Them're his ashes in that marble urn.

ALVARO: Ma! Scusatemi! Scusatemi! [*crossing himself*] – I hope he is resting in peace.

SERAFINA: It's him you reminded me of – when you opened

the shutters. Not the face but the body. – Please get me some
ice from the icebox in the kitchen. I had a – very bad day . . .

ALVARO: Oh, ice! Yes – ice – I'll get some . . . [*As he goes out,
she looks again through the broken spectacles at him.*]

SERAFINA: *Non posso crederlo!* – A clown of a face like that with
my husband's body!

[*There is the sound of ice being chopped in the kitchen. She
inserts a corkscrew in the bottle but her efforts to open it are
clumsily unsuccessful. Alvaro returns with a little bowl of ice.
He sets it down so hard on the table that a piece flies out. He
scrambles after it, retrieves it and wipes it off on his sweaty
undershirt.*]

SERAFINA: I think the floor would be cleaner!

ALVARO: Scusatemi! – I wash it again?

SERAFINA: Fa niente!

ALVARO: I am a – clean! – I . . .

SERAFINA: Fa niente, niente! – The bottle should be in the ice
but the next best thing is to pour the wine over the bottle.

ALVARO: You mean over the ice?

SERAFINA: I mean over the . . .

ALVARO: Let me open the bottle. Your hands are not used to
rough work. [*She surrenders the bottle to him and regards him
through the broken spectacles again.*]

SERAFINA: These little bits of white voile on the floor are not
from a snowstorm. I been making voile dresses for high school
graduation. – One for my daughter and for thirteen other
girls. – All of the work I'm not sure didn't kill me!

ALVARO: The wine will make you feel better.

[*There is a youthful cry from outside.*]

SERAFINA: There is a wild bunch of boys and girls in this town.
In Sicily the boys would dance with the boys because a girl
and a boy could not dance together unless they was going to

be married. But here they run wild on islands! – boys, girls, man-crazy teachers . . .

ALVARO: Ecco! [*The cork comes off with a loud pop. Serafina cries out and staggers against the table. He laughs. She laughs with him, helplessly, unable to stop, unable to catch her breath.*] – I like a woman that laughs with all her heart.

SERAFINA: And a woman that cries with her heart?

ALVARO: I like everything that a woman does with her heart.

[*Both are suddenly embarrassed and their laughter dies out. Serafina smooths down her rayon slip. He hands her a glass of the sparkling wine with ice in it. She murmurs 'Grazie'.*

Unconsciously the injured finger is lifted again to her lip and she wanders away from the table with the glass held shakily.]

ALVARO [*continuing nervously*]: I see you had a bad day.

SERAFINA: Sono cosi – stanca . . .

ALVARO [*suddenly springing to the window and shouting*]: Hey, you kids, git down off that truck! Keep your hands off them bananas! [*At the words 'truck' and 'bananas' Serafina gasps again and spills some wine on her slip.*] Little buggers! – Scusatemi . . .

SERAFINA: You haul – you haul bananas?

ALVARO: Si, Signora.

SERAFINA: Is it a 10-ton truck?

ALVARO: An 8-ton truck.

SERAFINA: My husband hauled bananas in a 10-ton truck.

ALVARO: Well, he was a baron.

SERAFINA: Do you haul just bananas?

ALVARO: Just bananas. What else would I haul?

SERAFINA: My husband hauled bananas, but underneath the bananas was something else. He was – wild like a – Gipsy. – 'Wild – like a – Gipsy'? Who said that? – I hate to start to remember, and then not remember . . .

[*The dialogue between them is full of odd hesitations, broken sentences and tentative gestures. Both are nervously exhausted*

*after their respective ordeals. Their fumbling communication
has a curious intimacy and sweetness, like the meeting of two
lonely children for the first time. It is oddly luxurious to them
both, luxurious as the first cool wind of evening after a scorching
day. Serafina idly picks up a little Sicilian souvenir cart from
a table.]*

SERAFINA: The priest was against it.

ALVARO: What was the priest against?

SERAFINA: Me keeping the ashes. It was against the Church
law. But I had to have something and that was all I could
have. [*She sets down the cart.*]

ALVARO: I don't see nothing wrong with it.

SERAFINA: You don't?

ALVARO: No! Niente! – The body would've decayed, but
ashes always stay clean.

SERAFINA [*eagerly*]: Si, si, bodies decay, but ashes always stay
clean! Come here. I show you this picture – my wedding.
[*She removes a picture tenderly from the wall.*] Here's me a bride
of fourteen, and this – this – this! [*drumming the picture with her
finger and turning her face to Alvaro with great lustrous eyes*] My
husband! [*There is a pause. He takes the picture from her hand
and holds it first close to his eyes, then far back, then again close
with suspirations of appropriate awe.*] Annnh? – Annnnh? –
Che dice!

ALVARO [*slowly, with great emphasis*]: Che bell'uomo! Che
bell'uomo!

SERAFINA [*replacing the picture*]: A rose of a man. On his chest
he had the tattoo of a rose. [*then, quite suddenly*] – Do you
believe strange things, or do you doubt them?

ALVARO: If strange things didn't happen, I wouldn't be
here. You wouldn't be here. We wouldn't be talking together.

SERAFINA: Davvero! I'll tell you something about the tattoo
of my husband. My husband, he had this rose tattoo on his

chest. One night I woke up with a burning pain on me here. I turn on the light. I look at my naked breast and on it I see the rose tattoo of my husband, on me, on *my* breast, *his* tattoo.

ALVARO: Strano!

SERAFINA: And that was the night that – I got to speak frankly to tell you . . .

ALVARO: Speak frankly! We're grown-up people.

SERAFINA: That was the night I conceived my son – the little boy that was lost when I lost my husband . . .

ALVARO: Che cosa – strana! – Would you be willing to show me the rose tattoo?

SERAFINA: Oh, it's gone now, it only lasted a moment. But I did see it. I saw it clearly. – Do you believe me?

ALVARO: Lo credo!

SERAFINA: I don't know why I told you. But I like what you said. That bodies decay but ashes always stay clean – immacolate! – But, you know, there are some people that want to make everything dirty. Two of them kind of people come in the house to-day and told me a terrible lie in front of the ashes. – So awful a lie that if I thought it was true – I would smash the urn – and throw the ashes away! [*She hurls her glass suddenly to the floor.*] Smash it, *smash it like that!*

ALVARO: Ma! – Baronessa!

[*Serafina seizes a broom and sweeps the fragments of glass away.*]

SERAFINA: And take this broom and sweep them out the back door like so much trash!

ALVARO [*impressed by her violence and a little awed*]: What lie did they tell you?

SERAFINA: No, no, no! I don't want to talk about it! [*She throws down the broom.*] I just want to forget it; it wasn't true, it was false, false, false! – as the hearts of the bitches that told it . . .

ALVARO: Yes. I would forget anything that makes you unhappy.

SERAFINA: The memory of a love don't make you unhappy
unless you believe a lie that makes it dirty. I don't believe in
the lie. The ashes are clean. The memory of the rose in my
heart is perfect! – Your glass is weeping . . .

ALVARO: *Your* glass is weeping too.

[*While she fills his glass, he moves about the room, looking here
and there. She follows him. Each time he picks up an article for
inspection she gently takes it from him and examines it herself
with fresh interest.*]

ALVARO: Cosy little homelike place you got here.

SERAFINA: Oh, it's – molto modesto. – You got a nice place
too?

ALVARO: I got a place with three dependants in it.

SERAFINA: What – dependants?

ALVARO [*counting them on his fingers*]: One old maid sister, one
feeble-minded grandmother, one lush of a pop that's not
worth the powder it takes to blow him to hell. – They got the
parchesi habit. They play the game of parchesi, morning,
night, noon. Passing a bucket of beer around the table . . .

SERAFINA: They got the beer habit, too?

ALVARO: Oh, yes. And the numbers habit. This spring the old
maid sister gets female trouble – mostly mental, I think – she
turns the housekeeping over to the feeble-minded grandmother, a very sweet old lady who don't think it is necessary
to pay the grocery bill so long as there's money to play the
numbers. She plays the numbers. She has a perfect system
except it don't ever work. And the grocery bill goes up, up,
up, up, up! – so high you can't even see it! – To-day the
Ideal Grocery Company garnishees my wages . . . There,
now! I've told you my life . . . [*The parrot squawks. He goes
over to the cage.*] Hello, Polly, how's tricks?

SERAFINA: The name ain't Polly. It ain't a she; it's a he.

ALVARO: How can you tell with all them tail feathers? [*He sticks his finger in the cage, pokes at the parrot and gets bitten.*] Owww!

SERAFINA [*vicariously*]: Ouuu ... [*Alvaro sticks his injured finger in his mouth. Serafina puts her corresponding finger in her mouth. He crosses to the telephone.*] I told you watch out. – What are you calling, a doctor?

ALVARO: I am calling my boss in Biloxi to explain why I'm late.

SERAFINA: The call to Biloxi is a ten-cent call.

ALVARO: Don't worry about it.

SERAFINA: I'm not worried about it. You will pay it.

ALVARO: You got a sensible attitude toward life ... Give me the Southern Fruit Company in Biloxi – seven-eight-seven!

SERAFINA: You are a bachelor. With three dependants? [*She glances below his belt.*]

ALVARO: I'll tell you my hopes and dreams!

SERAFINA: Who? Me?

ALVARO: I am hoping to meet some sensible older lady. Maybe a lady a little bit older than me. – I don't care if she's a little too plump or not such a stylish dresser! [*Serafina self-consciously pulls up a dangling strap.*] The important thing in a lady is understanding. Good sense. And I want her to have a well-furnished house and a profitable little business of some kind ... [*He looks about him significantly.*]

SERAFINA: And such a lady, with a well-furnished house and business, what does she want with a man with three dependants with the parchesi and the beer habit, playing the numbers!

ALVARO: Love and affection! – in a world that is lonely – and cold!

SERAFINA: It might be lonely but I would not say 'cold' on this particular day!

ALVARO: Love and affection is what I got to offer on hot or cold days in this lonely old world and is what I am looking for.

I got nothing else. Mangiacavallo has nothing. In fact, he is the grandson of the village idiot of Ribera!

SERAFINA [*uneasily*]: I see you like to make – jokes!

ALVARO: No, no joke! – Davvero! – He chased my grandmother in a flooded rice field. She slip on a wet rock. – Ecco! Here I am.

SERAFINA: You ought to be more respectful.

ALVARO: What have I got to respect? The rock my grandmother slips on?

SERAFINA: Yourself at least! Don't you work for a living?

ALVARO: If I *don't* work for a living I would respect myself *more*. Baronessa, I am a healthy young man, existing without no love life. I look at the magazine pictures. Them girls in the advertisement – you know what I mean? A little bitty thing here? A little bitty thing there?

[*He touches two portions of his anatomy. The latter portion embarrasses Serafina, who quietly announces:*]

SERAFINA: The call is ten cents for three minutes. Is the line busy?

ALVARO: Not the line, but the boss.

SERAFINA: And the charge for the call goes higher. That ain't the phone of a millionaire you're using!

ALVARO: I think you talk a poor mouth. [*He picks up the piggy bank and shakes it.*] This pig sounds well-fed to me.

SERAFINA: Dimes and quarters.

ALVARO: Dimes and quarters're better than nickels and dimes. [*Serafina rises severely and removes the piggy bank from his grasp.*] Ha, ha, ha! You think I'm a bank robber?

SERAFINA: I think you are maleducato! Just get your boss on the phone or hang the phone up.

ALVARO: What, what! Mr Siccardi? How tricks at the Southern Fruit Comp'ny this hot afternoon? Ha, ha, ha! – Mangiacavallo! – What? You got the complaint already? Sentite, per favore! This road hog was – Mr Siccardi? [*He jiggles the hook; then slowly hangs up.*] A man with three dependants! – out of a job . . . [*There is a pause.*]

SERAFINA: Well, you better ask the operator the charges.

ALVARO: Oofla! A man with three dependants – out of a job!

SERAFINA: I can't see to work no more. I got a suggestion to make. Open the bottom drawer of that there bureau and you will find a shirt in white tissue paper and you can wear that one while I am fixing this. And call for it later.[*He crosses to the bureau.*] – It was made for somebody that never called for it. [*He removes the package.*] Is there a name pinned to it?

ALVARO: Yes, it's . . .

SERAFINA [*fiercely, but with no physical movement*]: Don't tell me the name! Throw it away, out of the window!

ALVARO: Perchè?

SERAFINA: Throw it, throw it away!

ALVARO [*crumpling the paper and throwing it through the window*]: Ecco fatto! [*There is a distant cry of children as he unwraps the package and holds up the rose silk shirt, exclaiming in Latin delight at the luxury of it.*] Colore di rose! Seta! Seta pura! – Oh, this shirt is too good for Mangiacavallo! Everything here is too good for Mangiacavallo!

SERAFINA: Nothing's too good for a man if the man is good.

ALVARO: The grandson of a village idiot is not that good.

SERAFINA: No matter whose grandson you are, put it on; you are welcome to wear it.

ALVARO [*slipping voluptuously into the shirt*]: Sssssssss!

SERAFINA: How does it feel, the silk, on you?

ALVARO: It feels like a girl's hands on me! [*There is a pause, while he shows her the whiteness of his teeth.*]

SERAFINA [*holding up her broken spectacles*]: It will make you less trouble.

ALVARO: There is nothing more beautiful than a gift between people! – Now you are smiling! – You like me a little bit better?

SERAFINA [*slowly and tenderly*]: You know what they should

of done when you was a baby? They should of put tape on
your ears to hold them back so when you grow up they
wouldn't stick out like the wings of a little kewpie! [*She
touches his ear, a very slight touch, betraying too much of her heart.
Both laugh a little and she turns away, embarrassed.*]

[*Outside the goat bleats and there is the sound of splintering
timber. One of the children races into the front yard, crying
out.*]

SALVATORE: Mizz' Dell' Rose! The black goat's in your
yard!

SERAFINA: Il becco della strega!

[*Serafina dashes to the window, throws the shutters violently
open and leans way out. This time, she almost feels relief in this
distraction. The interlude of the goat chase has a quality of
crazed exaltation. Outside is heard the wild bleating of the
goat and the jingling of his harness.*]

SERAFINA: Miei pomodori! Guarda i miei pomodori!

THE STREGA [*entering the front yard with a broken length of rope,
calling out*]: Heyeh, Billy! Heyeh, Heyeh, Billy!

SERAFINA [*making the sign of horns with her fingers*]: There is the
Strega! She lets the goat in my yard to eat my tomatoes!
[*backing from the window*] She has the eye; she has the malocchio, and so does the goat! The goat has the evil eye, too.
He got in my yard the night that I lost Rosario and my boy!
Madonna, Madonna mia! Get that goat out of my yard! [*She
retreats to the Madonna, making the sign of the horns with her
fingers, while the goat chase continues outside.*]

ALVARO: Now take it easy! I will catch the black goat and give
him a kick that he will never forget!

[*Alvaro runs out the front door and joins in the chase. The little
boy is clapping together a pair of tin pan lids which sound like
symbals. The effect is weird and beautiful with the wild cries of*

the children and the goat's bleating. Serafina remains anxiously half way between the shutters and the protecting Madonna. She gives a furious imitation of the bleating goat, contorting her face with loathing. It is the fury of woman at the desire she suffers. At last the goat is captured.]

BRUNO: Got him, got him, got him!

ALVARO: Vieni presto, Diavolo!

[*Alvaro appears around the side of the house with a tight hold on the broken rope around the goat's neck. The boy follows behind, gleefully clapping the tin lids together, and farther back follows the Strega, holding her broken length of rope, her grey hair hanging into her face and her black skirts caught up in one hand, revealing bare feet and hairy legs. Serafina comes out on the porch as the grotesque little procession passes before it, and she raises her hand with the fingers making horns as the goat and the Strega pass her. Alvaro turns the goat over to the Strega and comes panting back to the house.*]

ALVARO: Niente paura! – I got to go now. – You have been troppo gentile, Mrs . . .

SERAFINA: I am the widow of the Baron Delle Rose. – Excuse the way I'm – not dressed . . . [*He keeps hold of her hand as he stands on the porch steps. She continues very shyly, panting a little.*] I am not always like this. – Sometimes I fix myself up! – When my husband was living, when my husband comes home, when he was living – I had a clean dress on! And sometimes even, I – put a rose in my hair . . .

ALVARO: A rose in your hair would be pretty!

SERAFINA: But for a widow – it ain't the time of roses . . .

[*The sound of music is heard, of a mandolin playing.*]

ALVARO: Naw, you make a mistake! It's always for everybody the time of roses! The rose is the heart of the world like the heart is the – heart of the – body? But you, Baronessa – you know what I think you have done?

SERAFINA: What – what have I – done?

ALVARO: You have put your heart in the marble urn with the ashes. [*Now singing is heard along with the music, which continues to the end of the scene.*] And if in a storm sometime, or sometime when a 10-ton truck goes down the highway – the marble urn was to *break*! [*He suddenly points up at the sky.*] Look! Look, Baronessa!

SERAFINA [*startled*]: Look? Look? I don't see!

ALVARO: I was pointing at your heart, broken out of the urn and away from the ashes! – *Rondinella felice!* [*He makes an airy gesture toward the fading sky.*]

SERAFINA: Oh! [*He whistles like a bird and makes graceful wing-like motions with his hands.*] Buffone, buffone – piantatela! I take you serious – then you make it a joke . . . [*She smiles involuntarily at his antics.*]

ALVARO: When can I bring the shirt back?

SERAFINA: When do you pass by again?

ALVARO: I will pass by to-night for supper. Volete?

SERAFINA: Then look at the window to-night. If the shutters are open and there is a light in the window, you can stop by for your – jacket – but if the shutters are closed, you better not stop because my Rosa will be home. Rosa's my daughter. She has gone to a picnic – maybe – home early – but you know how picnics are. They – wait for the moon to – start singing. – Not that there's nothing wrong in two grown-up people having a quiet conversation! – but Rosa's fifteen – I got to be careful to set her a perfect example.

ALVARO: I will look at the window. – I will look at the windooow! [*He imitates a bird flying off with gay whistles.*]

SERAFINA: Buffone!

ALVARO [*shouting from outside*]: Hey, you little buggers, climb down off that truck! Lay offa them bananas!

[*His truck is heard starting and pulling away. Serafina stands motionless on the porch, searching the sky with her eyes.*]

SERAFINA: Rosario, forgive me! Forgive me for thinking the awful lie could be true!

[*The light in the house dims out. A little boy races into the yard holding triumphantly-aloft a great golden bunch of bananas. A little girl pursues him with shrill cries. He eludes her. They dash around the house. The light fades and the curtain falls.*]

ACT THREE

SCENE I

It is the evening of the same day. The neighbourhood children are playing games around the house. One of them is counting by fives to a hundred, calling out the numbers, as he leans against the palm tree.

Serafina is in the parlour, sitting on the sofa. She is seated stiffly and formally, wearing a gown that she has not worn since the death of her husband, and with a rose in her hair. It becomes obvious from her movements that she is wearing a girdle that constricts her unendurably.

[*There is the sound of a truck approaching up on the highway. Serafina rises to an odd, crouching position. But the truck passes by without stopping. The girdle is becoming quite intolerable to Serafina and she decides to take it off, going behind the sofa to do so. With much grunting, she has gotten it down as far as her knees, when there is the sound outside of another truck approaching. This time the truck stops up on the highway, with a sound of screeching brakes. She realizes that Alvaro is coming, and her efforts to get out of the girdle, which is now pinioning her legs, become frantic. She hobbles from behind the sofa as Alvaro appears in front of the house.*]

ALVARO [*gaily*]: Rondinella felice! I will look at win-dooooo! Signora delle Rose!

[*Serafina's response to this salutation is a groan of anguish. She hobbles and totters desperately to the curtains between the rooms and reaches them just in time to hide herself as Alvaro comes into the parlour from the porch through the screen door. He is carrying a package and a candy box.*]

87

ALVARO: C'è nessuno?

SERAFINA [*at first inaudibly*]: Si, si, sono qui. [*then loudly and hoarsely, as she finally gets the girdle off her legs*] Si, si, sono qui! [*To cover her embarrassment, she busies herself with fixing wine glasses on a tray.*]

ALVARO: I hear the rattle of glasses! Let me help you! [*He goes eagerly through the curtain but stops short, astonished.*]

SERAFINA: Is – something the – matter?

ALVARO: I didn't expect to see you looking so pretty! You are a *young* little widow!

SERAFINA: You are – fix yourself up . . .

ALVARO: I been to The Ideal Barber's! I got the whole works!

SERAFINA [*faintly, retreating from him a little*]: You got – rose oil – in your hair . . .

ALVARO: Olio di rose! You like the smell of it? [*Outside there is a wild, distant cry of children, and inside a pause. Serafina shakes her head slowly with the infinite wound of a recollection.*] – You – don't – like – the smell of it? Oh, then I wash the smell *out*, I go and . . . [*He starts toward the back. She raises her hand to stop him.*]

SERAFINA: No, no, no, fa – niente. – I – *like* the smell of it . . .

[*A little boy races into the yard, ducks some invisible missile, sticks out his tongue and yells: 'Yahhhhh!' Then he dashes behind the house.*]

SERAFINA: Shall we – set down in the parlour?

ALVARO: I guess that's better than standing up in the dining-room. [*He enters formally.*] – Shall we set down on the sofa?

SERAFINA: You take the sofa. I will set down on this chair.

ALVARO [*disappointed*]: You don't like to set on a sofa?

SERAFINA: I lean back too far on that sofa. I like a straight back behind me . . .

ALVARO: That chair looks not comfortable to me.

SERAFINA: This chair is a comfortable chair.

ALVARO: But it's more easy to talk with two on a sofa!

SERAFINA: I talk just as good on a chair as I talk on a sofa . . . [*There is a pause. Alvaro nervously hitches his shoulder.*] Why do you hitch your shoulders like that?

ALVARO: Oh, that! – That's a – nervous – habit . . .

SERAFINA: I thought maybe the suit don't fit you good . . .

ALVARO: I bought this suit to get married in four years ago.

SERAFINA: But didn't get married?

ALVARO: I give her, the girl, a zircon instead of a diamond. She had it examined. The door was slammed in my face.

SERAFINA: I think that maybe I'd do the same thing myself.

ALVARO: Buy the zircon?

SERAFINA: No, slam the door.

ALVARO: Her eyes were not sincere looking. You've got sincere looking eyes. Give me your hand so I can tell your fortune! [*She pushes her chair back from him.*] I see two men in your life. One very handsome. One not handsome. His ears are too big but not as big as his heart! He has three dependants. – In fact he has four dependants! Ha, ha, ha!

SERAFINA: What is the fourth dependant?

ALVARO: The one that every man's got, his biggest expense, worst troublemaker, and chief liability! Ha, ha, ha!

SERAFINA: I hope you are not talking vulgar. [*She rises and turns her back to him. Then she discovers the candy box.*] What's that fancy red box?

ALVARO: A present I bought for a nervous but nice little lady!

SERAFINA: Chocolates? Grazie! But I'm too fat.

ALVARO: You are not fat, you are just pleasing and plump. [*He reaches way over to pinch the creamy flesh of her upper arm.*]

SERAFINA: No, please. Don't make me nervous. If I get nervous again I will start to cry . . .

ALVARO: Let's talk about something to take your mind off your troubles. You say you got a young daughter?

SERAFINA [*in a choked voice*]: Yes. I got a young daughter. Her name is Rosa.

ALVARO: Rosa, Rosa! She's pretty?

SERAFINA: She has the eyes of her father, and his wild, stubborn blood! To-day was the day of her graduation from high school. She looked so pretty in a white voile dress with a great big bunch of – roses . . .

ALVARO: Not no prettier than her Mama, I bet – with that rose in your hair!

SERAFINA: She's only fifteen.

ALVARO: Fifteen?

SERAFINA [*smoothing her blue silk lap with a hesitant hand*]: Yes, only fifteen . . .

ALVARO: But has a boyfriend, does she?

SERAFINA: She met a sailor.

ALVARO: Oh, Dio! No wonder you seem to be nervous.

SERAFINA: I didn't want to let her go out with this sailor. He had a gold ring in his ear.

ALVARO: Madonna Santa!

SERAFINA: This morning she cut her wrist – not much but enough to bleed – with a kitchen knife!

ALVARO: Tch, tch! A very wild girl!

SERAFINA: I had to give in and let her bring him to see me. He said he was Catholic. I made him kneel down in front of Our Lady there and give Her his promise that he would respect the innocence of my Rosa! – But how do I know that he was a Catholic, *really*?

ALVARO [*taking her hand*]: Poor little worried lady! But you got to face facts. Sooner or later the innocence of your daughter cannot be respected. – Did he – have a – tattoo?

SERAFINA [*startled*]: Did who have – what?

ALVARO: The sailor friend of your daughter, did he have a tattoo?

SERAFINA: Why do you ask me that?

ALVARO: Just because most sailors have a tattoo.

SERAFINA: How do I know if he had a tattoo or not!

ALVARO: *I* got a tattoo!

SERAFINA: *You* got a tattoo?

ALVARO: Sì, sì, veramente!

SERAFINA: What kind of tattoo you got?

ALVARO: What kind you think?

SERAFINA: Oh, I think – you have got – a South Sea girl without clothes on . . .

ALVARO: No South Sea girl.

SERAFINA: Well, maybe a big red heart with MAMA written across it.

ALVARO: Wrong again, Baronessa.

[*He takes off his tie and slowly unbuttons his shirt, gazing at her with an intensely warm smile. He divides the unbuttoned shirt, turning toward her his bare chest. She utters a gasp and rises.*]

SERAFINA: No, no, no! – *Not a rose!* [*She says it as if she were evading her feelings.*]

ALVARO: Si, si, una rosa!

SERAFINA: I – don't feel good! The air is . . .

ALVARO: Che fate, che fate, che dite?

SERAFINA: The house has a tin roof on it! – The air is – I got to go outside the house to breathe! Scu – scusatemi! [*She goes out onto the porch and clings to one of the spindling porch columns for support, breathing hoarsely with a hand to her throat. He comes out slowly.*]

ALVARO [*gently*]: I didn't mean to surprise you! – Mi dispiace molto!

SERAFINA [*with enforced calm*]: Don't – talk about it! Anybody could have a rose tattoo. – It don't mean nothing. – You know how a tin roof is. It catches the heat all day and it don't cool off until – midnight . . .

ALVARO: No, no, not until midnight. [*She makes a faint laughing sound, is quite breathless and leans her forehead against the porch column. He places his fingers delicately against the small of her back.*] It makes it hot in the bedroom – so that you got to sleep without nothing on you . . .

SERAFINA: No, you – can't stand the covers . . .

ALVARO: You can't even stand a – *nightgown!* [*His fingers press her back.*]

SERAFINA: Please. There is a strega next door; she's always watching!

ALVARO: It's been so long since I felt the soft touch of a woman! [*She gasps loudly and turns to the door.*] Where are you going?

SERAFINA: I'm going back in the house! [*She enters the parlour again, still with forced calm.*]

ALVARO [*following her inside*]: Now, now, what is the matter?

SERAFINA: I got a feeling like I have – forgotten something.

ALVARO: What?

SERAFINA: I can't remember.

ALVARO: It couldn't be nothing important if you can't remember. Let's open the chocolate box and have some candy.

SERAFINA [*eager for any distraction*]: Yes! Yes, open the box!

[*Alvaro places a chocolate in her hand. She stares at it blankly.*]

ALVARO: Eat it, eat the chocolate. If you don't eat it, it will melt in your hand and make your fingers all gooey!

SERAFINA: Please, I . . .

ALVARO: Eat it!

SERAFINA [*weakly and gagging*]: I can't, I can't, I would choke! Here, you eat it.

ALVARO: Put it in my mouth! [*She puts the chocolate in his mouth.*] Now, look. Your fingers are gooey!

SERAFINA: Oh! – I better go wash them! [*She rises unsteadily. He seizes her hands and licks her fingers.*]

ALVARO: Mmmm! Mmmmm! Good, very good!

SERAFINA: Stop that, stop that, stop that! That – ain't – nice . . .

ALVARO: I'll lick off the chocolate for you.

SERAFINA: No, no, no! – I am the mother of a fifteen-year-old girl!

ALVARO: You're as old as your arteries, Baronessa. Now set back down. The fingers are now white as snow!

SERAFINA: You don't – understand – how I feel . . .

ALVARO: You don't understand how *I* feel.

SERAFINA [*doubtfully*]: How do you – feel? [*In answer, he stretches the palms of his hands out toward her as if she were a fireplace in a freezing-cold room.*] – What does – *that* – mean?

ALVARO: The night is warm but I feel like my hands are – freezing!

SERAFINA: Bad – circulation . . .

ALVARO: No, too *much* circulation! [*Alvaro becomes tremulously pleading, shuffling forward a little, slightly crouched like a beggar.*] Across the room I feel the sweet warmth of a lady!

SERAFINA [*retreating, doubtfully*]: Oh, you talk a sweet mouth. I think you talk a sweet mouth to fool a woman.

ALVARO: No, no, I know – I know that's what warms the world, that is what makes it the summer! [*He seizes the hand she holds defensively before her and presses it to his own breast in a crushing grip.*] Without it, the rose – the rose would not grow on the bush; the fruit would not grow on the tree!

SERAFINA: I know, and the truck – the truck would not haul the bananas! But, Mr Mangiacavallo, that is my hand, not a sponge. I got bones in it. Bones break!

ALVARO: Scusatemi, Baronessa! [*He returns her hand to her with a bow.*] For me it is winter, because I don't have in my life the sweet warmth of a lady. I live with my hands in my pockets! [*He stuffs his hand violently into his pants' pockets, then jerks them out again. A small cellophane-wrapped disk falls on the floor, escaping his notice, but not Serafina's.*] – You don't like the poetry! – How can a man talk to you?

SERAFINA [*ominously*]: I like the poetry good. Is that a piece of the poetry that you dropped out of your pocket? [*He looks down.*] – No, no, right by your foot!

ALVARO [*aghast as he realizes what it is that she has seen*]: Oh, that's – that's nothing! [*He kicks it under the sofa.*]

SERAFINA [*fiercely*]: You talk a sweet mouth about women. Then drop such a thing from your pocket? – Va via, vigliacco! [*She marches grandly out of the room, pulling the curtains together behind her. He hangs his head despairingly between his hands. Then he approaches the curtains timidly.*]

ALVARO [*in a small voice*]: Baronessa?

SERAFINA: Pick up what you dropped on the floor and go to the Square Roof with it. Buona notte!

ALVARO: Baronessa! [*He parts the curtains and peeks through them.*]

SERAFINA: I told you good night. Here is no casa privata. Io, non sono puttana!

ALVARO: Understanding is – very – necessary!

SERAFINA: I understand plenty. You think you got a good thing, a thing that is cheap!

ALVARO: You make a mistake, Baronessa! [*He comes in and drops to his knees beside her, pressing his cheek to her flank. He speaks rhapsodically.*] So soft is a lady! So, so, so, so, so *soft* – is a lady!

SERAFINA: Andate via, sporcaccione, andate a casa! Lasciatemi! Lasciatemi stare!

[*She springs up and runs into the parlour. He pursues. The chase is grotesquely violent and comic. A floor lamp is overturned. She seizes the chocolate box and threatens to slam it into his face if he continues towards her. He drops to his knees, crouched way over, and pounds the floor with his fists, sobbing.*]

ALVARO: Everything in my life turns out like this!

SERAFINA: Git up, git up, git up! – you village idiot's grandson! There is people watching you through that window, the – strega next door . . . [*He rises slowly.*] And where is the shirt that I loaned you? [*He shuffles abjectly across the room, then hands her a neatly wrapped package.*]

ALVARO: My sister wrapped it up for you. – My sister was very happy I met this *nice* lady!

SERAFINA: Maybe she thinks I will pay the grocery bill while she plays the numbers!

ALVARO: She don't think nothing like that. She is an old maid, my sister. She wants – nephews – nieces . . .

SERAFINA: You tell her for me I don't give nephews and nieces!

[*Alvaro hitches his shoulders violently in his embarrassment and shuffles over to where he had left his hat. He blows the dust off it and rubs the crown on his sleeve. Serafina presses a knuckle to her lips as she watches his awkward gestures. She is a little abashed by his humility. She speaks next with the great dignity of a widow whose respectability has stood the test.*]

SERAFINA: Now, Mr Mangiacavallo, please tell me the truth about something. *When* did you get the tattoo put on your chest?

ALVARO [*shyly and sadly, looking down at his hat*]: I got it to-night – after supper . . .

SERAFINA: That's what I thought. You had it put on because I told you about my husband's tattoo.

ALVARO: I wanted to be – close to you . . . to make you – happy . . .

SERAFINA: Tell it to the marines! [*He puts on his hat with an apologetic gesture.*] You got the tattoo and the chocolate box after supper, and then you come here to fool me!

ALVARO: I got the chocolate box a long time ago.

SERAFINA: How long ago? If that is not too much a personal question!

ALVARO: I got it the night the door was slammed in my face by the girl that I give – the zircon . . .

SERAFINA: Let that be a lesson. Don't try to fool women. You are not smart enough! – Now take the shirt back. You can keep it.

ALVARO: Huh?

SERAFINA: Keep it. I don't want it back.

ALVARO: You just now said that you did.

SERAFINA: It's a man's shirt, ain't it?

95

ALVARO: You just now accused me of trying to steal it off you.

SERAFINA: Well, you been making me nervous!

ALVARO: Is it my fault you been a widow too long?

SERAFINA: You make a mistake!

ALVARO: *You* make a mistake!

SERAFINA: Both of us make a mistake!

[*There is a pause. They both sigh profoundly.*]

ALVARO: We should of have been friends, but I think we meet the wrong day. – Suppose I go out and come in the door again and we start all over?

SERAFINA: No, I think it's no use. The day was wrong to begin with, because of two women. Two women, they told me to–day that my husband had put on my head the nanny-goat's horns!

ALVARO: How is it possible to put horns on a widow?

SERAFINA: That was before, before! They told me my husband was having a steady affair with a woman at the Square Roof. What was the name on the shirt, on the slip of paper? Do you remember the name?

ALVARO: You told me to . . .

SERAFINA: Tell me! Do you remember?

ALVARO: I remember the name because I know the woman. The name was Estelle Hohengarten.

SERAFINA: Take me there! Take me to the Square Roof! – Wait, wait!

[*She plunges into the dining-room, snatches a knife out of the sideboard drawer and thrusts it in her purse. Then she rushes back, with the blade of the knife protruding from the purse.*]

ALVARO [*noticing the knife*]: They – got a cover charge there . . .

SERAFINA: I will charge them a cover! Take me there now, this minute!

ALVARO: The fun don't start till midnight.

SERAFINA: I will start the fun sooner.

ALVARO: The floor show commences at midnight.

SERAFINA: I will commence it! [*She rushes to the phone.*] Yellow Cab, please, Yellow Cab. I want to go to the Square Roof out of my house! Yes, you come to my house and take me to the Square Roof right this minute! My number is – what is my number? Oh my God, what is my number? – 64 is my number on Front Street! Subito, subito – quick!

[*The goat bleats outside.*]

ALVARO: Baronessa, the knife's sticking out of your purse. [*He grabs the purse.*] What do you want with this weapon?

SERAFINA: To cut the lying tongue out of a woman's mouth! Saying she has on her breast the tattoo of my husband because he had put on me the horns of a goat! I cut the heart out of that woman, she cut the heart out of me!

ALVARO: Nobody's going to cut the heart out of nobody!

[*A car is heard outside, and Serafina rushes to the porch.*]

SERAFINA [*shouting*]: Hey, Yellow Cab, Yellow Cab, Yellow – Cab . . . [*The car passes by without stopping. With a sick moan she wanders into the yard. He follows her with a glass of wine.*] – Something hurts – in my heart . . .

ALVARO [*leading her gently back to the house*]: Baronessa, drink this wine on the porch and keep your eyes on that star. [*He leads her to a porch pillar and places the glass in her trembling hand. She is now submissive.*] You know the name of that star? That star is Venus. She is the only female star in the sky. Who put her up there? Mr Siccardi, the transportation manager of the Southern Fruit Company? No. She was put there by God. [*He enters the house and removes the knife from her purse.*] And yet there's some people that don't believe in nothing. [*He picks up the telephone.*] Esplanade 9-7-0.

SERAFINA: What are you doing?

ALVARO: Drink that wine and I'll settle this whole problem for

97

you. [*on the telephone*] I want to speak to the blackjack dealer, please, Miss Estelle Hohengarten . . .

SERAFINA: Don't talk to that woman, she'll lie!

ALVARO: Not Estelle Hohengarten. She deals a straight game of cards. – Estelle? This is Mangiacavallo. I got a question to ask you which is a personal question. It has to do with a very good looking truck driver, not living now but once on a time thought to have been a very well-known character at the Square Roof. His name was . . . [*He turns questioningly to the door where Serafina is standing.*] What was his name, Baronessa?

SERAFINA [*hardly breathing*]: Rosario delle Rose!

ALVARO: Rosario delle Rose was the name. [*There is a pause.*] – È vero? – Mah! Che peccato . . .

[*Serafina drops her glass and springs into the parlour with a savage outcry. She snatches the phone from Alvaro and screams into it.*]

SERAFINA [*wildly*]: This is the wife that's speaking! What do you know of my husband, what is the lie?

[*A strident voice sounds over the wire.*]

THE VOICE [*loud and clear*]: Don't you remember? I brought you the rose-coloured silk to make him a shirt. You said, 'For a man?' and I said, 'Yes, for a man that's wild like a Gipsy!' But if you think I'm a liar, come here and let me show you his rose tattooed on my chest!

[*Serafina holds the phone away from her as though it had burst into flame. Then, with a terrible cry, she hurls it to the floor. She staggers dizzily toward the Madonna. Alvaro seizes her arm and pushes her gently onto the sofa.*]

ALVARO: Piano, piano, Baronessa! This will be gone, this will pass in a moment. [*He puts a pillow behind her, then replaces the telephone.*]

SERAFINA [*staggering up from the sofa*]: The room's – going round . . .

ALVARO: You ought to stay lying down a little while longer. I know, I know what you need! A towel with some ice in it to put on your forehead – Baronessa. – You stay right there while I fix it! [*He goes into the kitchen, and calls back.*] Torno subito, Baronessa!

[*The little boy runs into the yard. He leans against the bending trunk of the palm, counting loudly.*]

THE LITTLE BOY: Five, ten, fifteen, twenty, twenty-five, thirty . . .

[*There is the sound of ice being chopped in the kitchen.*]

SERAFINA: Dove siete, dove siete?

ALVARO: In cucina! – Ghiaccio . . .

SERAFINA: Venite qui!

ALVARO: Subito, subito . . .

SERAFINA [*turning to the shrine, with fists knotted*]: Non voglio, non voglio farlo!

[*But she crosses slowly, compulsively toward the shrine, with a trembling arm stretched out.*]

THE LITTLE BOY: Seventy-five, eighty, eighty-five, ninety, ninety-five, one hundred! [*then, wildly*] Ready or not you shall be caught!

[*At this cry, Serafina seizes the marble urn and hurls it violently into the farthest corner of the room. Then, instantly, she covers her face. Outside the mothers are heard calling their children home. Their voices are tender as music, fading in and out. The children appear slowly at the side of the house, exhausted from their wild play.*]

GIUSEPPINA: Vivi! Vi-vi!

PEPPINA: Salvatore!

VIOLETTA: Bruno! Come home, come home!

[*The children scatter. Alvaro comes in with the ice-pick.*]

ALVARO: I broke the point of the ice-pick.
SERAFINA [*removing her hands from her face*]: I don't want ice . . .
[*She looks about her, seeming to gather a fierce strength in her body. Her voice is hoarse, her body trembling with violence, eyes narrow and flashing, her fists clenched.*] Now I show you how wild and strong like a man a woman can be! [*She crosses to the screen door, opens it and shouts.*] Buona notte, Mr Mangiacavallo!
ALVARO: You – you make me go *home*, now?
SERAFINA: No, no; senti, cretino! [*in a strident whisper*] You make out like you are going. You drive the truck out of sight where the witch can't see it. Then you come back and I leave the back door open for you to come in. Now, tell me good-bye so all the neighbours can hear you! [*She shouts.*] Arrive-derci!
ALVARO: Ha, ha! Capish! [*He shouts too.*] Arrivederci! [*He runs to the foot of the embankment steps.*]
SERAFINA [*still more loudly*]: Buona notte!
ALVARO: Buona notte, Baronessa!
SERAFINA [*in a choked voice*]: Give them my love; give every-body – my love . . . Arrivederci!
ALVARO: Ciao!

[*Alvaro scrambles on down the steps and goes off. Serafina comes down into the yard. The goat bleats. She mutters savagely to herself.*]

SERAFINA: Sono una bestia, una bestia feroce!

[*She crosses quickly around to the back of the house. As she disappears, the truck is heard driving off; the lights sweep across the house. Serafina comes in through the back door. She is moving with great violence, gasping and panting. She rushes up to the Madonna and addresses her passionately with ex-*]

plosive gestures, leaning over so that her face is level with the statue's.]

SERAFINA: Ora, ascolta, Signora! You hold in the cup of your hand this little house and you smash it! You break this little house like the shell of a bird in your hand, because you have hate Serafina? – Serafina that *loved* you! – No, no, no, you don't speak! I don't believe in you, Lady! You're just a poor little doll with the paint peeling off, and now I blow out the light and I forget you the way you forget Serafina! [*She blows out the vigil light.*] *Ecco – fatto!*

[*But now she is suddenly frightened; the vehemence and boldness have run out. She gasps a little and backs away from the shrine, her eyes rolling apprehensively this way and that. The parrot squawks at her. The goat bleats. The night is full of sinister noises, harsh bird cries, the sudden flapping of wings in the cane-brake, a distant shriek of Negro laughter. Serafina retreats to the window and opens the shutters wider to admit the moonlight. She stands panting by the window with a fist pressed to her mouth. In the back of the house a door slams open. Serafina catches her breath and moves as though for protection behind the dummy of the bride. Alvaro enters through the back door, calling out softly and hoarsely, with great excitement.*]

ALVARO: Dove? Dove sei, cara?
SERAFINA [*faintly*]: Sono qui . . .
ALVARO: You have turn out the light!
SERAFINA: The moon is enough . . . [*He advances toward her. His white teeth glitter as he grins. Serafina retreats a few steps from him. She speaks tremulously, making an awkward gesture toward the sofa.*] Now we can go on with our – conversation . . . [*She catches her breath sharply.*]

[*The curtain comes down.*]

SCENE 2

It is just before daybreak of the next day. Rosa and Jack appear at the top of the embankment steps.

ROSA: I thought they would never leave. [*She comes down the steps and out in front of the house, then calls back to him.*] Let's go down there.

> [*He obeys hesitatingly. Both are very grave. The scene is played as close as possible to the audience. She sits very straight. He stands behind her with his hands on her shoulders.*]

ROSA [*leaning her head back against him*]: This was the happiest day of my life, and this is the saddest night . . . [*He crouches in front of her.*]

SERAFINA [*from inside the house*]: Aaaaaahhhhhhhh!

JACK [*springing up, startled*]: What's that?

ROSA [*resentfully*]: Oh! That's Mama dreaming about my father.

JACK: I – feel like a – *heel*! I feel like a rotten heel!

ROSA: Why?

JACK: That promise I made your mother.

ROSA: I hate her for it.

JACK: Honey – Rosa, she – wanted to protect you.

> [*There is a long-drawn cry from the back of the house: 'Ohhhh-Rosario!'*]

ROSA: She wanted me not to have what she's dreaming about . . .

JACK: Naw, naw, honey, she – wanted to – protect you . . .

> [*The cry from within is repeated softly.*]

ROSA: Listen to her making love in her sleep! Is that what she wants *me* to do, just – *dream* about it?

JACK [*humbly*]: She knows that her Rosa *is* a rose. And she wants her rose to have someone – better than *me* . . .

ROSA: *Better* than – *you*! [*She speaks as if the possibility were too preposterous to think of.*]

JACK: You see me through – rose-coloured – glasses . . .

ROSA: I see you with love!

JACK: Yes, but your Mama sees me with – common sense . . . [*Serafina cries out again.*] I got to be going! [*She keeps a tight hold on him. A rooster crows.*] Honey, it's so late the roosters are crowing!

ROSA: They're fools, they're fools, it's early!

JACK: Honey, on that island I almost forgot my promise. Almost, but not quite. Do you understand, honey?

ROSA: Forget the promise!

JACK: I made it on my knees in front of Our Lady. I've got to leave now, honey.

ROSA [*clasping him fiercely*]: You'd have to break my arms to!

JACK: Rosa, Rosa! You want to drive me crazy?

ROSA: I want you not to remember.

JACK: You're a very young girl! Fifteen – fifteen is too young!

ROSA: Caro, caro, carissimo!

JACK: You got to save some of those feelings for when you're grown up!

ROSA: Carissimo!

JACK: Hold some of it back until you're grown!

ROSA: I have been grown for two years!

JACK: No, no, that ain't what I . . .

ROSA: Grown enough to be married, and have a – baby!

JACK [*springing up*]: Oh, good – Lord! [*He circles around her, pounding his palm repeatedly with his fist and champing his teeth together with a grimace. Suddenly he speaks.*] I got to be going!

ROSA: You want me to scream? [*He groans and turns away from her to resume his desperate circle. Rosa is blocking the way with her body.*] – I know, I know! You don't want me! [*Jack groans through his gritting teeth.*] No, no, you don't want me . . .

JACK: Now you listen to me! You almost got into trouble to-day on that island! You almost did, but not quite! – But it didn't quite happen and no harm is done and you can just – forget it . . .

ROSA: It is the only thing in my life that I want to remember! – When are you going back to New Orleans?

JACK: To-morrow.

ROSA: When does your – ship sail?

JACK: To-morrow.

ROSA: Where to?

JACK: Guatemala.

SERAFINA [from the house]: Aahh!

ROSA: Is that a long trip?

JACK: After Guatemala, Buenos Aires. After Buenos Aires, Rio. Then around the Straits of Magellan and back up the west coat of South America, putting in at three ports before we dock at San Francisco.

ROSA: I don't think I will – ever see you again . . .

JACK: The ship won't sink!

ROSA [faintly and forlornly]: No, but – I think it could just happen once, and if it don't happen that time, it never can – later . . . [A rooster crows. They face each other sadly and quietly.] You don't need to be very old to understand how it works out. One time, one time, only once, it could be – God! – to remember. – Other times? Yes – they'd be something. – But only once, God – to remember . . . [With a little sigh she crosses to pick up his white cap and hand it gravely to him.] – I'm sorry to you it didn't – mean – that much . . .

JACK [taking the cap and hurling it to the ground]: Look! Look at my knuckles! You see them scabs on my knuckles? You know how them scabs got there? They got there because I banged my knuckles that hard on the deck of the sailboat!

ROSA: Because it – didn't quite happen? [Jack jerks his head up and down in grotesquely violent assent to her question. Rosa picks up his cap and returns it to him again.] – Because of the promise to Mama! I'll never forgive her ... [*There is a pause.*] What time in the afternoon must you be on the boat?

JACK: Why?

ROSA: Just tell me what time.

JACK: Five! – Why?

ROSA: What will you be doing till five?

JACK: Well, I could be a goddam liar and tell you I was going to – pick me a hatful of daisies in Audubon Park. – Is that what you want me to tell you?

ROSA: No, tell me the truth.

JACK: All right, I'll tell you the truth. I'm going to check in at some flea-bag hotel on North Rampart Street. Then I'm going to get loaded! And then I'm going to get ... [*He doesn't complete the sentence but she understands him. She places the hat more becomingly on his blond head.*]

ROSA: Do me a little favour. [*Her hand slides down to his cheek and then to his mouth.*] Before you get loaded and before you – before you –

JACK: Huh?

ROSA: Look in the waiting room at the Greyhound bus station, please. At twelve o'clock, noon!

JACK: Why?

ROSA: You might find me there, waiting for you ...

JACK: What – what good would that do?

ROSA: I never been to a hotel but I know they have numbers on doors and sometimes – numbers are – lucky. – Aren't they? – Sometimes? – Lucky?

JACK: You want to buy me a ten-year stretch in the brig?

ROSA: I want you to give me that little gold ring on your ear to put on my finger. – I want to give you my heart to keep forever! And ever! And ever! [*Slowly and with a barely audible sigh she leans her face against him.*] Look for me! I will be there!

JACK [*breathlessly*]: In all of my life, I never felt nothing so sweet as the feel of your little warm body in my arms ...

[*He breaks away and runs toward the road. From the foot of the steps he glares fiercely back at her like a tiger through the bars of a cage. She clings to the two porch pillars, her body leaning way out.*]

ROSA: Look for me! I will be there!

[*Jack runs away from the house. Rosa returns inside. Listlessly she removes her dress and falls on the couch in her slip, kicking off her shoes. Then she begins to cry, as one cries only once in a lifetime, and the scene dims out.*]

SCENE 3

The time is three hours later.

We see first the exterior view of the small frame building against a night sky which is like the starry blue robe of Our Lady. It is growing slightly paler.

[*The faint light discloses Rosa asleep on the couch. The covers are thrown back for it has been a warm night, and on the concave surface of the white cloth, which is like the dimly lustrous hollow of a shell, is the body of the sleeping girl which is clad only in a sheer white slip.*

A cock crows. A gentle wind stirs the white curtains inward and the tendrils of vine at the windows, and the sky lightens enough to distinguish the purple trumpets of the morning glory against the very dim blue of the sky in which the planet Venus remains still undimmed.

In the back of the cottage someone is heard coughing hoarsely and groaning in the way a man does who has drunk very heavily the night before. Bedsprings creak as a heavy figure rises. Light spills dimly through the curtains, now closed, between the two front rooms.]

There are heavy, padding footsteps and Alvaro comes stumbling rapidly into the dining-room with the last bottle of Spumanti in the crook of an arm, his eyes barely open, legs rubbery, saying, 'Wuh-wuh-wuh-wuh-wuh-wuh . . .' like the breathing of an old dog. The scene should be played with the pantomimic lightness, almost fantasy, of an early Chaplin comedy. He is wearing only his trousers and his chest is bare. As he enters he collides with the widow dummy, staggers back, pats her inflated bosom in a timid, apologetic way, remarking:]

ALVARO: Scusami, Signora, I am the grandson of the village idiot of Ribera!

[Alvaro backs into the table and is propelled by the impact all the way to the curtained entrance to the parlour. He draws the curtains apart and hangs onto them, peering into the room. Seeing the sleeping girl, he blinks several times, suddenly makes a snoring sound in his nostrils and waves one hand violently in front of his eyes as if to dispel a vision. Outside the goat utters a long 'Baaaaaaaaaaa!' As if in response, Alvaro whispers, in the same basso key, 'Che bella!' The first vowel of 'bella' is enormously prolonged like the 'baaa' of the goat. On his rubbery legs he shuffles forward a few steps and leans over to peer more intently at the vision. The goat bleats again. Alvaro whispers more loudly: 'Che bel-la!' He drains the Spumanti, then staggers to his knees, the empty bottle rolling over the floor. He crawls on his knees to the foot of the bed, then leans against it like a child peering into a candy shop window, repeating: 'Che bel-la, che bel-la!' with antiphonal responses from the goat outside. Slowly, with tremendous effort, as if it were the sheer side of a precipice, he clambers upon the couch and crouches over the sleeping girl in a leap-frog position, saying 'Che bel-la!' quite loudly, this time, in a tone of innocently joyous surprise. All at once Rosa wakens. She screams, even before she is quite awake, and springs from the couch so violently that Alvaro topples over to the floor.]

Serafina cries out almost instantly after Rosa. She lunges through the dining-room in her torn and disordered nightgown. At the sight of the man crouched by the couch a momentary stupefaction turns into a burst of savage fury. She flies at him like a great bird, tearing and clawing at his stupefied figure. With one arm Alvaro wards off her blows, plunging to the floor and crawling into the dining-room. She seizes a broom with which she flails him about the head, buttocks, and shoulders while he scrambles awkwardly away. The assault is nearly wordless. Each time she strikes at him she hisses: 'Sporcaccione!' He continually groans: 'Dough, dough, dough!' At last he catches hold of the widow dummy which he holds as a shield before him while he entreats the two women.]

ALVARO: Senti, Baronessa! Signorina! I didn't know what I was doin', I was dreamin', I was just dreamin'! I got turn around in the house; I got all twisted! I thought that you was your Mama! – Sono ubriaco! Per favore!

ROSA [*seizing the broom*]: That's enough, Mama!

SERAFINA [*rushing to the phone*]: Police!

ROSA [*seizing the phone*]: No, no, no, no, no, no! – You want everybody to know?

SERAFINA [*weakly*]: Know? – Know *what*, cara?

ROSA: Just give him his clothes, now, Mama, and let him get out! [*She is clutching a bedsheet about herself.*]

ALVARO: Signorina – young lady! I swear I was *dreaming*!

SERAFINA: Don't speak to my daughter! [*then, turning to Rosa*] – Who is this man? How did this man get here?

ROSA [*coldly*]: Mama, don't say any more. Just give him his clothes in the bedroom so he can get out!

ALVARO [*still crouching*]: I am so sorry, so sorry! I don't remember a thing but that I was dreaming!

SERAFINA [*shoving him toward the back of the room with her broom*]: Go on, get your clothes on, you – idiot's grandson, you! – Svelto, svelto, più svelto! [*Alvaro continues his apolo-*

getic mumbling in the back room.] Don't talk to me, don't say nothing! Or I will kill you!

[*A few moments later Alvaro rushes around the side of the house, his clothes half buttoned and his shirt-tails out.*]

ALVARO: But, Baronessa, I *love* you! [*A tea kettle sails over his head from behind the house. The Strega bursts into laughter. Despairingly Alvaro retreats, tucking his shirt-tails in and shaking his head.*] Baronessa, Baronessa, I love you!

[*As Alvaro runs off, the Strega is heard cackling:*]

THE STREGA'S VOICE: The Wops are at it again. Had a truck-driver in the house all night!

[*Rosa is feverishly dressing. From the bureau she has snatched a shimmering white satin slip, disappearing for a moment behind a screen to put it on as Serafina comes padding sheepishly back into the room, her nightgown now covered by a black rayon kimono sprinkled with poppies, her voice tremulous with fear, shame, and apology.*]

ROSA [*behind the screen*]: Has the man gone?
SERAFINA: That – man?
ROSA: Yes, 'that man'!
SERAFINA [*inventing desperately*]: I don't know how he got in. Maybe the back door was open.
ROSA: Oh, yes, maybe it was!
SERAFINA: Maybe he – climbed in a window . . .
ROSA: Or fell down the chimney, maybe! [*She comes from behind the screen, wearing the white bridal slip.*]
SERAFINA: Why you put on the white things I save for your wedding?
ROSA: Because I want to. That's a good enough reason. [*She combs her hair savagely.*]
SERAFINA: I want you to understand about that man. That was a man that – that was – that was a man that . . .

ROSA: You can't think of a lie?

SERAFINA: He was a – truckdriver, cara. He got in a fight, he was chase by – policemen!

ROSA: They chased him into your bedroom?

SERAFINA: I took pity on him, I give him first aid, I let him sleep on the floor. He give me his promise – he . . .

ROSA: Did he kneel in front of Our Lady? Did he promise that he would respect your innocence?

SERAFINA: Oh, cara, cara! [*abandoning all pretence*] He was Sicilian; he had rose oil in his hair and the rose tattoo of your father. In the dark room I couldn't see his clown face. I closed my eyes and dreamed that he was your father! I closed my eyes! I dreamed that he was your father . . .

ROSA: Basta, basta, non voglio sentire più niente! The only thing worse than a liar is a liar that's also a hypocrite!

SERAFINA: Senti, per favore! [*Rosa wheels about from the mirror and fixes her mother with a long and withering stare. Serafina cringes before it.*] Don't look at me like that with the eyes of your father! [*She shields her face as from a terrible glare.*]

ROSA: Yes, I am looking at you with the eyes of my father. I see you the way *he* saw you. [*She runs to the table and seizes the piggy bank.*] Like this, this pig! [*Serafina utters a long, shuddering cry like a cry of childbirth.*] I need five dollars. I'll take it out of this! [*Rosa smashes the piggy bank to the floor and ⁓akes some coins into her purse. Serafina stoops to the floor. There is the sound of a train whistle. Rosa is now fully dressed, but she hesitates, a little ashamed of her cruelty – but only a little. Serafina cannot meet her daughter's eyes. At last the girl speaks.*]

SERAFINA: How beautiful – is my daughter! Go to the boy!

ROSA [*as if she might be about to apologize*]: Mama? He didn't touch me – he just said – 'Che bella!'

[*Serafina turns slowly, shamefully, to face her. She is like a peasant in the presence of a young princess. Rosa stares at her a*

*moment longer, then suddenly catches her breath and runs out
of the house. As the girl leaves, Serafina calls:*]

SERAFINA: Rosa, Rosa, the – wrist watch! [*Serafina snatches up
the little gift box and runs out onto the porch with it. She starts to
call her daughter again, holding the gift out toward her, but her
breath fails her.*] Rosa, Rosa, the – wrist watch . . . [*Her arms
fall to her side. She turns, the gift still ungiven. Senselessly,
absently, she holds the watch to her ear again. She shakes it a
little, then utters a faint, startled laugh.*]

[*Assunta appears beside the house and walks directly in, as
though Serafina had called her.*]

SERAFINA: Assunta, the urn is broken. The ashes are spilt on
the floor and I can't touch them.

[*Assunta stoops to pick up the pieces of the shattered urn.
Serafina has crossed to the shrine and relights the candle before
the Madonna.*]

ASSUNTA: There are no ashes.
SERAFINA: Where – where are they? Where have the ashes
gone?
ASSUNTA [*crossing the shrine*]: The wind has blown them
away.

[*Assunta places what remains of the broken urn in Serafina's
hands. Serafina turns it tenderly in her hands and then replaces
it on the top of the prie-dieu before the Madonna.*]

SERAFINA: A man, when he burns, leaves only a handful of
ashes. No woman can hold him. The wind must blow him
away.

[*Alvaro's voice is heard, calling from the top of the highway
embankment.*]

ALVARO'S VOICE: Rondinella felice!

[*The neighbourhood women hear Alvaro calling, and there is a burst of mocking laughter from some of them. Then they all converge on the house from different directions and gather before the porch.*]

PEPPINA: Serafina delle Rose!

GIUSEPPINA: Baronessa! Baronessa delle Rose!

PEPPINA: There is a man on the road without the shirt!

GIUSEPPINA [*with delight*]: Si, si! Senza camicia!

PEPPINA: All he got on his chest is a rose tattoo! [*to the women*] She lock up his shirt so he can't go to the high school?

[*The women shriek with laughter. In the house Serafina snatches up the package containing the silk shirt, while Assunta closes the shutters of the parlour windows.*]

SERAFINA: Un momento! [*She tears the paper off the shirt and rushes out onto the porch, holding the shirt above her head defiantly.*] Ecco la camicia!

[*With a soft cry, Serafina drops the shirt, which is immediately snatched up by Peppina. At this point the music begins again, with a crash of percussion, and continues to the end of the play. Peppina flourishes the shirt in the air like a banner and tosses it to Giuseppina, who is now on the embankment. Giuseppina tosses it on to Mariella, and she in her turn to Violetta, who is above her, so that the brilliantly coloured shirt moves in a zig-zag course through the pampas grass to the very top of the embankment, like a streak of flame shooting up a dry hill. The women call out as they pass the shirt along:*]

PEPPINA: Guardate questa camicia! Colore di rose!

MARIELLA [*shouting up to Alvaro*]: Coraggio, signor!

GIUSEPPINA: Avanti, avanti, signor!

VIOLETTA [*at the top of the embankment, giving the shirt a final flourish above her*]: Coraggio, coraggio! The Baronessa is waiting!

[*Bursts of laughter are mingled with the cries of the women. Then they sweep away like a flock of screaming birds, and Serafina is left upon the porch, her eyes closed, a hand clasped to her breast. In the meanwhile, inside the house, Assunta has poured out a glass of wine. Now she comes to the porch, offering the wine to Serafina and murmuring:*]

ASSUNTA: Stai tranquilla.

SERAFINA [*breathlessly*]: Assunta, I'll tell you something that maybe you won't believe.

ASSUNTA [*with tender humour*]: It is impossible to tell me anything that I don't believe.

SERAFINA: Just now I felt on my breast the burning again of the rose. I know what it means. It means that I have conceived! [*She lifts the glass to her lips for a moment and then returns it to Assunta.*] Two lives again in the body! Two, two lives again, two!

ALVARO'S VOICE [*nearer now, and sweetly urgent*]: Rondinella felice!

[*Alvaro is not visible on the embankment but Serafina begins to move slowly toward his voice.*]

ASSUNTA: Dove vai, Serafina?

SERAFINA [*shouting now, to Alvaro*]: Vengo, vengo, amore!

[*She starts up the embankment toward Alvaro and the curtain falls as the music rises with her in great glissandi of sound.*]

CAMINO REAL*

In the middle of the journey of our life I came to myself in a dark wood where the straight way was lost.

CANTO I, DANTE'S *Inferno*

FOR ELIA KAZAN

*Use Anglicized pronunciation: *Cá*-mino *Ré*al

CAMINO REAL

An Appreciation

The *Camino Real* is at the frontiers of experience. The sudden movement, the mysterious and savage violence, and the silence cannot at
once be comprehended but must be accepted. As in life the moments
of beauty, when we are frightened and lonely, are not moments of
reality.

Reality is the known, the understood. Let me put it this way. You
are a stranger alone in an unshuttered room in a Southern city. There
is a shout in the street. There are running footsteps. Beyond the door
of the room two unknown people are quietly speaking together in an
unknown language. They may be lovers or they may be plotting your
death. There is distant music. Later, you go out of the room and into
the streets. Across the way words are chalked on a wall: an unknown
name. A plane passes over towards an unknown destination. An old
woman getting down from a train is in tears. These incidents can
only be accepted. They happen, but it is impossible to trace each to its
source and discover why they happen. They cannot be related to
personal experience which finds that the street ends, bringing you to
the outskirts of the city to look out far over the inland plains. The way
still to be travelled. You hesitate. You turn back. And that is the reality.
So it is on the *Camino Real*.

It is a play of the middle years. Don Quixote's lance droops and
Marguerite's camellias are all white now. It is a play of the decision to
be taken in the middle years. The way to be taken. Throw off the
idealism, the romanticism of youth. Be realistic. But absolute realism
leads to absolute disgust. Mankind is rubbish. Witness: the street
cleaners. Very well. Keep the romantic ideals of youth beyond their
time. Desperately stay young. With the young. But this is very sad.
Witness: the ageing voluptuary surrounded by the paraphernalia
needed to whip up the flagging senses.

Yet in the middle years there is a middle way, not at all a com-
promise. It is found on the *Camino Real*. The *terra incognita* of age can
be crossed in the light of that discovery. But if the winds blow too
harshly, and if the barrenness of the body and the land seem unbearable,
well, there is always the gas oven. And the street cleaners.

Recently the play was summarily dismissed by a young English writer as a literary exercise, and a failure at that. The question the play poses cannot be the immediate concern of youth, but it is as well to remember that even the young grow old. If they are lucky.

JOHN WHITING

AUTHOR'S FOREWORD*

It is amazing and frightening how completely one's whole being becomes absorbed in the making of a play. It is almost as if you were frantically constructing another world while the world that you live in dissolves beneath your feet, and that your survival depends on completing this construction at least one second before the old habitation collapses.

More than any other work that I have done, this play has seemed to me like the construction of another world, a separate existence. Of course, it is nothing more nor less than my conception of the time and world that I live in, and its people are mostly archetypes of certain basic attitudes and qualities with those mutations that would occur if they had continued along the road to this hypothetical terminal point in it.

A convention of the play is existence outside of time in a place of no specific locality. If you regard it that way, I suppose it becomes an elaborate allegory, but in New Haven we opened directly across the street from a movie theatre that was showing *Peter Pan* in Technicolor and it did not seem altogether inappropriate to me. Fairy tales nearly always have some simple moral lesson of good and evil, but that is not the secret of their fascination any more, I hope, than the philosophical import that might be distilled from the fantasies of *Camino Real* is the principal element of its appeal.

To me the appeal of this work is its unusual degree of freedom. When it began to get under way I felt a new sensation of release, as if I could 'ride out' like a tenor sax taking the breaks in a Dixieland combo or a piano in a bop session. You may call it self-indulgence, but I was not doing it merely for myself. I could not have felt a purely private thrill of release unless I had hope of sharing this experience with lots and lots of audiences to come.

My desire was to give these audiences my own sense of something wild and unrestricted that ran like water in the mountains, or clouds changing shape in a gale, or the continually dissolving and transforming images of a dream. This sort of freedom is not chaos nor anarchy.

*Written prior to the Broadway premiere of *Camino Real* and published in the New York *Times* on Sunday, 15 March 1953.

On the contrary, it is the result of painstaking design, and in this work I have given more conscious attention to form and construction than I have in any work before. Freedom is not achieved simply by working freely.

Elia Kazan was attracted to this work mainly, I believe, for the same reason – its freedom and mobility of form. I know that we have kept saying the word 'flight' to each other as if the play were merely an abstraction of the impulse to fly, and most of the work out of town, his in staging, mine in cutting and revising, has been with this impulse in mind: the achievement of a continual flow. Speech after speech and bit after bit that were nice in themselves have been remorselessly blasted out of the script and its staging wherever they seemed to obstruct or divert this flow.

There have been plenty of indications already that this play will exasperate and confuse a certain number of people which we hope is not so large as the number it is likely to please. At each performance a number of people have stamped out of the auditorium, with little regard for those whom they have had to crawl over, almost as if the building had caught on fire, and there have been sibilant noises on the way out and demands for money back if the cashier was foolish enough to remain in his box.

I am at a loss to explain this phenomenon, and if I am being facetious about one thing, I am being quite serious about another when I say that I had never for one minute supposed that the play would seem obscure and confusing to anyone who was willing to meet it even less than halfway. It was a costly production, and for this reason I had to read it aloud, together with a few of the actors on one occasion, before large groups of prospective backers, before the funds to produce it were in the till. It was only then that I came up against the disconcerting surprise that some people would think that the play needed clarification.

My attitude is intransigent. I still don't agree that it needs any explanation. Some poet has said that a poem should not mean but be. Of course, a play is not a poem, not even a poetic play has quite the same licence as a poem. But to go to *Camino Real* with the inflexible demands of a logician is unfair to both parties.

In Philadelphia a young man from a literary periodical saw the play and then cross-examined me about all its dream-like images. He had made a list of them while he watched the play, and afterward at my hotel he brought out the list and asked me to explain the meaning of each one. I can't deny that I used a lot of those things called symbols but being a self-defensive creature, I say that symbols are nothing but the natural speech of drama.

We all have in our conscious and unconscious minds a great vocabulary of images, and I think all human communication is based on these images as are our dreams; and a symbol in a play has only one legitimate purpose which is to say a thing more directly and simply and beautifully than it could be said in words.

I hate writing that is a parade of images for the sake of images; I hate it so much that I close a book in disgust when it keeps on saying one thing is like another; I even get disgusted with poems that make nothing but comparisons between one thing and another. But I repeat that symbols, when used respectfully, are the purest language of plays. Sometimes it would take page after tedious page of exposition to put across an idea that can be said with an object or a gesture on the lighted stage.

To take one case in point: the battered portmanteau of Jacques Casanova is hurled from the balcony of a luxury hotel when his remittance cheque fails to come through. While the portmanteau is still in the air, he shouts: 'Careful, I have – ' – and when it has crashed to the street he continues – 'fragile – mementoes . . . ' I suppose that is a symbol, at least it is an object used to express as directly and vividly as possible certain things which could be said in pages of dull talk.

As for those patrons who departed before the final scene, I offer myself this tentative bit of solace: that these theatregoers may be a little domesticated in their theatrical tastes. A cage represents security as well as confinement to a bird that has grown used to being in it; and when a theatrical work kicks over the traces with such apparent insouciance, security seems challenged and, instead of participating in its sense of freedom, one out of a certain number of playgoers will rush back out to the more accustomed implausibility of the street he lives on.

To modify this effect of complaisance I would like to admit to you quite frankly that I can't say with any personal conviction that I have written a good play, I only know that I have felt a release in this work which I wanted you to feel with me.

AFTERWORD

Once in a while someone will say to me that he would rather wait for a play to come out as a book than see a live performance of it, where he would be distracted from its true values, if it has any, by so much that is mere spectacle and sensation and consequently must be meretricious and vulgar. There are plays meant for reading. I have read them. I have read the works of 'thinking playwrights' as distinguished from us who are permitted only to feel, and probably read them earlier and appreciated them as much as those who invoke their names nowadays like the incantation of Aristophanes' frogs. But the incontinent blaze of a live theatre, a theatre meant for seeing and for feeling, has never been and never will be extinguished by a bucket brigade of critics, new or old, bearing vessels that range from cut-glass punch bowl to Haviland tea-cup. And in my dissident opinion, a play in a book is only the shadow of a play and not even a clear shadow of it. Those who did not like *Camino Real* on the stage will not be likely to form a higher opinion of it in print, for of all the works I have written, this one was meant most for the vulgarity of performance. The printed script of a play is hardly more than an architect's blueprint of a house not yet built or built and destroyed.

The colour, the grace and levitation, the structural pattern in motion, the quick interplay of live beings, suspended like fitful lightning in a cloud, these things are the play, not words on paper, nor thoughts and ideas of an author, those shabby things snatched off basement counters at Gimbels.

My own creed as a playwright is fairly close to that expressed by the painter in Shaw's play *The Doctor's Dilemma*: 'I believe in Michelangelo, Velasquez, and Rembrandt; in the might of design, the mystery of colour, the redemption of all things by beauty everlasting and the message of art that has made these hands blessed. Amen.'

How much art his hands were blessed with or how much mine are, I don't know, but that art is a blessing is certain and that it contains its message is also certain, and I feel, as the painter did, that the message lies in those abstract beauties of form and colour and line, to which I would add light and motion.

AFTERWORD

In these following pages are only the formulas by which a play could exist.

Dynamic is a word in disrepute at the moment, and so, I suppose, is the word *organic*, but those terms still define the dramatic values that I value most and which I value more as they are more deprecated by the ones self-appointed to save what they have never known.

1 June 1953   TENNESSEE WILLIAMS

CAMINO REAL

This play was first performed in England at the Phoenix Theatre on 8 April 1957, with the following cast:

DON QUIXOTE	John Wood
SANCHO PANZA	Ronald Barker
GUTMAN	Harold Kasket
CASANOVA	Harry Andrews
OLYMPE	Isla Cameron
ROSITA	Golda Casimir
THE DREAMER	Leslie Bravery
LA MADRECITA	Eileen Way
THE GIPSY	Freda Jackson
KILROY	Denholm Elliott
NURSIE	Ronald Barker
A. RATT	Gordon Gostelow
BARON DE CHARLUS	Martin Miller
ESMERALDA	Elizabeth Seal
LORD MULLIGAN	John Nettleton
LADY MULLIGAN	Lally Bowers
MARGUERITE GAUTIER	Diana Wynyard
BYRON	Robert Hardy

Produced by Peter Hall

PROLOGUE

As the curtain rises, on an almost lightless stage, there is a loud singing of wind, accompanied by distant, measured reverberations like pounding surf or distant shellfire. Above the ancient wall that backs the set and the perimeter of mountains visible above the wall, are flickers of a white radiance as though daybreak were a white bird caught in a net and struggling to rise.

The plaza is seen fitfully by this light. It belongs to a tropical seaport that bears a confusing, but somehow harmonious, resemblance to such widely scattered ports as Tangiers, Havana, Vera Cruz, Casablanca, Shanghai, New Orleans.

On stage left is the luxury side of the street, containing the façade of the Siete Mares hotel and its low terrace on which are a number of glass-topped white iron tables and chairs. In the downstairs there is a great bay window in which are seen a pair of elegant 'dummies', one seated, one standing behind, looking out into the plaza with painted smiles. Upstairs is a small balcony and behind it a large window exposing a wall on which is hung a phoenix painted on silk: this should be softly lighted now and then in the play, since resurrections are so much a part of its meaning.

Opposite the hotel is Skid Row which contains the Gipsy's gaudy stall, the Loan Shark's establishment with a window containing a variety of pawned articles, and the 'Ritz Men Only' which is a flea-bag hotel or flophouse and which has a practical window above its downstairs entrance, in which a bum will appear from time to time to deliver appropriate or contrapuntal song titles.

Upstage is a great flight of stairs that mount the ancient wall to a sort of archway that leads out into 'Terra Incognita', as it is called in the play, a wasteland between the walled town and the distant perimeter of snow-topped mountains.

Downstage right and left are a pair of arches which give entrance to dead-end street.

[*Immediately after the curtain rises a shaft of blue light is thrown down a central aisle of the theatre, and in this light, advancing from the back of the house, appears Don Quixote de la Mancha, dressed like an old 'desert rat'. As he enters the aisle he shouts, 'Hola!', in a cracked old voice which is still full of energy and is answered by another voice which is impatient and tired, that of his squire, Sancho Panza. Stumbling with a fatigue which is only physical, the old knight comes down the aisle, and Sancho follows a couple of yards behind him, loaded down with equipment that ranges from a medieval shield to a military canteen or Thermos bottle. Shouts are exchanged between them.*]

QUIXOTE [*ranting above the wind in a voice which is nearly as old*]: Blue is the colour of distance!

SANCHO [*wearily behind him*]: Yes, distance is blue.

QUIXOTE: Blue is also the colour of nobility.

SANCHO: Yes, nobility's blue.

QUIXOTE: Blue is the colour of distance and nobility, and that's why an old knight should always have somewhere about him a bit of blue ribbon. . . .

[*He jostles the elbow of an aisle-sitter as he staggers with fatigue; he mumbles an apology.*]

SANCHO: Yes, a bit of blue ribbon.

QUIXOTE: A bit of faded blue ribbon, tucked away in whatever remains of his armour, or borne on the tip of his lance, his – unconquerable lance! It serves to remind an old knight of distance that he has gone and distance he has yet to go. . . .

[*Sancho mutters the Spanish word for excrement as several pieces of rusty armour fall into the aisle.*

Quixote has now arrived at the foot of the steps on to the forestage. He pauses there as if wandering out of or into a dream. Sancho draws up clanking behind him.

Mr Gutman, a lordly fat man wearing a linen suit and a pith helmet, appears dimly on the balcony of the Siete Mares, a white cockatoo on his wrist. The bird cries out harshly.]

GUTMAN: Hush, Aurora.

QUIXOTE: It also reminds an old knight of that green country he lived in which was the youth of his heart, before such singing words as *Truth!*

SANCHO [*panting*]: – Truth.

QUIXOTE: *Valour!*

SANCHO: – Valour.

QUIXOTE [*elevating his lance*]: *Devoir!*

SANCHO: – Devoir . . .

QUIXOTE: – turned into the meaningless mumble of some old monk hunched over cold mutton at supper!

[*Gutman alerts a pair of Guards in the plaza, who cross with red lanterns to either side of the proscenium where they lower black and white striped barrier gates as if the proscenium marked a frontier. One of them, with a hand on his holster, advances toward the pair on the steps.*]

GUARD: Vien aquí.

[*Sancho hangs back but Quixote stalks up to the barrier gate. The Guard turns a flashlight on his long and exceedingly grave red face, 'frisks' him casually for concealed weapons, examines a rusty old knife and tosses it contemptuously away.*]

Sus papeles! Sus documentos!

[*Quixote fumblingly produces some tattered old papers from the lining of his hat.*]

GUTMAN [*impatiently*]: Who is it?

GUARD: An old desert rat named Quixote.

GUTMAN: Oh! – Expected! – Let him in.

[*The Guards raise the barrier gate and one sits down to smoke on the terrace. Sancho hangs back still. A dispute takes place on the forestage and steps into the aisle.*]

QUIXOTE: Forward!

SANCHO: Aw, naw. I know this place. [*He produces a crumpled parchment.*] Here it is on the chart. Look, it says here: 'Continue until you come to the square of a walled town which is the end of the Camino Real and the beginning of the Camino Real. Halt there,' it says, 'and turn back, Traveller, for the spring of humanity has gone dry in this place and –'

QUIXOTE [*he snatches the chart from him and reads the rest of the inscription*]: ' – there are no birds in the country except wild birds that are tamed and kept in –' [*He holds the chart close to his nose.*] – Cages!

SANCHO [*urgently*]: Let's go back to La Mancha!

QUIXOTE: Forward!

SANCHO: The time has come for retreat! . . .

QUIXOTE: The time for retreat never comes!

SANCHO: *I'm going back to La Mancha!*

[*He dumps the knightly equipment into the orchestra pit.*]

QUIXOTE: *Without me?*

SANCHO [*bustling up the aisle*]: With you or without you, old tireless and tiresome master!

QUIXOTE [*imploringly*]: *Saaaaaan–chooooooooo!*

SANCHO [*near the top of the aisle*]: I'm going back to La Maaaa–aaaaan–chaaaaaaa. . . .

[*He disappears as the blue light in the aisle dims out.. The Guard puts out his cigarette and wanders out of the plaza. The wind moans and Gutman laughs softly as the Ancient Knight enters the plaza with such a desolate air.*]

QUIXOTE [*looking about the plaza*]: – Lonely . . .

[*To his surprise the word is echoed softly by almost unseen figures huddled below the stairs and against the wall of the town. Quixote leans upon his lance and observes with a wry smile –*]

– When so many are lonely as seem to be lonely, it would be inexcusably selfish to be lonely alone.

[*He shakes out a dusty blanket. Shadowy arms extend toward him and voices murmur.*]

VOICE: Sleep. Sleep. Sleep.

QUIXOTE [*arranging his blanket*]: Yes, I'll sleep for a while, I'll sleep and dream for a while against the wall of this town ...

[*A mandolin or guitar plays 'The Nightingale of France'.*]

– And my dream will be a pageant, a masque in which old meanings will be remembered and possibly new ones discovered, and when I wake from this sleep and this disturbing pageant of a dream, I'll choose one among its shadows to take along with me in the place of Sancho ...

[*He blows his nose between his fingers and wipes them on his shirt tail.*]

– For new companions are not as familiar as old ones but all the same – they're old ones with only slight differences of face and figure, which may or may not be improvements, and it would be selfish of me to be lonely alone. ...

[*He stumbles down the incline into the Pit below the stairs where most of the Street People huddle beneath awnings of open stalls. The white cockatoo squawks.*]

GUTMAN: Hush, Aurora.

QUIXOTE: And to-morrow at this same hour, which we call madrugada, the loveliest of all words, except the word alba, and that word also means daybreak –

– Yes, at daybreak to-morrow I will go on from there with a new companion and this old bit of blue ribbon to keep me in mind of distance that I have gone and distance I have yet to go, and also to keep me in mind of –

[*The cockatoo cries wildly.*

Quixote nods as if in agreement with the outcry and folds himself into his blanket below the great stairs.]

GUTMAN [*stroking the cockatoo's crest*]: Be still, Aurora. I know it's morning, Aurora.

[*Daylight turns the plaza silver and slowly gold. Vendors rise beneath white awnings of stalls. The Gipsy's stall opens. A tall, courtly figure, in his latemiddle years (Jacques Casanova) crosses from the Siete Mares to the Loan Shark's, removing a silver snuff box from his pocket as Gutman speaks. His costume, like that of all the legendary characters in the play (except perhaps Quixote) is generally 'modern' but with vestigial touches of the period to which he was actually related. The cane and the snuff box and perhaps a brocaded vest may be sufficient to give this historical suggestion in Casanova's case. He bears his hawk-like head with a sort of anxious pride on most occasions, a pride maintained under a steadily mounting pressure.*]

– It's morning and after morning. It's afternoon, ha, ha! And now I must go downstairs to announce the beginning of that old wanderer's dream. . . .

[*He withdraws from the balcony as oid Prudence Duvernoy stumbles out of the hotel, as if not yet quite awake from an afternoon siesta. Chattering with beads and bracelets, she wanders vagely down into the plaza, raising a faded green silk parasol, damp henna-streaked hair slipping under a monstrous hat of faded silk roses; she is searching for a lost poodle.*]

PRUDENCE: Trique? Trique?

[*Jacques comes out of the Loan Shark's replacing his case angrily in his pocket.*]

JACQUES: Why, I'd rather give it to a street beggar! This case is a Boucheron, I won it at faro at the summer palace, at Tsarskeo Selo in the winter of –

[*The Loan Shark slams the door. Jacques glares, then shrugs and starts across the plaza. Old Prudence is crouched over the filthy grey bundle of a dying mongrel by the fountain.*]

PRUDENCE: Trique, oh, Trique!

[*The Gipsy's son, Abdullah, watches, giggling.*]

JACQUES [*reproving*]: It is a terrible thing for an old woman to outlive her dogs.

[*He crosses to Prudence and gently disengages the animal from her grasp.*]

Madam, that is not Trique.

PRUDENCE: – When I woke up she wasn't in her basket. . . .

JACQUES: Sometimes we sleep too long in the afternoon and when we wake we find things changed, Signora.

PRUDENCE: Oh, you're Italian!

JACQUES: I am from Venice, Signora.

PRUDENCE: Ah, Venice, city of pearls! I saw you last night on the terrace dining with – Oh, I'm so worried about her! I'm an old friend of hers, perhaps she's mentioned me to you. Prudence Duvernoy? I was her best friend in the old days in Paris, but now she's forgotten so much. . . .

I hope you have influence with her!

[*A waltz of Camille's time in Paris is heard.*]

I want you to give her a message from a certain wealthy old gentleman that she met at one of those watering places she used to go to for her health. She resembled his daughter who died of consumption and so he adored Camille, lavished everything on her! What did she do? Took a young lover who hadn't a couple of pennies to rub together, disinherited by his father because of *her*! Oh, you can't do that, not now, not any more, you've got to be realistic on the Camino Real!

[*Gutman has come out on the terrace: he announces quietly – *]

GUTMAN: Block One on the Camino Real.

PRUDENCE [*continuing*]: Yes, you've got to be practical on it!
Well, give her this message, please, Sir. He wants her back
on any terms whatsoever! [*Her speech gathers furious
momentum.*] Her evenings will be free. He wants only her
mornings, mornings are hard on old men because their
hearts beat slowly, and he wants only her mornings! Well,
that's how it should be! A sensible arrangement! Elderly
gentlemen have to content themselves with a lady's spare
time before supper! Isn't that so? Of course so! And so I told
him! I told him, Camille isn't well! She requires delicate
care! Has many debts, creditors storm her doors! 'How
much does she owe?' he asked me, and, oh, did I do some
lightning mathematics! Jewels in pawn, I told him, pearls,
rings, necklaces, bracelets, diamond eardrops are in pawn!
Horses put up for sale at a public auction!

JACQUES [*appalled by this torrent*]: Signora, Signora, all of these
things are –

PRUDENCE: – What?

JACQUES: *Dreams!*

[*Gutman laughs. A woman sings at a distance.*]

PRUDENCE [*continuing with less assurance*]: – You're not so
young as I thought when I saw you last night on the terrace
by candlelight on the – Oh, but – Ho ho! – I bet there is *one*
old fountain in this plaza that hasn't gone dry!

[*She pokes him obscenely. He recoils. Gutman laughs. Jacques
starts away but she seizes his arm again, and the torrent of speech
continues.*]

PRUDENCE: Wait, wait, listen! Her candle is burning low. But how can you tell? She might have a lingering end, and charity hospitals? Why, you might as well take a flying leap into the Streetcleaners' barrel. Oh, I've told her and told her not to live in a dream! A dream is nothing to live in, why, it's gone like a –

Don't let her elegance fool you! That girl has done the Camino in carriages but she has also done it on foot! She knows every stone the Camino is paved with! So tell her this. You tell her, she won't listen to me! – Times and conditions have undergone certain changes since we were friends in Paris, and now we dismiss young lovers with skins of silk and eyes like a child's first prayer, we put them away as lightly as we put away white gloves meant only for summer, and pick up a pair of black ones, suitable for winter. . . .

[*The singing voice rises: then subsides.*]

JACQUES: Excuse me, Madam.

[*He tears himself from her grasp and rushes into the Siete Mares.*]

PRUDENCE [*dazed, to Gutman*]: – What block is this?
GUTMAN: Block One.
PRUDENCE: I didn't hear the announcement. . . .
GUTMAN [*coldly*]: Well, now you do.

[*Olympe comes out of the lobby with a pale orange silk parasol like a floating moon.*]

OLYMPE: Oh, there you are, I've looked for you high and low! – mostly low. . . .

[*They float vaguely out into the dazzling plaza as though a*

133

capricious wind took them, finally drifting through the Moorish arch downstage right.

The song dies out.]

GUTMAN [*lighting a thin cigar*]: Block Two on the Camino Real.

BLOCK TWO

After Gutman's announcement, a hoarse cry is heard. A figure in rags, skin blackened by the sun, tumbles crazily down the steep alley to the plaza. He turns about blindly, murmuring: 'Adonde la fuente?' He stumbles against the hideous old prostitute Rosita who grins horribly and whispers something to him, hitching up her ragged, filthy skirt. Then she gives him a jocular push toward the fountain. He falls upon his belly and thrusts his hands into the dried-up basin. Then he staggers to his feet with a despairing cry.

THE SURVIVOR: La fuente está seca!

[*Rosita laughs madly but the other Street People moan. A dry gourd rattles.*]

ROSITA: The fountain is dry, but there's plenty to drink in the Siete Mares!

[*She shoves him toward the hotel. The proprietor, Gutman, steps out, smoking a thin cigar, fanning himself with a palm leaf. As The Survivor advances, Gutman whistles. A man in military dress comes out upon the low terrace.*]

OFFICER: Go back!

[*The Survivor stumbles forward. The Officer fires at him. He lowers his hands to his stomach, turns slowly about with a lost expression, looking up at the sky, and stumbles toward the fountain. During the scene that follows, until the entrance of La Madrecita and her Son, The Survivor drags himself slowly about the concrete rim of the fountain, almost entirely ignored, as a dying pariah dog in a starving country. Jacques Casanova comes out upon the terrace of the Siete Mares. Now he passes the hotel proprietor's impassive figure, descending a step beneath and a little in advance of him, and without looking at him.*]

JACQUES [*with infinite weariness and disgust*]: What has happened?

GUTMAN [*serenely*]: We have entered the second in a progress of sixteen blocks on the Camino Real. It's five o'clock. That angry old lion, the Sun, looked back once and growled and then went switching his tail toward the cool shade of the Sierras. Our guests have taken their afternoon siestas. . . .

[*The Survivor has come out upon the forestage, now, not like a dying man but like a shy speaker who has forgotten the opening line of his speech. He is only a little crouched over with a hand obscuring the red stain over his belly. Two or three Street People wander about calling their wares: 'Tacos, tacos, fritos . . .' – 'Loteria, loteria' – Rosita shuffles around, calling 'Love? Love?' – pulling down the filthy décolletage of her blouse to show more of her sagging bosom. The Survivor arrives at the top of the stairs descending into the orchestra of the theatre, and hangs on to it, looking out reflectively as a man over the rail of a boat coming into a somewhat disturbingly strange harbour.*]

GUTMAN [*continuing*]: – They suffer from extreme fatigue, our guests at the Siete Mares, all of them have a degree or two of fever. Questions are passed amongst them like something illicit and shameful, like counterfeit money or drugs or indecent postcards –

[*He leans forward and whispers*]: – 'What is this place?
Where are we? What is the meaning of – *Shhhh!*' – Ha ha . . .

THE SURVIVOR [*very softly to the audience*]: I once had a pony
named Peeto. He caught in his nostrils the scent of thunder-
storms coming even before the clouds had crossed the
Sierra. . . .

VENDOR: Tacos, tacos, fritos. . . .

ROSITA: Love? Love?

LADY MULLIGAN [*to waiter on terrace*]: Are you sure no one
called me? I was expecting a call. . . .

GUTMAN [*smiling*]: My guests are confused and exhausted but
at this hour they pull themselves together, and drift downstairs on the wings of gin and the lift, they drift into the public
rooms and exchange notes again on fashionable couturiers
and custom tailors, restaurants, vintages of wine, hair-
dressers, plastic surgeons, girls and young men susceptible
to offers. . . .

[*There is a hum of light conversation and laughter within.*]

– Hear them? They're exchanging notes. . . .

JACQUES [*striking the terrace with his cane*]: I asked you what has
happened in the plaza!

GUTMAN: Oh, in the plaza, ha ha! – Happenings in the plaza
don't concern us. . . .

JACQUES: I heard shots fired.

GUTMAN: Shots were fired to remind you of your good
fortune in staying here. The public fountains have gone dry,
you know, but the Siete Mares was erected over the only
perpetual never-dried-up spring in Tierre Caliente, and of
course that advantage has to be – protected – sometimes by –
martial law. . . .

[*The guitar resumes.*]

THE SURVIVOR: When Peeto, my pony, was born – he stood

on his four legs at once, and accepted the world! – He was wiser than I. . . .

VENDOR: Fritos, fritos, tacos!

ROSITA: Love!

THE SURVIVOR: – When Peeto was one year old he was wiser than God!

[*A wind sings across the plaza; a dry gourd rattles.*]

'Peeto, Peeto!' the Indian boys call after him, trying to stop him – trying to stop the wind!

[*The Survivor's head sags forward. He sits down as slowly as an old man on a park bench. Jacques strikes the terrace again with his cane and starts toward The Survivor. The Guard seizes his elbow.*]

JACQUES: Don't put your hand on *me*!

GUARD: *Stay here.*

GUTMAN: Remain on the terrace, please, Signor Casanova.

JACQUES [*fiercely*]: *Cognac!*

[*The Waiter whispers to Gutman. Gutman chuckles.*]

GUTMAN: The Maître 'D' tells me that your credit has been discontinued in the restaurant and bar, he says that he has enough of your tabs to pave the terrace with!

JACQUES: What a piece of impertinence! I told the man that the letter that I'm expecting has been delayed in the mail. The postal service in this country is fantastically disorganized, and you know it! You also know that Mlle Gautier will guarantee my tabs!

GUTMAN: Then let her pick them up at dinner to-night if you're hungry!

JACQUES: I'm not accustomed to this kind of treatment on the Camino *Real*!

GUTMAN: Oh, you'll be, you'll be, after a single night at the 'Ritz Men Only'. That's where you'll have to transfer your patronage if the letter containing the remittance cheque doesn't arrive to-night.

JACQUES: I assure you that I shall do nothing of the sort! – To-night or ever!

GUTMAN: Watch out, old hawk, the wind is ruffling your feathers!

[*Jacques sinks trembling into a chair.*]

– Give him a thimble of brandy before he collapses . . . Fury is a luxury of the young, their veins are resilient, but his are brittle. . . .

JACQUES: Here I sit, submitting to insult for a thimble of brandy while directly in front of me –

[*The singer, La Madrecita, enters the plaza. She is a blind woman led by a ragged Young Man. The Waiter brings Jacques a brandy.*]

– a man in the plaza dies like a pariah dog! – I take the brandy! I sip it! – My heart is too tired to break, my heart is too tired to – break. . . .

[*La Madrecita chants softly. She slowly raises her arm to point at The Survivor crouched on the steps from the plaza.*]

GUTMAN [*suddenly*]: Give me the phone! Connect me with the Palace. Get me the Generalissimo, quick, quick, quick!

[*The Survivor rises feebly and shuffles very slowly toward the extended arms of 'The Little Blind One'.*]

Generalissimo? Gutman speaking! Hello, sweetheart. There has been a little incident in the plaza. You know that party of young explorers that attempted to cross the desert on foot? Well, one of them's come back. He was very thirsty. He found the fountain dry. He started toward the hotel. He was politely advised to advance no farther. But he disregarded this advice. Action had to be taken. And now, and now – that old blind woman they call 'La Madrecita'? – She's come into the plaza with the man called 'The Dreamer' . . .

THE SURVIVOR: Donde?

THE DREAMER: Aquí!

GUTMAN [*continuing*]: You remember those two! I once mentioned them to you. You said 'They're harmless dreamers and they're loved by the people.' – 'What,' I asked you, 'is harmless about a dreamer, and what,' I asked you, 'is harmless about the love of the people? – Revolution only needs good dreamers who remember their dreams, and the love of the people belongs safely only to you – their Generalissimo!' – Yes, now the blind woman has recovered her sight and is extending her arms to the wounded Survivor, and the man with the guitar is leading him to her. . . .

[*The described action is being acted.*]

Wait one moment! There's a possibility that the forbidden word may be spoken! Yes! The forbidden word is about to be spoken!

[*The Dreamer places an arm about the blinded Survivor, and cries out.*]

THE DREAMER: *Hermano!*

[*The cry is repeated like springing fire and a loud murmur sweeps the crowd. They push forward with cupped hands extended and the gasping cries of starving people at the sight of bread. Two Military Guards herd them back under the colonnades with clubs and drawn revolvers.*

La Madrecita chants softly with her blind eyes lifted. A guard starts towards her. The People shout 'NO!']

LA MADRECITA [*chanting*]: 'Rojo está el sol! Rojo está el sol de sangre! Blanca está la luna! Blanca está la luna de miedo!'

[*The crowd makes a turning motion.*]

GUTMAN [*to the Waiter*]: Put up the ropes!

[*Velvet ropes are strung very quickly about the terrace of the Siete Mares. They are like the ropes on decks of steamers in rough waters. Gutman shouts into the phone again.*]

The word was spoken. The crowd is agitated. Hang on!

[*He lays down instrument.*]

JACQUES [*hoarsely, shaken*]: He said 'Hermano'. That's the word for brother.

GUTMAN [*calmly*]: Yes, the most dangerous word in any human tongue is the word for brother. It's inflammatory. – I don't suppose it can be struck out of the language altogether but it must be reserved for strictly private usage in back of sound-proof walls. Otherwise it disturbs the population. . . .

JACQUES: The people need the word. They're thirsty for it!

GUTMAN: What are these creatures; Mendicants. Prostitutes. Thieves and petty vendors in a bazaar where the human heart is a part of the bargain.

JACQUES: Because they need the word and the word is forbidden!

GUTMAN: The word is said in pulpits and at tables of council where its volatile essence can be contained. But on the lips of these creatures, what is it? A wanton incitement to riot, without understanding. For what is a brother to them but someone to get ahead of, to cheat, to lie to, to undersell in the market. Brother, you say to a man whose wife you sleep with! – But now, you see, the word has disturbed the people and made it necessary to invoke martial law!

[*Meanwhile The Dreamer has brought The Survivor to La Madrecita, who is seated on the cement rim of the fountain. She has cradled the dying man in her arms in the attitude of a Pietà.*
The Dreamer is crouched beside them, softly playing a guitar. Now he springs up with a harsh cry.]

THE DREAMER: *Muerto!*

[*The Streetcleaners' piping commences at a distance. Gutman seizes the phone again.*]

GUTMAN [*into phone*]: Generalissimo, the Survivor is no longer surviving. I think we'd better have some public diversion right away. Put the Gipsy on! Have her announce the Fiesta!

LOUDSPEAKER [*responding instantly*]: Damas y Caballeros! The next voice you hear will be the voice of – the Gipsy!

GIPSY [*over loudspeaker*]: Hoy! Noche de Fiesta! To-night the moon will restore the virginity of my daughter!

GUTMAN: Bring on the Gipsy's daughter, Esmeralda. Show the virgin-to-be!

[*Esmeralda is led from the Gipsy's stall by a severe duenna, 'Nursie', out upon the forestage. She is manacled by the wrist to the duenna. Her costume is vaguely Levantine.*
Guards are herding the crowd back again.]

GUTMAN: Ha ha! Ho ho ho! Music!

[*There is gay music. Rosita dances.*]

Abdullah! You're on!

[*Abdullah skips into the plaza, shouting histrionically.*]

ABDULLAH: To-night the moon will restore the virginity of my sister, Esmeralda!

GUTMAN: *Dance, boy!*

[*Esmeralda is led back into the stall. Throwing off his burnoose, Abdullah dances with Rosita. Behind their dance, armed Guards force La Madrecita and The Dreamer to retreat from the fountain, leaving the lifeless body of The Survivor. All at once there is a discordant blast of brass instruments.*
Kilroy comes into the plaza. He is a young American vagrant, about twenty-seven. He wears dungarees and a skivvy shirt, the

*pants faded nearly white from long wear and much washing,
fitting him as closely as the clothes of sculpture. He has a pair of
golden boxing gloves slung about his neck and he carries a small
duffle bag. His belt is ruby-and-emerald-studded with the word
CHAMP in bold letters. He stops before a chalked inscription
on a wall downstage which says: 'Kilroy Is Coming!' He
scratches out 'Coming' and over it prints 'Here!']*

GUTMAN: Ho ho! – a clown! The Eternal Punchinella! That's
exactly what's needed in a time of crisis!
Block Three on the Camino Real.

BLOCK THREE

KILROY [*genially, to all present*]: Ha ha!

[*Then he walks up to the Officer by the terrace of the Siete
Mares.*]

Buenas dias, señor.

[*He gets no response – barely even a glance.*]

Habla Inglesia? Usted?
OFFICER: What is it you want?
KILROY: Where is Western Union or Wells-Fargo? I got to
send a wire to some friends in the States.
OFFICER: No hay Western Union, no hay Wells-Fargo.
KILROY: That is very peculiar. I never struck a town yet that
didn't have one or the other. I just got off a boat. Lousiest
frigging tub I ever shipped on, one continual hell it was, all
the way up from Rio. And me sick, too. I picked up one of

those tropical fevers. No sick-bay on that tub, no doctor, no medicine or nothing, not even one quinine pill, and I was burning up with Christ knows how much fever. I couldn't make them understand I was sick. I got a bad heart, too. I had to retire from the prize ring because of my heart. I was the light heavyweight champion of the West Coast, won these gloves! – before my ticker went bad. – Feel my chest! Go on, feel it! Feel it. I've got a heart in my chest as big as the head of a baby. Ha ha! They stood me in front of a screen that makes you transparent and that's what they seen inside me, a heart in my chest as big as the head of a baby! With something like that you don't need the Gipsy to tell you, 'Time is short, Baby – get ready to hitch on wings!' The medics wouldn't okay me for no more fights. They said to give up liquor and smoking and sex! – To give up sex! – I used to believe a man couldn't live without sex – but he can – if he wants to! My real true woman, my wife, she would of stuck with me, but it was all spoiled with her being scared and me, too, that a real hard kiss would kill me! – So one night while she was sleeping I wrote her good-bye. . . .

[*He notices a lack of attention in the Officer: he grins.*]

No comprendo the lingo?

OFFICER: What is it you want?

KILROY: Excuse my ignorance, but what place is this? What is this country and what is the name of this town? I know it seems funny of me to ask such a question. Loco! But I was so glad to get off that rotten tub that I didn't ask nothing of no one except my pay – and I got short-changed on that. I have trouble counting these pesos or Whatzit-you-call-'em.

[*He jerks out his wallet.*]

All-a-this-here. In the States that pile of lettuce would make you a plutocrat! – But I bet you this stuff don't add up to fifty dollars American coin. Ha ha!

OFFICER: Ha ha.
KILROY: Ha ha!
OFFICER [*making it sound like a death-rattle*]: Ha-ha-ha-ha-ha.

[*He turns and starts into the cantina. Kilroy grabs his arm.*]

KILROY: Hey!
OFFICER: What is it you want?
KILROY: What is the name of this country and this town?

[*The Officer thrusts his elbow in Kilroy's stomach and twists his
arm loose with a Spanish curse. He kicks the swinging doors open
and enters the cantina.*]

Brass hats are the same everywhere.

[*As soon as the Officer goes, the Street People come forward and
crowd about Kilroy with their wheedling cries.*]

STREET PEOPLE: Dulces, dulces! Loteria! Loteria! Pasteles,
café con leche!
KILROY: No caree, no caree!

[*The Prostitute creeps up to him and grins.*]

ROSITA: Love? Love?
KILROY: What did you say?
ROSITA: *Love?*
KILROY: Sorry – I don't feature that. [*To Audience.*] I have
ideals.

[*The Gipsy appears on the roof of her establishment with
Esmeralda whom she secures by handcuffs to the iron railing.*]

GIPSY: Stay there while I give the pitch!

[*She then advances with a portable microphone.*]

Testing! One, two, three, four!
NURSIE [*from offstage*]: You're on the air!

GIPSY'S LOUDSPEAKER: Are you perplexed by something? Are you tired out and confused? Do you have a fever?

[*Kilroy looks around for the source of the voice.*]

Do you feel yourself to be spiritually unprepared for the age of exploding atoms? Do you distrust the newspapers? Are you suspicious of governments? Have you arrived at a point on the Camino Real where the walls converge not in the distance but right in front of your nose? Docs further progress appear impossible to you? Are you afraid of anything at all? Afraid of your heartbeat? Or the eyes of strangers! Afraid of breathing? Afraid of not breathing? Do you wish that things could be straight and simple again as they were in your childhood? Would you like to go back to Kindy Garten?

[*Rosita has crept up to Kilroy while he listens. She reaches out to him. At the same time a Pickpocket lifts his wallet.*]

KILROY [*catching the whore's wrist*]: Keep y'r hands off me, y' dirty ole bag! No caree putas! No loteria, no dulces, nada – so get away! Vamoose! All of you! Quit picking at me!

[*He reaches in his pocket and jerks out a handful of small copper and silver coins which he flings disgustedly down the street. The grotesque people scramble after it with their inhuman cries. Kilroy goes on a few steps – then stops short – feeling the back pocket of his dungarees. Then he lets out a startled cry.*]

Robbed! My God, I've been robbed!

[*The Street People scatter to the walls.*]

Which of you got my wallet? *Which* of you dirty – ? Shh – Uh!

[*They mumble with gestures of incomprehension. He marches back to the entrance to the hotel.*]

Hey! Officer! Official! – General!

[*The Officer finally lounges out of the hotel entrance and glances at Kilroy.*]

Tiende? One of them's got my wallet! Picked it out of my pocket while that old whore there was groping me! Don't you comprendo?

OFFICER: Nobody rob you. You don't have no pesos.

KILROY: Huh?

OFFICER: You just dreaming that you have money. You don't ever have money. Nunca! Nada!

[*He spits between his teeth.*]

Loco . . .

[*The Officer crosses to the fountain. Kilroy stares at him, then bawls out.*]

KILROY [*to the Street People*]: We'll see what the American Embassy has to say about this! I'll go to the American Consul. Whichever of you rotten spivs lifted my wallet is going to jail – calaboose! I hope I have made myself plain. If not, I will make myself plainer!

[*There are scattered laughs among the crowd. He crosses to the fountain. He notices the body of the no longer Survivor, kneels beside it, shakes it, turns it over, springs up and shouts:*]

Hey! This guy is dead!

[*There is the sound of the Streetcleaners' piping. They trundle their white barrel into the plaza from one of the downstage arches. The appearance of these men undergoes a progressive alteration through the play. When they first appear they are almost like any such public servants in a tropical country; their white jackets are dirtier than the musicians' and some of the stains are red. They have on white caps with black visors. They are continually exchanging sly jokes and giggling unpleasantly*]

together. Lord Mulligan has come out upon the terrace and as
they pass him, they pause for a moment, point at him, snicker.
He is extremely discomfited by this impertinence, touches his
chest as if he felt a palpitation and turns back inside.

Kilroy yells to the advancing Streetcleaners.]

There's a dead man layin' here!

[*They giggle again. Briskly they lift the body and stuff it into the*
barrel; then trundle it off, looking back at Kilroy, giggling,
whispering. They return under the downstage arch through
which they entered. Kilroy, in a low, shocked voice:]

What *is* this place? What kind of a hassle have I got myself
into?

LOUDSPEAKER: If anyone on the Camino is bewildered, come
to the Gipsy. A poco dinero will tickle the Gipsy's palm and
give her visions!

ABDULLAH [*giving Kilroy a card*]: If you got a question, ask my
mama, the Gipsy!

KILROY: Man, whenever you see those three brass balls on a
street, you don't have to look a long way for a Gipsy. Now
le' me think. I am faced with three problems. One: I'm
hungry. Two: I'm lonely. Three: I'm in a place where I don't
know what it is or how I got there! First action that's indicated is to – cash in on something – Well . . . let's see. . . .

[*Honky-tonk music fades in at this point and the Skid Row*
façade begins to light up for the evening. There is the Gipsy's
stall with its cabalistic devices, its sectional cranium and palm,
three luminous brass balls overhanging the entrance to the Loan
Shark and his window filled with a vast assortment of hocked
articles for sale: trumpets, banjos, fur coats, tuxedos, a gown of
scarlet sequins, loops of pearls and rhinestones. Dimly behind
this display is a neon sign in three pastel colours, pink, green, and
blue. It fades softly in and out and it says: 'Magic Tricks Jokes.'
There is also the advertisement of a flea-bag hotel or flophouse

*called 'Ritz Men Only'. This sign is also pale neon or luminous
paint, and only the entrance is on the street floor, the rooms are
above the Loan Shark and Gipsy's stall. One of the windows of
this upper storey is practical. Figures appear in it sometimes,
leaning out as if suffocating or to hawk and spit into the street
below.*

*This side of the street should have all the colour and animation
that are permitted by the resources of the production. There may
be moments of dancelike action, a fight, a seduction, sale of
narcotics, arrest, etc.]*

KILROY [*to the audience from the apron*]: What've I got to cash in
on? My golden gloves? Never! I'll say that once more,
never! That silver-framed photo of my One True Woman?
Never! Repeat that! Never! What else have I got of a
detachable and a negotiable nature? Oh! My ruby-and-
emerald-studded belt with the word CHAMP on it.

[*He whips it off his pants.*]

This is not necessary to hold on my pants, but this is a precious
reminder of the sweet used-to-be. Oh, well. Sometimes a
man has got to hock his sweet used-to-be in order to finance
his present situation. . . .

[*He enters the Loan Shark's. A Drunken Bum leans out of the
practical window of the 'Ritz Men Only' and shouts.*]

BUM: O Jack o' Diamonds you robbed my pockets, you robbed
my pockets of silver and gold!

[*He jerks the window shade down.*]

GUTMAN [*on the terrace*]: Block Four on the Camino Real!

BLOCK FOUR

There is a phrase of light music as the Baron de Charlus, an elderly foppish sybarite in a light silk suit, a carnation in his lapel, crosses from the Siete Mares to the honky-tonk side of the street. On his trail is a wild-looking young man of startling beauty called Lobo. Charlus is aware of the follower and, during his conversation with A. Ratt, he takes out a pocket mirror to inspect him while pretending to comb his hair and point his moustache. As Charlus approaches, the Manager of the flea-bag puts up a vacancy sign and calls out.

A. RATT: Vacancy here! A bed at the 'Ritz Men Only'! A little white ship to sail the dangerous night in. . . .

THE BARON: Ah, bon soir, Mr Ratt.

A. RATT: Cruising?

THE BARON: No, just – walking!

A. RATT: That's all you need to do.

THE BARON: I sometimes find it suffices. You have a vacancy, do you?

A. RATT: For you?

THE BARON: And a possible guest. You know the requirements. An iron bed with no mattress and a considerable length of stout knotted rope. No! Chains this evening, metal chains. I've been very bad, I have a lot to atone for. . . .

A. RATT: Why don't you take these joy-rides at the Siete Mares?

THE BARON [*with the mirror focused on Lobo*]: They don't have Ingreso Libero at the Siete Mares. Oh, I don't like places in the haute saison, the alta staggione, and yet if you go between the fashionable seasons, it's too hot or too damp or appallingly overrun by all the wrong sort of people who rap on

149

the wall if canaries sing in your bed-springs after midnight. I don't know why such people don't stay at home. Surely a Kodak, a Brownie, or even a Leica works just as well in Milwaukee or Sioux City as it does in these places they do on their whirlwind summer tours, and don't look now, but I think I am being followed!

A. RATT: Yep, you've made a pickup!

THE BARON: Attractive?

A. RATT: That depends on who's driving the bicycle, Dad.

THE BARON: Ciao, Caro! Expect me at ten.

[*He crosses elegantly to the fountain.*]

A. RATT: Vacancy here! A little white ship to sail the dangerous night in!

[*The music changes. Kilroy backs out of the Loan Shark's, belt unsold, engaged in a violent dispute. The Loan Shark is haggling for his golden gloves. Charlus lingers, intrigued by the scene.*]

LOAN SHARK: I don't want no belt! I want the gloves! Eight-fifty!

KILROY: No dice.

LOAN SHARK: Nine, nine-fifty!

KILROY: Nah, nah, nah!

LOAN SHARK: Yah, yah, yah.

KILROY: I say nah.

LOAN SHARK: I say yah.

KILROY: The nahs have it.

LOAN SHARK: Don't be a fool. What can you do with a pair of golden gloves?

KILROY: I can remember the battles I fought to win them! I can remember that I used to be – CHAMP!

[*Fade in Band Music: 'March of the Gladiators' – ghostly cheers, etc.*]

LOAN SHARK: You can remember that you *used to be* – Champ?

KILROY: Yes! I used to be – CHAMP!

THE BARON: Used to be is the past tense, meaning useless.

KILROY: Not to me, Mister. These are my gloves, these gloves are gold, and I fought a lot of hard fights to win 'em! I broke clean from the clinches. I never hit a low blow, the referee never told me to mix it up! And the fixers never got to me!

LOAN SHARK: In other words, a sucker!

KILROY: Yep, I'm a sucker that won the golden gloves!

LOAN SHARK: Congratulations. My final offer is a piece of green paper with Alexander Hamilton's picture on it. Take it or leave it.

KILROY: I leave it for you to *stuff* it! I'd hustle my heart on this street, I'd peddle my heart's true blood before I'd leave my golden gloves hung up in a loan shark's window between a rusted trombone and some poor lush's long ago mildewed tuxedo!

LOAN SHARK: So you say but I will see you later.

THE BARON: The name of the Camino is not unreal!

[*The Bum sticks his head out of the window and shouts.*]

BUM: Pa dam, Pa dam, Pa dam!

THE BARON [*continuing the Bum's song*]: Echoes the beat of my heart! Pa dam, Pa dam – *hello!*

[*He has crossed to Kilroy as he sings and extends his hand to him.*]

KILROY [*uncertainly*]: Hey, mate. It's wonderful to see you.

THE BARON: Thanks, but why?

KILROY: A normal American. In a clean white suit.

THE BARON: My suit is pale yellow. My nationality is French, and my normality has been often subject to question.

KILROY: I still say your suit is clean.

THE BARON: Thanks. That's more than I can say for your apparel.

KILROY: Don't judge a book by the covers. I'd take a shower if I could locate the 'Y'.

THE BARON: What's the 'Y'?

KILROY: Sort of a Protestant church with a swimmin' pool in it. Sometimes it also has an employment bureau. It does good in the community.

THE BARON: Nothing in this community does much good.

KILROY: I'm getting the same impression. This place is confusing to me. I think it must be the after effects of fever. Nothing seems real. Could you give me the scoop?

THE BARON: Serious questions are referred to the Gipsy. Once upon a time. Oh, once upon a time. I used to wonder. Now I simply wander. I stroll about the fountain and hope to be followed. Some people call it corruption. I call it – simplification. . . .

BUM [very softly at the window]: I wonder what's become of Sally, that old gal of mine?

[He lowers the blind.]

THE BARON: Well, anyhow?

KILROY: How about the hot-spots in this town?

THE BARON: Oh, the hot-spots, ho ho! There's the Pink Flamingo, the Yellow Pelican, the Blue Heron, and the Prothonotary Warbler! They call it the Bird Circuit. But I don't care for such places. They stand three-deep at the bar and look at themselves in the mirror and what they see is depressing. One sailor comes in – they faint! My choice of resorts is the Bucket of Blood downstairs from the 'Ritz Men Only'. How about a match?

KILROY: Where's your cigarette?

THE BARON [gently and sweetly]: Oh, I don't smoke. I just wanted to see your eyes more clearly. . . .

KILROY: Why?

THE BARON: The eyes are the windows of the soul, and yours are too gentle for someone who has as much as I have to atone for.

[He starts off.]

Au revoir. . . .

KILROY: A very unusual type character. . . .

[*Casanova is on the steps leading to the arch, looking out at the desert beyond. Now he turns and descends a few steps, laughing with a note of tired incredulity. Kilroy crosses to him.*]

Gee, it's wonderful to see you, a normal American in a –

[*There is a strangulated outcry from the arch under which the Baron has disappeared.*]

Excuse me a minute!

[*He rushes toward the source of the outcry. Jacques crosses to the bench before the fountain. Rhubarb is heard through the arch. Jacques shrugs wearily as if it were just a noisy radio. Kilroy comes plummeting out backwards, all the way to Jacques.*]

I tried to interfere, but what's th' use?!

JACQUES: No use at all!

[*The Streetcleaners come through the arch with the Baron doubled up in their barrel. They pause and exchange sibilant whispers, pointing and snickering at Kilroy.*]

KILROY: Who are they pointing at? At me, Kilroy?

[*The Bum laughs from the window. A. Ratt laughs from his shadowy doorway. The Loan Shark laughs from his.*]

Kilroy is here and he's not about to be here! – If he can help it. . . .

[*He snatches up a rock and throws it at the Streetcleaners. Everybody laughs louder and the laughter seems to reverberate from the mountains. The light changes, dims a little in the plaza.*]

Sons a whatever you're sons of! Don't look at me, I'm not about to take a ride in the barrel!

[*The Baron, his elegant white shoes protruding from the barrel, is wheeled up the Alleyway Out. Figures in the square resume their dazed attitudes and one or two Guests return to the terrace of the Siete Mares as –*]

GUTMAN: Block Five on the Camino Real!

[*He strolls off.*]

BLOCK FIVE

KILROY [*to Jacques*]: Gee, the blocks go fast on this street!

JACQUES: Yes. The blocks go fast.

KILROY: My name's Kilroy. I'm here.

JACQUES: Mine is Casanova. I'm here, too.

KILROY: But you been here longer than me and maybe could brief me on it. For instance, what do they do with a stiff picked up in this town?

[*The Guard stares at them suspiciously from the terrace.*
  Jacques whistles 'La Golondrina' and crosses downstage. Kilroy follows.]

Did I say something untactful?

JACQUES [*smiling into a sunset glow*]: The exchange of serious questions and ideas, especially between persons from opposite sides of the plaza, is regarded unfavourably here. You'll notice I'm talking as if I had acute laryngitis. I'm gazing into the sunset. If I should start to whistle 'La Golondrina' it means we're being overheard by the Guards on the terrace. Now you want to know what is done to a body from which the soul has departed on the Camino Real! – It's disposition depends on what the Streetcleaners happen to find in its pockets. If its pockets are empty as the unfortunate Baron's turned out to be, and as mine are at this moment – the 'stiff' is wheeled straight off to the Laboratory. And there the individual becomes an undistinguished member of a collectivist state. His chemical components are separated and poured into vats containing the corresponding elements of countless others. If any of his vital organs or parts are at all unique in size or structure, they're placed on exhibition in bottles containing a very foul-smelling solution called formaldehyde. There is a charge of admission to this museum. The proceeds go to the maintenance of the military police.

[*He whistles 'La Golondrina' till the Guard turns his back again. He moves toward the front of the stage.*]

KILROY [*following*]: – I guess that's – sensible. . . .

JACQUES: Yes, but not romantic. And romance is important. Don't you think?

KILROY: Nobody thinks romance is more important than me!

JACQUES: Except possibly me!

KILROY: Maybe that's why fate has brung us together! We're buddies under the skin!

JACQUES: Travellers born?

KILROY: Always looking for something!

JACQUES: Satisfied by nothing!

KILROY: Hopeful?

JACQUES: Always!

OFFICER: Keep moving!

[*They move apart till the Officer exits.*]

KILROY: And when a joker on the Camino gets fed up with one continual hassle – how does he get *off* it?

JACQUES: You see the narrow and very steep stairway that passes under what is described in the travel brochures as a

'Magnificent Arch of Triumph'? – Well, that's the Way Out!

KILROY: That's the way out?

[*Kilroy without hesitation plunges right up to almost the top step; then pauses with a sound of squealing brakes. There is a sudden loud wind.*]

JACQUES [*shouting with hand cupped to mouth*]: Well, how does the prospect please you, Traveller born?

KILROY [*shouting back in a tone of awe*]: It's too unknown for my blood. Man, I seen nothing like it except through a telescope once on the pier on Coney Island. 'Ten cents to see the craters and plains of the moon!' – And there's the same view in three dimensions for nothing!

[*The desert wind sings loudly: Kilroy mocks it.*]

JACQUES: Are you – ready to cross it?

KILROY: Maybe sometime with someone but not right now and alone! How about you?

JACQUES: I'm not alone.

KILROY: You're with a party?

JACQUES: No, but I'm sweetly encumbered with a – lady....

KILROY: It wouldn't do with a lady. I don't see nothing but nothing – and then more nothing. And then I see some mountains. But the mountains are covered with snow.

JACQUES: Snowshoes would be useful!

[*He observes Gutman approaching through the passage at upper left. He whistles 'La Golondrina' for Kilroy's attention and points with his cane as he exits.*]

KILROY [*descending steps disconsolately*]: Mush, mush.

[*The Bum comes to his window. A. Ratt enters his doorway. Gutman enters below Kilroy.*]

BUM: It's sleepy time down South!

GUTMAN [*warningly as Kilroy passes him*]: Block Six in a progress of sixteen blocks on the Camino Real.

BLOCK SIX

KILROY [*from the stairs*]: Man, I could use a bed now. – I'd like to make me a cool pad on this camino now and lie down and sleep and dream of being with someone – friendly. . . .

[*He crosses to the 'Ritz Men Only'.*]

A. RATT [*softly and sleepily*]: Vacancy here! I got a single bed at the 'Ritz Men Only', a little white ship to sail the dangerous night in.

[*Kilroy crosses down to his doorway.*]

KILROY: – You got a vacancy here?

A. RATT: I got a vacancy here if you got the one-fifty there.

KILROY: Ha ha! I been in countries where money was not legal tender. I mean it was legal but it wasn't tender.

[*There is a loud groan from offstage above.*]

– Somebody dying on you or just drunk?

A. RATT: Who knows or cares in this pad, Dad?

KILROY: I heard once that a man can't die while he's drunk. Is that a fact or a fiction?

A. RATT: Strictly a fiction.

VOICE ABOVE: *Stiff in number seven! Call the Streetcleaners!*

A. RATT [*with absolutely no change in face or voice*]: Number seven vacant.

[*Streetcleaners' piping is heard. The Bum leaves the window.*]

KILROY: Thanks, but to-night I'm going to sleep under the stars.

[*A. Ratt gestures 'Have it your way' and exits.*
Kilroy, left alone, starts downstage. He notices that La Madrecita is crouched near the fountain, holding something up, inconspicuously, in her hand. Coming to her he sees that it's a piece of food. He takes it, puts it in his mouth, tries to thank her but her head is down, muffled in her rebozo and there is no way for him to acknowledge the gift. He starts to cross. Street People raise up their heads in their Pit and motion him invitingly to come in with them. They call softly, 'Sleep, sleep. . . .']

GUTMAN [*from his chair on the terrace*]: Hey, Joe.

[*The Street People duck immediately.*]

KILROY: Who? Me?
GUTMAN: Yes, you, Candy Man. Are you disocupado?
KILROY: – That means – unemployed, don't it?

[*He sees Officers converging from right.*]

GUTMAN: Jobless. On the bum. Carrying the banner!
KILROY: – Aw, no, aw, no, don't try to hang no vagrancy rap on me! I was robbed on this square and I got plenty of witnesses to prove it.
GUTMAN [*with ironic courtesy*]: Oh?

[*He makes a gesture asking 'Where?'*]

KILROY [*coming down to apron left and crossing to the right*]: Witnesses! Witness! Witnesses!

[*He comes to La Madrecita.*]

You were a witness!

158

[*A gesture indicates that he realizes her blindness. Opposite the Gipsy's balcony he pauses for a second.*]

Hey, Gipsy's daughter!

[*The balcony is dark. He continues up to the Pit. The Street People duck as he calls down:*]

You were witnesses!

[*An Officer enters with a Patsy outfit. He hands it to Gutman.*]

GUTMAN: Here, Boy! Take these.

[*Gutman displays and then tosses on the ground at Kilroy's feet the Patsy outfit – the red fright wig, the big crimson nose that lights up and has horn rimmed glasses attached, a pair of clown pants that have a huge footprint on the seat.*]

KILROY: What is this outfit?
GUTMAN: The uniform of a Patsy.
KILROY: I know what a Patsy is – he's a clown in the circus who takes prat-falls but *I'm no Patsy!*
GUTMAN: Pick it up.
KILROY: Don't give me orders. Kilroy is a free agent –
GUTMAN [*smoothly*]: But a Patsy isn't. Pick it up and put it on, Candy Man. You are now the Patsy.
KILROY: So you say but you are completely mistaken.

[*Four Officers press it on him.*]

And don't crowd me with your torpedoes! I'm a stranger here but I got a clean record in all the places I been, I'm not in the books for nothin' but vagrancy and once when I was hungry I walked by a truck-load of pineapples without picking one, because I was brought up good –

[*Then with a pathetic attempt at making friends with the Officer to his right.*]

and there was a cop on the corner!

OFFICER: Ponga selo!

KILROY: What'd you say? [*Desperately to audience he asks:*] What did he say?

OFFICER: Ponga selo!

KILROY: What'd you say?

[*The Officer shoves him down roughly to the Patsy outfit. Kilroy picks up the pants, shakes them out carefully as if about to step into them and says very politely:*]

Why, surely. I'd be delighted. My fondest dreams have come true.

[*Suddenly he tosses the Patsy dress into Gutman's face and leaps into the aisle of the theatre.*]

GUTMAN: Stop him! Arrest that vagrant! Don't let him get away!

LOUDSPEAKER: Be on the lookout for a fugitive Patsy. The Patsy has escaped. Stop him, stop that Patsy!

[*A wild chase commences. The two Guards rush madly down either side to intercept him at the back of the house. Kilroy wheels about at the top of the centre aisle, and runs back down it, panting, gasping out questions and entreaties to various persons occupying aisle seats, such as:*]

KILROY: How do I git out? Which way do I go, which way do I get out? Where's the Greyhound depot? Hey, do you know where the Greyhound bus depot is? What's the best way out, if there is any way out? I got to find one. I had enough of this place. I had too much of this place. I'm free. I'm a free man with equal rights in this world! You better believe it because that's news for you and you had better believe it! Kilroy's a free man with equal rights in this world! All right, now, help me, somebody, help me find a way out,

I got to find one, I don't like this place! It's not for me and I
am not buying any! Oh! Over there! I see a sign that says
EXIT. That's a sweet word to me, man, that's a lovely
word, EXIT! That's the entrance to paradise for Kilroy!
Exit, I'm coming, Exit, I'm coming!

[*The Street People have gathered along the forestage to watch
the chase. Esmeralda, barefooted, wearing only a slip, bursts out
of the Gipsy's establishment like an animal broken out of a cage,
darts among the Street People to the front of the Crowd which is
shouting like the spectators at the climax of a corrida. Behind her,
Nursie appears, a male actor, wigged and dressed austerely as a
duenna, crying out in both languages.*]

NURSIE: Esmeralda! Esmeralda!
GIPSY: Police!
NURSIE: Come back here, Esmeralda!
GIPSY: Catch her, idiot!
NURSIE: Where is my lady bird, where is my precious treasure?
GIPSY: Idiot! I told you to keep her door locked!
NURSIE: She jimmied the lock. Esmeralda!

[*These shouts are mostly lost in the general rhubarb of the chase
and the shouting Street People. Esmeralda crouches on the forestage, screaming encouragement in Spanish to the fugitive.
Abdullah catches sight of her, seizes her wrist, shouting.*]

ABDULLAH: Here she is! I got her!

[*Esmeralda fights savagely. She nearly breaks loose, but Nursie
and the Gipsy close upon her, too, and she is overwhelmed and
dragged back, fighting all the way, toward the door from which
she escaped.*

*Meanwhile – timed with the above action – shots are fired in
the air by Kilroy's pursuers. He dashes, panting, into the boxes
of the theatre, darting from one box to another, shouting in-
coherently, now, sobbing for breath, crying out.*]

KILROY: *Mary, help a Christian! Help a Christian, Mary!*

ESMERALDA: *Yankee! Yankee, jump!*

[*The Officers close upon him in the box nearest the stage. A dazzling spot of light is thrown on him. He lifts a little gilded chair to defend himself. The chair is torn from his grasp. He leaps upon the ledge of the box.*]

Jump! Jump, Yankee!

[*The Gipsy is dragging the girl back by her hair.*]

KILROY: *Watch out down there! Geronimo!*

[*He leaps on to the stage and crumples up with a twisted ankle. Esmeralda screams demoniacally, breaks from her mother's grasp and rushes to him, fighting off his pursuers who have leapt after him from the box. Abdullah, Nursie, and the Gipsy seize her again, just as Kilroy is seized by his pursuers. The Officers beat him to his knees. Each time he is struck, Esmeralda screams as if she received the blow herself. As his cries subside into sobbing, so do hers, and at the end, when he is quite helpless, she is also overcome by her captors and as they drag her back to the Gipsy's she cries to him.*]

ESMERALDA: *They've got you! They've got me!*

[*Her mother slaps her fiercely.*]

Caught! Caught! We're caught!

[*She is dragged inside. The door is slammed shut on her continuing outcries. For a moment nothing is heard but Kilroy's hoarse panting and sobbing. Gutman takes command of the situation, thrusting his way through the crowd to face Kilroy who is pinioned by two Guards.*]

GUTMAN [*smiling serenely*]: Well, well, how do you do! I understand that you're seeking employment here. We need a Patsy and the job is yours for the asking!

162

KILROY: I don't. Accept. This job. I been. Shanghied!

[*Kilroy dons Patsy outfit.*]

GUTMAN: Hush! The Patsy doesn't talk. He lights his nose, that's all!

GUARD: Press the little button at the end of the cord.

GUTMAN: That's right. Just press the little button at the end of the cord!

[*Kilroy lights his nose. Everybody laughs.*]

GUTMAN: Again, ha ha! Again, ha ha! Again!

[*The nose goes off and on like a firefly as the stage dims out. The curtain falls. There is a short intermission.*]

BLOCK SEVEN

The Dreamer is singing with mandolin, 'Noche de Ronde'. The Guests murmur, 'cool – cool. . . .' Gutman stands on the podiumlike elevation downstage right, smoking a long thin cigar, signing an occasional tab from the bar or café. He is standing in an amber spot. The rest of the stage is filled with blue dusk. At the signal the song fades to a whisper and Gutman speaks.

GUTMAN: Block Seven on the Camino Real –
I like this hour.

[*He gives the audience a tender gold-toothed smile.*]

The fire's gone out of the day but the light of it lingers. . . .
In Rome the continual fountains are bathing stone heroes

with silver, in Copenhagen the Tivoli gardens are lighted, they're selling the lottery on San Juan de Latrene. . . .

[*The Dreamer advances a little, playing the mandolin softly.*]

LA MADRECITA [*holding up glass beads and shell necklaces*]: Recuerdos, recuerdos?

GUTMAN: And these are the moments when we look into ourselves and ask with a wonder which never is lost altogether: 'Can this be all? Is there nothing more? Is this what the glittering wheels of the heavens turn for?'

[*He leans forward as if conveying a secret.*]

– Ask the Gipsy! Un poco dinero will tickle the Gipsy's palm and give her visions!

[*Abdullah emerges with a silver tray, calling.*]

ABDULLAH: Letter for Signor Casanova, letter for Signor Casanova!

[*Jacques springs up but stands rigid.*]

GUTMAN: Casanova, you have received a letter. Perhaps it's the letter with the remittance cheque in it!

JACQUES [*in a hoarse, exalted voice*]: Yes! It is! The letter! With the remittance cheque in it!

GUTMAN: Then why don't you take it so you can maintain your residence at the Siete Mares and so avoid the more sombre attractions of the 'Ritz Men Only'?

JACQUES: My hand is –

GUTMAN: Your hand is paralysed? . . . By what? *Anxiety? Apprehension?* . . . Put the letter in Signor Casanova's pocket so he can open it when he recovers the use of his digital extremities. Then give him a shot of brandy on the house before he falls on his face!

[*Jacques has stepped down into the plaza. He looks down at Kilroy crouched to the right of him and wildly blinking his nose.*]

JACQUES: Yes. I know the Morse code.

[*Kilroy's nose again blinks on and off.*]

Thank you, brother.

[*This is said as if acknowledging a message.*]

I knew without asking the Gipsy that something of this sort would happen to you. You have a spark of anarchy in your spirit and that's not to be tolerated. Nothing wild or honest is tolerated here! It has to be extinguished or used only to light up your nose for Mr Gutman's amusement. . . .

[*Jacques saunters around Kilroy whistling 'La Golondrina'. Then satisfied that no one is suspicious of this encounter . . .*]

Before the final block we'll find some way out of here! Meanwhile, patience and courage, little brother!

[*Jacques feeling he's been there too long starts away giving Kilroy a reassuring pat on the shoulder and saying:*]

Patience! . . . Courage!

LADY MULLIGAN [*from the Mulligans' table*]: Mr Gutman!

GUTMAN: Lady Mulligan! And how are you this evening, Lord Mulligan?

LADY MULLIGAN [*interrupting Lord Mulligan's rumblings*]: He's not at all well. This . . . climate is so enervating!

LORD MULLIGAN: I was so weak this morning . . . I couldn't screw the lid on my toothpaste!

LADY MULLIGAN: Raymond, tell Mr Gutman about those two impertinent workmen in the square! . . . These two idiots pushing a white barrel! Pop up every time we step outside the hotel!

LORD MULLIGAN: – point and giggle at me!

LADY MULLIGAN: Can't they be discharged?

GUTMAN: They can't be discharged, disciplined nor bribed! All you can do is pretend to ignore them.

LADY MULLIGAN: I can't eat! . . . Raymond, stop stuffing!

LORD MULLIGAN: *Shut up!*

GUTMAN [*to the audience*]: When the big wheels crack on this street it's like the fall of a capital city, the destruction of Carthage, the sack of Rome by the white-eyed giants from the North! I've seen them fall! I've seen the destruction of them! Adventurers suddenly frightened of a dark room! Gamblers unable to choose between odd and even! Con men and pitchmen and plume-hatted cavaliers turned baby-soft at one note of the Streetcleaners' pipes! When I observe this change, I say to myself: 'Could it happen to ME?' – The answer is 'YES!' and that's what curdles my blood like milk on the doorstep of someone gone for the summer!

[*A Hunchback Mummer somersaults through his hoop of silver bells, springs up and shakes it excitedly toward a downstage arch which begins to flicker with a diamond-blue radiance; this marks the advent of each legendary character in the play. The music follows: a waltz from the time of Camille in Paris.*]

GUTMAN [*downstage to the audience*]: Ah, there's the music of another legend, one that everyone knows, the legend of the sentimental whore, the courtesan who made the mistake of love. But now you see her coming into this plaza not as she was when she burned with a fever that cast a thin light over Paris, but changed, yes, faded as lanterns and legends fade when they burn into day!

[*He turns and shouts*]:

Rosita, sell her a flower!

[*Marguerite has entered the plaza. A beautiful woman of indefinite age. The Street People cluster about her with wheed-*

ling cries, holding up glass beads, shell necklaces and so forth.
She seems confused, lost, half-awake. Jacques has sprung up at
her entrance but has difficulty making his way through the
cluster of vendors. Rosita has snatched up a tray of flowers and
cries out.]

ROSITA: Camellias, camellias! Pink or white, whichever a
lady finds suitable to the moon!

GUTMAN: That's the ticket!

MARGUERITE: Yes, I would like a camellia.

ROSITA [*in a bad French accent*]: Rouge ou blanc ce soir?

MARGUERITE: It's always a white one, now . . . but there used
to be five evenings out of the month when a pink camellia,
instead of the usual white one, let my admirers know that the
moon those nights was unfavourable to pleasure, and so they
called me – Camille . . .

JACQUES: Mia cara!

[*Imperiously, very proud to be with her, he pushes the Street*
People aside with his cane.]

Out of the way, make way, let us through, please!

MARGUERITE: Don't push them with your cane.

JACQUES: If they get close enough they'll snatch your purse.

[*Marguerite utters a low, shocked cry.*]

What is it?

MARGUERITE: *My purse is gone! It's lost! My papers were in it!*

JACQUES: Your passport was in it?

MARGUERITE: My passport and my permiso de residencia!

[*She leans faint against the arch during the following scene.*
Abdullah turns to run. Jacques catches him.]

JACQUES [*seizing Abdullah's wrist*]: Where did you take her?

ABDULLAH: Oww! – P'tit Zoco.

167

JACQUES: The Souks?
ABDULLAH: The Souks!
JACQUES: Which cafés did she go to?
ABDULLAH: Ahmed's, she went to –
JACQUES: Did she smoke at Ahmed's?
ABDULLAH: Two kif pipes!
JACQUES: Who was it took her purse? Was it *you*? We'll see!

[*He strips off the boy's burnoose. He crouches whimpering, shivering in a ragged slip.*]

MARGUERITE: Jacques, let the boy go, he didn't take it!
JACQUES: He doesn't have it on him but knows who does!
ABDULLAH: No, no, I don't know!
JACQUES: You little son of a Gipsy! Senta! . . . You know who I am? I am Jacques Casanova! I belong to the Secret Order of the Rose-coloured Cross! . . . Run back to Ahmed's. Contact the spiv that took the lady's purse. Tell him to keep it but give her back her papers! There'll be a large reward.

[*He thumps his cane on the ground to release Abdullah from the spell. The boy dashes off. Jacques laughs and turns triumphantly to Marguerite.*]

LADY MULLIGAN: Waiter! That adventurer and his mistress must not be seated next to Lord Mulligan's table!
JACQUES [*loudly enough for Lady Mulligan to hear*]: This hotel has become a mecca for black marketeers and their expensively kept women?
LADY MULLIGAN: Mr Gutman!
MARGUERITE: Let's have dinner upstairs!
WAITER [*directing them to terrace table*]: *This* way, M'sieur.
JACQUES: We'll take our usual table.

[*He indicates one.*]

MARGUERITE: Please!

WAITER [*overlapping Marguerite's 'please!'*]: This table is reserved for Lord Byron!

JACQUES [*masterly*]: This table is always our table.

MARGUERITE: I'm not hungry.

JACQUES: Hold out the lady's chair, cretino!

GUTMAN [*darting over to Marguerite's chair*]: Permit me!

[*Jacques bows with mock gallantry to Lady Mulligan as he turns to his chair during seating of Marguerite.*]

LADY MULLIGAN: We'll move to *that* table!

JACQUES: – You must learn how to carry the banner of Bohemia into the enemy camp.

[*A screen is put up around them.*]

MARGUERITE: Bohemia has no banner. It survives by discretion.

JACQUES: I'm glad that you value discretion. *Wine list!* Was it discretion that led you through the bazaars this afternoon wearing your cabochon sapphire and diamond ear-drops! You were fortunate that you lost only your purse and papers!

MARGUERITE: Take the wine list.

JACQUES: Still or sparkling?

MARGUERITE: Sparkling.

GUTMAN: May I make a suggestion, Signor Casanova?

JACQUES: Please do.

GUTMAN: It's a very cold and dry wine from only ten metres below the snowline in the mountains. The name of the wine is Quando! – meaning when! Such as 'When are remittances going to be received?' 'When are accounts to be settled?' Ha ha ha! Bring Signor Casanova a bottle of Quando with the compliments of the house!

JACQUES: I'm sorry this had to happen in – your presence. . . .

MARGUERITE: That doesn't matter, my dear. But why don't you *tell* me when you are short of money?

JACQUES: I thought the fact was apparent. It is to everyone else.

MARGUERITE: The letter you were expecting, it still hasn't come?

JACQUES [*removing it from his pocket*]: It came this afternoon – Here it is!

MARGUERITE: You haven't opened the letter!

JACQUES: I haven't had the nerve to! I've had so many unpleasant surprises that I've lost faith in my luck.

MARGUERITE: Give the letter to me. Let me open it for you.

JACQUES: Later, a little bit later, after the – wine. . . .

MARGUERITE: Old hawk, anxious old hawk!

[*She clasps his hand on the table: he leans toward her: she kisses her fingertips and places them on his lips.*]

JACQUES: Do you call that a kiss?

MARGUERITE: I call it the ghost of a kiss. It will have to do for now.

[*She leans back, her blue-tinted eyelids closed.*]

JACQUES: Are you tired? Are you tired, Marguerite? You know you should have rested this afternoon.

MARGUERITE: I looked at silver and rested.

JACQUES: You looked at silver at Ahmed's?

MARGUERITE: No, I rested at Ahmed's, and had mint-tea.

[*The Dreamer accompanies their speech with his guitar. The duologue should have the style of an antiphonal poem, the cues picked up so that there is scarcely a separation between the speeches, and the tempo quick and the voices edged.*]

JACQUES: You had mint-tea downstairs?

MARGUERITE: No, upstairs.

JACQUES: Upstairs where they burn the poppy?

MARGUERITE: Upstairs where it's cool and there's music and

the haggling of the bazaar is soft as the murmur of pigeons.

JACQUES: That sounds restful. Reclining among silk pillows on a divan, in a curtained and perfumed alcove above the bazaar?

MARGUERITE: Forgetting for a while where I am, or that I don't know where I am. . . .

JACQUES: Forgetting alone or forgetting with some young companion who plays the lute or the flute or who had silver to show you? Yes. That sounds very restful. And yet you do seem tired.

MARGUERITE: If I seem tired, it's your insulting solicitude that I'm tired of!

JACQUES: Is it insulting to feel concern for your safety in this place?

MARGUERITE: Yes, it is. The implication is.

JACQUES: What is the implication?

MARGUERITE: You know what it is: that I am one of those *age-ing – voluptuaries* – who used to be paid for pleasure but now have to pay! – Jacques, I won't be followed, I've gone too far to be followed! – *What is it?*

[*The Waiter has presented an envelope on a salver.*]

WAITER: A letter for the lady.

MARGUERITE: How strange to receive a letter in a place where nobody knows I'm staying! Will you open it for me?

[*The Waiter withdraws. Jacques takes the letter and opens it.*]

Well! What is it?

JACQUES: Nothing important. An illustrated brochure from some resort in the mountains.

MARGUERITE: What is it called?

JACQUES: Bide-a-While.

[*A chafing dish bursts into startling blue flame at the Mulligans' table. Lady Mulligan clasps her hands and exclaims with affected delight, the Waiter and Mr Gutman laugh agreeably. Marguerite springs up and moves out upon the forestage. Jacques goes to her.*]

Do you know this resort in the mountains?

MARGUERITE: Yes. I stayed there once. It's one of those places with open sleeping verandas, surrounded by snowy pine woods. It has rows and rows of narrow white iron beds as regular as tombstones. The invalids smile at each other when axes flash across valleys, ring, flash, ring again! Young voices shout across valleys Hola! And mail is delivered. The friend that used to write you ten-page letters contents himself now with a postcard bluebird that tells you to 'Get well Quick!'

[*Jacques throws the brochure away.*]

— And when the last bleeding comes, not much later nor earlier than expected, you're wheeled discreetly into a little tent of white gauze, and the last thing you know of this world, of which you've known so little and yet so much, is the smell of an empty ice box.

[*The blue flame expires in the chafing dish. Gutman picks up the brochure and hands it to the Waiter, whispering something.*]

JACQUES: You won't go back to that place.

[*The Waiter places the brochure on the salver again and approaches behind them.*]

MARGUERITE: I wasn't released. I left without permission. They sent me this to remind me.

WAITER [*presenting the salver*]: You dropped this.

JACQUES: We threw it away!

WAITER: Excuse me.

JACQUES: Now, from now on, Marguerite, you must take better care of yourself. Do you hear me?

MARGUERITE: I hear you. No more distractions for me? No more entertainers in curtained and perfumed alcoves above the bazaar, no more young men that a pinch of white powder or a puff of grey smoke can almost turn to someone devoutly remembered?

JACQUES: No, from now on –

MARGUERITE: What 'from now on,' old hawk?

JACQUES: Rest. Peace.

MARGUERITE: Rest in peace is that final bit of advice they carve on gravestones, and I'm not ready for it! Are you? Are *you* ready for it?

[*She returns to the table. He follows her.*]

Oh, Jacques, when are we going to leave here, how are we going to leave here, you've got to tell me!

JACQUES: I've told you all I know.

MARGUERITE: Nothing, you've given up hope!

JACQUES: I haven't, that's not true.

[*Gutman has brought out the white cockatoo which he shows to Lady Mulligan at her table.*]

GUTMAN [*his voice rising above the murmurs*]: Her name is Aurora.

LADY MULLIGAN: Why do you call her Aurora?

GUTMAN: She cries at daybreak.

LADY MULLIGAN: Only at daybreak?

GUTMAN: Yes, at daybreak only.

[*Their voices and laughter fade under.*]

MARGUERITE: How long is it since you've been to the travel agencies?

JACQUES: This morning I made the usual round of Cook's, American Express, Wagon-lits Universal, and it was the same story. There are no flights out of here till further orders from someone higher up.

MARGUERITE: Nothing, nothing at all?

JACQUES: Oh, there's a rumour of something called the Fugitivo but –

MARGUERITE: The What!!!?

JACQUES: The Fugitivo. It's one of those non-scheduled things that –

MARGUERITE: When, when, when?

JACQUES: I told you it was non-scheduled. Non-scheduled means it comes and goes at no predictable –

MARGUERITE: Don't give me the dictionary! I want to know how does one get on it? Did you bribe them? Did you offer them money? No. Of course you didn't! And I know why! You really don't want to leave here. You *think* you don't want to go because you're brave as an old hawk. But the truth of the matter – the real not the royal truth – is that you're terrified of the Terra Incognita outside that wall.

JACQUES: You've hit upon the truth. I'm terrified of the unknown country inside or outside this wall or any place on earth without you with me! The only country, known or unknown that I can breathe in, or care to, is the country in which we breathe together, as we are now at this table. And later, a little while later, even closer than this, the sole inhabitants of a tiny world whose limits are those of the light from a rose-coloured lamp – beside the sweetly, completely known country of your cool bed!

MARGUERITE: The little comfort of love?

JACQUES: Is that comfort so little?

MARGUERITE: Caged birds accept each other but flight is what they long for.

JACQUES: I want to stay here with you and love you and guard you until the time or way comes that we both can leave with honour.

MARGUERITE: 'Leave with honour'? Your vocabulary is almost as out-of-date as your cape and your cane. How could anyone quit this field with honour, this place where there's nothing but the gradual wasting away of everything decent in us . . . the sort of desperation that comes after even desperation has been worn out through long wear! . . . Why have they put these screens around the table?

[*She springs up and knocks one of them over.*]

LADY MULLIGAN: There! You see? I don't understand why you let such people stay here.
GUTMAN: They pay the price of admission the same as you.
LADY MULLIGAN: What price is that?
GUTMAN: Desperation! – With cash here!

[*He indicates the Siete Mares.*]

Without cash there!

[*He indicates Skid Row.*]

Block Eight on the Camino Real!

BLOCK EIGHT

There is the sound of loud desert wind and a flamenco cry followed by a dramatic phrase of music.

A flickering diamond blue radiance floods the hotel entrance. The crouching, grimacing Hunchback shakes his hoop of bells which is the convention for the appearance of each legendary figure.

Lord Byron appears in the doorway readied for departure.

Gutman raises his hand for silence.

GUTMAN: You're leaving us, Lord Byron?

BYRON: Yes, I'm leaving you, Mr Gutman.

GUTMAN: What a pity! But this is a port of entry and departure. There are no permanent guests. Possibly you are getting a little restless?

BYRON: The luxuries of this place have made me soft. The metal point's gone from my pen, there's nothing left but the feather.

GUTMAN: That may be true. But what can you do about it?

BYRON: Make a departure!

GUTMAN: From yourself?

BYRON: From my present self to myself as I used to be!

GUTMAN: *That's* the *farthest* departure a man could make! I guess you're sailing to Athens? There's another war there and like all wars since the beginning of time it can be interpreted as a – struggle for *what*?

BYRON: – For *freedom*! You may laugh at it, but it still means something to *me*!

GUTMAN: Of course it does! I'm not laughing a bit, I'm beaming with admiration.

BYRON: I've allowed myself many distractions.

GUTMAN: Yes, indeed!

BYRON: But I've never altogether forgotten my old devotion to the –

GUTMAN: – To the *what*, Lord Byron?

[*Byron passes nervous fingers through his hair.*]

You can't remember the object of your one-time devotion?

[*There is a pause. Byron limps away from the terrace and goes toward the fountain.*]

BYRON: When Shelley's corpse was recovered from the sea . . .

[*Gutman beckons The Dreamer who approaches and accompanies Byron's speech.*]

– It was burned on the beach at Viareggio. – I watched the spectacle from my carriage because the stench was revolting . . . Then it – fascinated me! I got out of my carriage. Went nearer, holding a handkerchief to my nostrils! – I saw that the front of the skull had broken away in the flames, and there –

[*He advances out upon the stage apron, followed by Abdullah with a pine torch or lantern.*]

And there was the brain of Shelley, indistinguishable from a cooking stew! – *boiling, bubbling, hissing!* – in the *blackening – cracked – pot – of* his skull!

[*Marguerite rises abruptly. Jacques supports her.*]

– Trelawney, his friend, Trelawney, threw salt and oil and frankincense in the flames and finally the almost intolerable stench –

[*Abdullah giggles. Gutman slaps him.*]

– was *gone* and the burning was *pure?* – as a man's burning should be. . . .

A man's burning *ought* to be pure! – *not* like mine – (a crepe suzette – burned in brandy . . .).

Shelley's burning was finally very *pure!*

But the body, the corpse, split open like a grilled pig!

[*Abdullah giggles irrepressibly again. Gutman grips the back of his neck and he stands up stiff and assumes an expression of exaggerated solemnity.*]

– And then Trelawney – as the ribs of the corpse unlocked – reached into them as a baker reaches quickly into an oven!

[*Abdullah almost goes into another convulsion.*]

– And snatched out – as a baker would a biscuit! – the *heart* of Shelley! Snatched the heart of Shelley out of the blistering corpse! – Out of the purifying – blue-flame. . . .

[*Marguerite resumes her seat; Jacques his.*]

– And it was *over*! – I thought –

[*He turns slightly from the audience and crosses upstage from the apron. He faces Jacques and Marguerite.*]

– I thought it was a disgusting thing to do, to snatch a man's heart from his body! What can one man do with another man's heart?

[*Jacques rises and strikes the stage with his cane.*]

JACQUES [*passionately*]: He can do this with it!

[*He seizes a loaf of bread on his table, and descends from the terrace.*]

He can twist it like this!

[*He twists the loaf.*]

He can tear it like this!

[*He tears the loaf in two.*]

He can crush it under his foot!

[*He drops the bread and stamps on it.*]

– *And kick it away – like this!*

[*He kicks the bread off the terrace. Lord Byron turns away from him and limps again out upon the stage apron and speaks to the audience.*]

BYRON: That's very true, Senor. But a poet's vocation, which used to be my vocation, is to influence the heart in a gentler fashion than you have made your mark on that loaf of bread. He ought to purify it and lift it above its ordinary level. For what is the heart but a sort of –

[He makes a high, groping gesture in the air.]

– A sort of – *instrument!* – that translates *noise* into *music*, chaos into – *order. . . .*

[Abdullah ducks almost to the earth in an effort to stifle his mirth. Gutman coughs to cover his own amusement.]

– *a mysterious order!*

[He raises his voice till it fills the plaza.]

– That was my vocation once upon a time, before it was obscured by vulgar plaudits! – Little by little it was lost among gondolas and palazzos! – masked balls, glittering salons, huge shadowy courts and torch-lit entrances! – Baroque façades, canopies and carpets, candelabra and gold plate among snowy damask, ladies with throats as slender as flower-stems, bending and breathing toward me their fragrant breath –

– Exposing their breasts to me!

Whispering, half-smiling! – And everywhere marble, the visible grandeur of marble, pink and grey marble, veined and tinted as flayed corrupting flesh – all these provided agreeable distractions from the rather frightening solitude of a poet. Oh, I wrote many cantos in Venice and Constantinople and in Ravenna and Rome on all of those Latin and Levantine excursions that my twisted foot led me into – but I wonder about them a little. They seem to improve as the wine in the bottle – dwindles. . . . *There is a passion for declivity in this world!*

And lately I've found myself listening to hired musicians behind a row of artificial palm trees – instead of the single – pure-stringed instrument of my heart. . . .

Well, then, it's time to leave here!

[He turns back to the stage.]

179

– There is a time for departure even when there's no certain place to go!

I'm going to look for one, now. I'm sailing to Athens. At least I can look up at the Acropolis, I can stand at the foot of it and look up at broken columns on the crest of a hill – if not purity, at least its recollection. . . .

I can sit quietly looking for a long, long time in absolute silence, and possibly, yes, *still* possibly –

The old pure music will come to me again. Of course on the other hand I may hear only the little noise of insects in the grass. . . .

But I am sailing to Athens! *Make voyages! – Attempt them! –* there's nothing else. . . .

MARGUERITE [*excitedly*]: *Watch where he goes!*

[*Lord Byron limps across the plaza with his head bowed, making slight, apologetic gestures to the wheedling Beggars who shuffle about him. There is music. He crosses toward the steep Alleyway Out. The following is played with a quiet intensity so it will be in a lower key than the later Fugitivo Scene.*]

Watch him, watch him, see which way he goes. Maybe he knows of a way that we haven't found out.

JACQUES: Yes, I'm watching him, Cara.

[*Lord and Lady Mulligan half rise, staring anxiously through monocle and lorgnon.*]

MARGUERITE: Oh, my God, I believe he's going up that alley.
JACQUES: Yes, he is. He has.
LORD and LADY MULLIGAN: Oh, the fool, the idiot, he's going under the arch!
MARGUERITE: Jacques, run after him, warn him, tell him about the desert he has to cross.
JACQUES: I think he knows what he's doing.
MARGUERITE: I can't look!

[*She turns to the audience, throwing back her head and closing her eyes. The desert wind sings loudly as Byron climbs to the top of the steps.*]

BYRON [*to several porters carrying luggage – which is mainly caged birds*]: THIS WAY!

[*He exits.*
  Kilroy starts to follow. He stops at the steps, cringing and looking at Gutman. Gutman motions him to go ahead. Kilroy rushes up the stairs. He looks out, loses his nerve and sits – blinking his nose. Gutman laughs as he announces –]

GUTMAN: Block Nine on the Camino Real!

[*He goes into the hotel.*]

BLOCK NINE

Abdullah runs back to the hotel with the billowing flambeau. A faint and far away humming sound becomes audible. . . . Marguerite opens her eyes with a startled look. She searches the sky for something. A very low percussion begins with the humming sound, as if excited hearts are beating.

MARGUERITE: Jacques! I hear something in the sky!
JACQUES: I think what you hear is –
MARGUERITE [*with rising excitement*]: – No, – it's a plane, a great one. I see the lights of it, now!
JACQUES: Some kind of fireworks, Cara.
MARGUERITE: Hush! LISTEN!

[*She blows out the candle to see better above it. She rises, peering into the sky.*]

I see it! I see it! There! It's circling over us!

LADY MULLIGAN: Raymond, Raymond, sit down, your face is flushed!

HOTEL GUESTS [*overlapping*]: – What is it?
– The FUGITIVO!
– THE FUGITIVO! THE FUGITIVO!
– Quick, get my jewellery from the hotel safe!
– Cash a cheque!
– Throw some things in a bag! I'll wait here!
– Never mind luggage, we have our money and papers!
– Where is it now?
– There, there!
– It's turning to land!
– To go like this?
– Yes, go anyhow, just go anyhow, just go!
– Raymond! Please!
– Oh, it's rising again!
– Oh, it's – SHH! MR GUTMAN!

[*Gutman appears in the doorway. He raises a hand in a commanding gesture.*]

GUTMAN: Signs in the sky should not be mistaken for wonders!

[*The Voices modulate quickly.*]

Ladies, gentlemen, please resume your seats!,

[*Places are resumed at tables, and silver is shakily lifted. Glasses are raised to lips, but the noise of concerted panting of excitement fills the stage and a low percussion echoes frantic heart beats.*

Gutman descends to the plaza, shouting furiously to the Officer.]

Why wasn't I told the Fugitivo was coming?

[*Everyone, almost as a man, rushes into the hotel and reappears almost at once with hastily collected possessions. Marguerite rises but appears stunned.*

There is a great whistling and screeching sound as the aerial transport halts somewhere close by, accompanied by rainbow splashes of light and cries like children's on a roller-coaster. Some incoming Passengers approach the stage down an aisle of the theatre, preceded by Redcaps with luggage.]

PASSENGERS: – What a heavenly trip!
– The scenery was thrilling!
– It's so quick!
– The only way to travel! Etc., etc.

[*A uniformed man, the Pilot, enters the plaza with a megaphone.*]

PILOT [*through the megaphone*]: Fugitivo now loading for departure! Fugitivo loading immediately for departure! Northwest corner of the plaza!

MARGUERITE: Jacques, it's the Fugitivo, it's the non-scheduled thing you heard of this afternoon!

PILOT: All out-going passengers on the Fugitivo are requested to present their tickets and papers immediately at this station.

MARGUERITE: He said 'out-going passengers'!

PILOT: Out-going passengers on the Fugitivo report immediately at this station for customs inspection.

MARGUERITE [*with a forced smile*]: Why are you just standing there?

JACQUES [*with an Italian gesture*]: Che cosa possa fare!

MARGUERITE: Move, move, do something!

JACQUES: *What!*

MARGUERITE: Go to them, ask, find out!

JACQUES: I have no idea what the damned thing is!

MARGUERITE: I do, I'll tell you! It's a way to escape from this abominable place!

JACQUES: Forse, forse, non so!

MARGUERITE: It's a way *out* and *I'm* not going to miss it!

PILOT: Ici la Douane! Customs inspection here!

MARGUERITE: Customs. That means luggage. Run to my room! Here! Key! Throw a few things in a bag, my jewels, my furs, but hurry! Vite, vite, vite! I don't believe there's much time! No, everybody is –

[*Outgoing Passengers storm the desk and table.*]

– Clamouring for tickets! There must be limited space! Why don't you do what I tell you?

[*She rushes to a man with a rubber stamp and a roll of tickets.*]

Monsieur! Senor! Pardonnez-moi! I'm going, I'm going out! I want my ticket!

PILOT [*coldly*]: Name, please.

MARGUERITE: Mademoiselle – Gautier – but I –

PILOT: Gautier? Gautier? We have no Gautier listed.

MARGUERITE: I'm – *not* listed! I mean I'm – travelling under another name.

TRAVEL AGENT: What name are you travelling under?

[*Prudence and Olympe rush out of the hotel half dressed, dragging their furs. Meanwhile Kilroy is trying to make a fast buck or two as a Redcap. The scene gathers wild momentum, is punctuated by crashes of percussion. Grotesque mummers act as demon custom inspectors and immigration authorities, etc. Baggage is tossed about, ripped open, smuggled goods seized, arrests made, all amid the wildest importunities, protests, threats, bribes, entreaties; it is a scene for improvisation.*]

PRUDENCE: Thank God I woke up!

OLYMPE: Thank God I wasn't asleep!

PRUDENCE: I knew it was non-scheduled but I *did* think they'd give you time to get in your girdle.

OLYMPE: Look who's trying to crash it! I know damned well *she* don't have a reservation!

PILOT [*to Marguerite*]: What name did you say, Mademoiselle? Please! People are waiting, you're holding up the line!

MARGUERITE: I'm so confused! Jacques! What name did you make my reservation under?

OLYMPE: She has no reservation!

PRUDENCE: *I have, I got mine!*

OLYMPE: *I got mine!*

PRUDENCE: *I'm next!*

OLYMPE: Don't push *me*, you old bag!

MARGUERITE: I was here first! I was here before anybody! Jacques, quick! Get my money from the hotel safe!

[*Jacques exits.*]

AGENT: *Stay in line!*

[*There is a loud warning whistle.*]

PILOT: Five minutes. The Fugitivo leaves in five minutes. Five, five minutes only!

[*At this announcement the scene becomes riotous.*]

TRAVEL AGENT: *Four minutes! The Fugitivo leaves in four minutes!*

[*Prudence and Olympe are shrieking at him in French. The warning whistle blasts again.*]

Three minutes, the Fugitivo leaves in three minutes!

MARGUERITE [*topping the turmoil*]: Monsieur! Please! I was here first, I was here before anybody! Look!

[*Jacques returns with her money.*]

I have thousands of francs! Take whatever you want! Take all of it, it's yours!

PILOT: Payment is only accepted in pounds sterling or dollars. Next, please.

MARGUERITE: You don't accept francs? They do at the hotel! They accept my francs at the Siete Mares!

PILOT: Lady, don't argue with me, I don't make the rules!

MARGUERITE [*beating her forehead with her fist*]: Oh, God, Jacques! Take these back to the cashier!

[*She thrusts the bills at him.*]

Get them changed to dollars or – *Hurry! Tout de suite!* I'm – going to faint. . . .

JACQUES: But Marguerite –

MARGUERITE: *Go! Go! Please!*

PILOT: Closing, we're closing now! The Fugitivo leaves in two minutes!

[*Lord and Lady Mulligan rush forward.*]

LADY MULLIGAN: Let Lord Mulligan through.

PILOT [*to Marguerite*]: You're standing in the way.

[*Olympe screams as the Customs Inspector dumps her jewels on the ground. She and Prudence butt heads as they dive for the gems: the fight is renewed.*]

MARGUERITE [*detaining the Pilot*]: Oh, look, Monsieur! Regardez ça! My diamond, a solitaire – two carats! Take that as security!

PILOT: Let me go. The Loan Shark's across the plaza!

[*There is another warning blast. Prudence and Olympe seize hat boxes and rush toward the whistle.*]

MARGUERITE [*clinging desperately to the Pilot*]: You don't understand! Senor Casanova has gone to change money! He'll be here in a second. And I'll pay five, ten, twenty times the price of – JACQUES! JACQUES! WHERE ARE YOU?

VOICE [*back of auditorium*]: We're closing the gate!

MARGUERITE: You can't close the gate!

PILOT: Move, Madame!

MARGUERITE: I won't move!

LADY MULLIGAN: I tell you, Lord Mulligan is the Iron & Steel man from Cobh! Raymond! They're closing the gate!

LORD MULLIGAN: I can't seem to get through!

GUTMAN: Hold the gate for Lord Mulligan!

PILOT [*to Marguerite*]: Madame, stand back or I will have to use force!

MARGUERITE: Jacques! Jacques!

LADY MULLIGAN: Let us through! We're clear!

PILOT: Madame! Stand back and let these passengers through!

MARGUERITE: No, No! I'm first! I'm next!

LORD MULLIGAN: Get her out of our way! That woman's a whore!

LADY MULLIGAN: How dare you stand in our way?

PILOT: Officer, take this woman!

LADY MULLIGAN: Come on, Raymond!

MARGUERITE [*as the Officer pulls her away*]: Jacques! Jacques! Jacques!

[*Jacques returns with changed money.*]

Here! Here is the money!

PILOT: All right, give me your papers.

MARGUERITE: – My papers? Did you say my papers?

PILOT: Hurry, hurry, your passport!

MARGUERITE: – Jacques! He wants my papers! Give him my papers, Jacques!

JACQUES: – The lady's papers are lost!

MARGUERITE [*wildly*]: No, no, no, THAT IS NOT TRUE! HE WANTS TO KEEP ME HERE! HE'S LYING ABOUT IT!

JACQUES: Have you forgotten that your papers were stolen?

MARGUERITE: I gave you my papers, I gave you my papers to keep, you've got my papers.

[*Screaming, Lady Mulligan breaks past her and descends the stairs.*]

LADY MULLIGAN: Raymond! Hurry!

LORD MULLIGAN [*staggering on the top step*]: I'm sick! I'm sick!

[*The Streetcleaners disguised as expensive morticians in swallow tail coats come rapidly up the aisle of the theatre and wait at the foot of the stairway for the tottering tycoon.*]

LADY MULLIGAN: You cannot be sick till we get on the Fugitivo!

LORD MULLIGAN: Forward all cables to Guaranty Trust in Paris.

LADY MULLIGAN: Place de la Concorde.

LORD MULLIGAN: Thank you! All purchases C.O.D. to Mulligan Iron & Steel Works in Cobh – Thank you!

LADY MULLIGAN: Raymond! Raymond! Who are these men?

LORD MULLIGAN: I know these men! I recognize their faces!

LADY MULLIGAN: Raymond! They're the Streetcleaners!

[*She screams and runs up the aisle screaming repeatedly, stopping halfway to look back. The Two Streetcleaners seize Lord Mulligan by either arm as he crumples.*]

Pack Lord Mulligan's body in dry ice! Ship Air Express to Cobh care of Mulligan Iron & Steel Works, in Cobh!

[*She runs sobbing out of the back of the auditorium as the whistle blows repeatedly and a Voice shouts:*]

I'm coming! I'm coming!

MARGUERITE: Jacques! Jacques! Oh, God!

PILOT: The Fugitivo is leaving, all aboard!

[*He starts toward the steps. Marguerite clutches his arm.*]

Let go of me!

MARGUERITE: You can't go without me!

PILOT: Officer, hold this woman!

JACQUES: Marguerite, let him go!

[*She releases the Pilot's arm and turns savagely on Jacques. She tears his coat open, seizes a large envelope of papers and rushes after the Pilot who has started down the steps over the orchestra pit and into a centre aisle of the house. Timpani build up as she starts down the steps, screaming* –]

MARGUERITE: Here! I have them here! Wait! I have my papers now, I have my papers!

[*The Pilot runs cursing up the centre aisle as the Fugitivo whistle gives repeated short, shrill blasts; timpani and dissonant brass are heard. Outgoing Passengers burst into hysterical song, laughter, shouts of farewell. These can come over a loudspeaker at the back of the house.*]

VOICE IN DISTANCE: Going! Going! Going!

MARGUERITE [*attempting as if half-paralysed to descend the steps*]: NOT WITHOUT ME, NO, NO, NOT WITHOUT ME!

[*Her figure is caught in the dazzling glacial light of the follow-spot. It blinds her. She makes violent, crazed gestures, clinging to the railing of the steps; her breath is loud and hoarse as a dying person's, she holds a blood-stained handkerchief to her lips.*

There is a prolonged, gradually fading, rocketlike roar as the Fugitivo takes off. Shrill cries of joy from departing passengers; something radiant passes above the stage and streams of confetti and tinsel fall into the plaza. Then there is a great calm, the ship's receding roar diminished to the hum of an insect.]

GUTMAN [*somewhat compassionately*]: Block Ten on the Camino Real.

There is something about the desolation of the plaza that suggests a city devastated by bombardment. Reddish lights flicker here and there as if ruins were smouldering and wisps of smoke rise from them.

LA MADRECITA [*almost inaudibly*]: Donde?
THE DREAMER: Aquí. Aquí, Madrecita.
MARGUERITA: Lost! Lost! Lost! Lost!

[*She is clinging brokenly to the railing of the steps. Jacques descends to her and helps her back up the steps.*]

JACQUES: Lean against me, Cara. Breathe quietly, now.
MARGUERITE: Lost!
JACQUES: Breathe quietly, quietly, and look up at the sky.
MARGUERITE: Lost . . .
JACQUES: These tropical nights are so clear. There's the Southern Cross. Do you see the Southern Cross, Marguerite?

[*He points through the proscenium. They are now on the bench before the fountain; she is resting in his arms.*]

And there, over there, is Orion, like a fat, golden fish swimming North in the deep clear water, and we are together, breathing quietly together, leaning together, quietly, quietly together, completely, sweetly together, not frightened, now, not alone, but completely quietly together. . . .

[*La Madrecita, led into the centre of the plaza by her son, has begun to sing very softly; the reddish flares dim out and the smoke disappears.*]

All of us have a desperate bird in our hearts, a memory of – an expectant mother with – wings. . . .

MARGUERITE: I would have – left – without you. . . .

JACQUES: I know, I know!

MARGUERITE: Then how can you – still – ?

JACQUES: Hold you?

[*Marguerite nods slightly.*]

Because you've taught me that part of love which is tender. I never knew it before. Oh, I had – mistresses that circled me like moons! I scrambled from one bed-chamber to another bed-chamber with shirt-tails always aflame, from girl to girl, like buckets of coal-oil poured on a conflagration! But never loved until now with the part of love that's tender. . . .

MARGUERITE: – We're used to each other. That's what you think is love. . . . You'd better leave me now, you'd better go and let me go because there's a cold wind blowing out of the mountains and over the desert and into my heart, and if you stay with me now, I'll say cruel things, I'll wound your vanity, I'll taunt you with the decline of your male vigour!

JACQUES: Why does disappointment make people unkind to each other?

MARGUERITE: Each of us is very much alone.

JACQUES: Only if we distrust each other.

MARGUERITE: We have to distrust each other. It is our only defence against betrayal.

JACQUES: I think our defence is love.

MARGUERITE: Oh, Jacques, we're used to each other, we're a pair of captive hawks caught in the same cage, and so we've grown used to each other. That's what passes for love at this dim, shadowy end of the Camino Real. . . .

What are we sure of? Not even of our existence, dear comforting friend! And whom can we ask the questions that torment us? 'What is this place?' 'Where are we?' – a fat old man who gives sly hints that only bewilder us more, a fake of a Gipsy squinting at cards and tea-leaves. What else are we offered? The never-broken procession of little events that assure us that we and strangers about us are still going on? Where? Why? and the perch that we hold is unstable!

We're threatened with eviction, for this is a port of entry and departure, there are no permanent guests! And where else have we to go when we leave here? Bide-a-While? 'Ritz Men Only'? Or under that ominous arch into Terra Incognita? We're lonely. We're frightened.

We hear the streetcleaners' piping not far away. So now and then, although we've wounded each other time and again – we stretch out hands to each other in the dark that we can't escape from – we huddle together for some dim communal comfort – and that's what passes for love on this terminal stretch of the road that used to be royal. What is it, this feeling between us? When you feel my exhausted weight against your shoulder – when I clasp your anxious old hawk's head to my breast, what is it we feel in whatever is left of our hearts? Something, yes, something – delicate, unreal, bloodless! The sort of violets that could grow on the moon, or in the crevices of those far away mountains, fertilized by the droppings of carrion birds. Those birds are familiar to us. Their shadows inhabit the plaza. I've heard them flapping their wings like old charwomen beating worn-out carpets with grey brooms. . . . But tenderness, the violets in the mountains – can't break the rocks!

JACQUES: The violets in the mountains can break the rocks if you believe in them and allow them to grow!

[*The plaza has resumed its usual aspect. Abdullah enters through one of the downstage arches.*]

ABDULLAH: Get your carnival hats and nosemakers here! To-night the moon will restore the virginity of my sister!

MARGUERITE [*almost tenderly touching his face*]: Don't you know that to-night I am going to betray you?

JACQUES: – Why would you do that?

MARGUERITE: Because I've out-lived the tenderness of my heart. Abdullah, come here! I have an errand for you! Go to Ahmed's and deliver a message!

ABDULLAH: I'm working for Mama, making the Yankee dollar! Get your carnival hats and –

MARGUERITE: *Here, boy!*

[*She snatches a ring off her finger and offers it to him.*]

JACQUES: – Your cabochon sapphire?

MARGUERITE: Yes, my cabochon sapphire!

JACQUES: Are you mad?

MARGUERITE: Yes, I'm mad, or nearly! The spectre of lunacy's at my heels to-night!

[*Jacques drives Abdullah back with his cane.*]

Catch, boy! The other side of the fountain! Quick!

[*The guitar is heard molto vivace. She tosses the ring across the fountain. Jacques attempts to hold the boy back with his cane Abdullah dodges in and out like a little terrier, laughing. Marguerite shouts encouragement in French. When the boy is driven back from the ring, she snatches it up and tosses it to him again, shouting:*]

Catch, boy! Run to Ahmed's! Tell the charming young man that the French lady's bored with her company to-night! Say that the French lady missed the Fugitivo and wants to forget she missed it! Oh, and reserve a room with a balcony so I can watch your sister appear on the roof when the moonrise makes her a virgin!

[*Abdullah skips shouting out of the plaza. Jacques strikes the stage with his cane. She says, without looking at him:*]

Time betrays us and we betray each other.

JACQUES: Wait, Marguerite.

MARGUERITE: No! I can't! The wind from the desert is sweeping me away!

[*A loud singing wind sweeps her toward the terrace, away from him. She looks back once or twice as if for some gesture of leave-taking but he only stares at her fiercely, striking the stage at intervals with his cane, like a death-march. Gutman watches, smiling, from the terrace, bows to Marguerite as she passes into the hotel. The drum of Jacques' cane is taken up by other percussive instruments, and almost unnoticeably at first, weird-looking celebrants or carnival mummers creep into the plaza, silently as spiders descending a wall.*

A sheet of scarlet and yellow rice paper bearing some cryptic device is lowered from the centre of the plaza. The percussive effects become gradually louder. Jacques is oblivious to the scene behind him, standing in front of the plaza, his eyes closed.]

GUTMAN: Block Eleven on the Camino Real.

BLOCK ELEVEN

GUTMAN: The Fiesta has started. The first event is the coronation of the King of Cuckolds.

[*Blinding shafts of light are suddenly cast upon Casanova on the forestage. He shields his face, startled, as the crowd closes about him.*

The blinding shafts of light seem to strike him like savage blows and he falls to his knees as —

The Hunchback scuttles out of the Gipsy's stall with a crown

*of gilded antlers on a velvet pillow. He places it on Jacques'
head. The celebrants form a circle about him chanting.*]

JACQUES: What is this? – a crown –

GUTMAN: A crown of horns!

CROWD: Cornudo! Cornudo! Cornudo! Cornudo!
Cornudo!

GUTMAN: Hail, all hail, the King of Cuckolds on the Camino
Real!

[*Jacques springs up, first striking out at them with his cane.
Then all at once he abandons self-defence, throws off his cape,
casts away his cane, and fills the plaza with a roar of defiance
and self-derision.*]

ACQUES: Si, si, sono cornudo! Cornudo! Cornudo! Casan-
ova is the King of Cuckolds on the Camino Real! Show me
crowned to the world! Announce the honour! Tell the
world of the honour bestowed on Casanova, Chevalier de
Seingalt! Knight of the Golden Spur by the Grace of His
Holiness the Pope . . . . Famous adventurer! Con man
Extraordinary! Gambler! Pitch-man par excellence! Shill!
Pimp! Spiv! *And – great – lover.* . . .

[*The Crowd howls with applause and laughter but his voice
rises above them with sobbing intensity.*]

Yes, I said GREAT LOVER! The greatest lover wears the
longest horns on the Camino! GREAT LOVER!

GUTMAN: Attention! Silence! The moon is rising! The res-
toration is about to occur!

[*A white radiance is appearing over the ancient wall of the town.
The mountains become luminous. There is music. Everyone
with breathless attention, faces the light.*

*Kilroy crosses to Jacques and beckons him out behind the
crowd. There he snatches off the antlers and returns him his
fedora. Jacques reciprocates by removing Kilroy's fright wig and*

electric nose. They embrace as brothers. In a Chaplinesque dumb-play, Kilroy points to the wildly flickering three brass balls of the Loan Shark and to his golden gloves: then with a terrible grimace he removes the gloves from about his neck, smiles at Jacques and indicates that the two of them together will take flight over the wall. Jacques shakes his head sadly, pointing to his heart and to the Siete Mares. Kilroy nods with regretful understanding of a human and manly folly. A Guard has been silently approaching them in a soft shoe dance. Jacques whistles 'La Golondrina'. Kilroy assumes a very nonchalant pose. The Guard picks up curiously the discarded fright wig and electric nose. Then glancing suspiciously at the pair, he advances. Kilroy makes a run for it. He does a baseball slide into the Loan Shark's welcoming doorway. The door slams. The Cop is about to crash it when a gong sounds and Gutman shouts.]

GUTMAN: SILENCE! ATTENTION! THE GIPSY!

GIPSY [*appearing on the roof with a gong*]: The moon has restored the virginity of my daughter Esmeralda!

[*The gong sounds.*]

STREET PEOPLE: Ahh!

GIPSY: The moon in its plenitude has made her a virgin!

[*The gong sounds.*]

STREET PEOPLE: Ahh!

GIPSY: Praise her, celebrate her, give her suitable homage!

[*The gong sounds.*]

STREET PEOPLE: Ahh!

GIPSY: Summon her to the roof!

[*She shouts:*]

ESMERALDA!

[*Dancers shout the name in rhythm.*]

RISE WITH THE MOON, MY DAUGHTER! CHOOSE THE HERO!

[*Esmeralda appears on the roof in dazzling light. She seems to be dressed in jewels. She raises her jewelled arms with a harsh flamenco cry.*]

ESMERALDA: OLÉ!
DANCERS: OLÉ!

[*The details of the Carnival are a problem for director and choreo-grapher but it has already been indicated in the script that the Fiesta is a sort of serio-comic, grotesque-lyric 'Rites of Fertility' with roots in various pagan cultures.*

It should not be over-elaborated or allowed to occupy much time. It should not be more than three minutes from the appear-ance of Esmeralda on the Gipsy's roof till the return of Kilroy from the Loan Shark's.

Kilroy emerges from the Pawn Shop in grotesque disguise, a turban, dark glasses, a burnoose and an umbrella or sunshade.]

KILROY [*to Jacques*]: So long, pal, I wish you could come with me.

[*Jacques claps his cross in Kilroy's hands.*]

ESMERALDA: Yankee!
KILROY [*to the audience*]: So long, everybody. Good luck to you all on the Camino! I hocked my golden gloves to finance this expedition. I'm going. Hasta luega. I'm going. I'm gone!
ESMERALDA: Yankee!

[*He has no sooner entered the plaza than the riotous women strip off everything but the dungarees and skivvy which he first appeared in.*]

KILROY [*to the women*]: Let me go. Let go of me! Watch out for my equipment!

ESMERALDA: Yankee! Yankee!

[*He breaks away from them and plunges up the stairs of the ancient wall. He is half-way up them when Gutman shouts out.*]

GUTMAN: Follow-spot on that gringo, light the stairs!

[*The light catches Kilroy. At the same instant Esmeralda cries out to him.*]

ESMERALDA: *Yankee! Yankee!*

GIPSY: What's goin' on down there?

[*She rushes into the plaza.*]

KILROY: Oh, no, I'm on my way out!

ESMERALDA: Espere un momento!

[*The Gipsy calls the police, but is ignored in the crowd.*]

KILROY: Don't tempt me, baby! I hocked my golden gloves to finance this expedition!

ESMERALDA: Querido!

KILROY: Querido means sweetheart, a word which is hard to resist but I must resist it.

ESMERALDA: Champ!

KILROY: I used to be Champ but why remind me of it?

ESMERALDA: Be champ again! Contend in the contest! Compete in the competition!

GIPSY [*shouting*]: *Naw, naw, not eligible!*

ESMERALDA: *Pl-eeeeeeze!*

GIPSY: Slap her, Nursie, she's flippin'.

[*Esmeralda slaps Nursie instead.*]

198

ESMERALDA: Hero! Champ!

KILROY: I'm not in condition!

ESMERALDA: You're still the Champ, the undefeated Champ of the golden gloves!

KILROY: Nobody's called me that in a long, long time!

ESMERALDA: Champ!

KILROY: My resistance is crumbling!

ESMERALDA: Champ!

KILROY: It's crumbled!

ESMERALDA: Hero!

KILROY: GERONIMO!

[*He takes a flying leap from the stairs into the centre of the plaza. He turns toward Esmeralda and cries.*]

DOLL!

[*Kilroy surrounded by cheering Street People goes into a triumphant eccentric dance which reviews his history as fighter, traveller, and lover.*

At finish of the dance, the music is cut off, as Kilroy lunges, arm uplifted toward Esmeralda, and cries:]

KILROY: *Kilroy the Champ!*

ESMERALDA: *KILROY the Champ!*

[*She snatches a bunch of red roses from the stunned Nursie and tosses them to Kilroy.*]

CROWD [*sharply*]: OLÉ.

[*The Gipsy, at the same instant, hurls her gong down, creating a resounding noise.*

Kilroy turns and comes down towards the audience, saying to them:]

KILROY: Y'see.

[*Cheering Street People surge towards him and lift him in the air. The lights fade as the curtain descends.*]

CROWD [*in a sustained yell*]: OLÉ!

[*The curtain falls. There is a short intermission.*]

BLOCK TWELVE

The stage is in darkness except for a spotlight which picks out Esmeralda on the Gipsy's roof.

ESMERALDA: Mama, what happened? – Mama, the lights went out! – Mama, where are you? It's so dark I'm scared! – MAMA!

[*The lights are turned on displaying a deserted plaza. The Gipsy is seated at a small table before her stall.*]

GIPSY: Come on downstairs, Doll. The mischief is done. You've chosen your hero!

GUTMAN [*from the balcony of the Siete Mares*]: Block Twelve on the Camino Real.

NURSIE [*at the fountain*]: Gipsy, the fountain is still dry!

GIPSY: What d'yuh expect? There's nobody left to uphold the old traditions! You raise a girl. She watches television. Plays be-bop. Reads *Screen Secrets*. Comes the Big Fiesta. The moonrise makes her a virgin – which is the neatest trick of the week! And what does she do! Chooses a Fugitive Patsy for the Chosen Hero! Well, show him in! Admit the joker and get the virgin ready!

NURSIE: You're going through with it?

GIPSY: Look, Nursie! I'm operating a legitimate joint! This joker'll get the same treatment he'd get if he breezed down the Camino in a blizzard of G-notes! Trot, girl! Lubricate your means of locomotion!

[*Nursie goes into the Gipsy's stall. The Gipsy rubs her hands together and blows on the crystal ball, spits on it and gives it the old one-two with a 'shammy' rag. . . . She mutters 'Crystal ball, tell me all . . . crystal ball tell me all' . . . as:*

Kilroy bounds into the plaza from her stall . . . a rose between his teeth.]

GIPSY: Siente se, por favor.

KILROY: No comprendo the lingo.

GIPSY: Put it down!

NURSIE [*offstage*]: Hey, Gipsy!

GIPSY: Address me as Madam!

NURSIE [*entering*]: *Madam!* Winchell has scooped you!

GIPSY: In a pig's eye!

NURSIE: The Fugitivo has '*fftt* . . .'!

GIPSY: In Elizabeth, New Jersey . . . ten fifty seven P.M. . . . Eastern Standard Time – while you were putting them kiss-me-quicks in your hair-do! Furthermore, my second exclusive is that the solar system is drifting towards the constellation of Hercules: *Skiddoo!*

[*Nursie exits. Stamping is heard offstage.*]

Quiet, back there! God damn it!

NURSIE [*offstage*]: She's out of control!

GIPSY: Give her a double-bromide! [*To Kilroy*] Well, how does it feel to be the Chosen Hero?

KILROY: I better explain something to you.

GIPSY: Save your breath. You'll need it.

KILROY: I want to level with you. Can I level with you?

GIPSY [*rapidly stamping some papers*]: How could you help but level with the Gipsy?

KILROY: I don't know what the hero is chosen for.

[*Esmeralda and Nursie shriek offstage.*]

GIPSY: Time will brief you. . . . Aw, I hate paper work! . . . NURSEHH!

[*Nursie comes out and stands by the table.*]

This filing system is screwed up six ways from Next Sunday. . . . File this crap under crap! – [*To Kilroy*] The smoking lamp is lit. Have a stick on me!

[*She offers him a cigarette.*]

KILROY: No thanks.

GIPSY: Come on, indulge yourself. You got nothing to lose that won't be lost.

KILROY: If that's a professional opinion, I don't respect it.

GIPSY: Resume your seat and give me your full name.

KILROY: Kilroy.

GIPSY [*writing all this down*]: Date of birth and place of that disaster?

KILROY: Both unknown.

GIPSY: Address?

KILROY: Traveller.

GIPSY: Parents?

KILROY: Anonymous.

GIPSY: Who brought you up?

KILROY: I was brought up and down by an eccentric old aunt in Dallas.

GIPSY: Raise both hands simultaneously and swear that you have not come here for the purpose of committing an immoral act.

ESMERALDA [*from offstage*]: Hey, Chico!

GIPSY: *QUIET!* Childhood diseases?

KILROY: Whooping cough, measles, and mumps.

GIPSY: Likes and dislikes?

KILROY: I like situations I can get out of. I don't like cops and –

GIPSY: Immaterial! Here! Signature on this!

[*She hands him a blank.*]

KILROY: What is it?

GIPSY: You always sign something, don't you?

KILROY: Not till I know what it is.

GIPSY: It's just a little formality to give a tone to the establishment and make an impression on our out-of-town trade. Roll up your sleeve.

KILROY: What for?

GIPSY: A shot of some kind.

KILROY: What kind?

GIPSY: Any kind. Don't they always give you some kind of a shot?

KILROY: 'They'?

GIPSY: Brass-hats, Americanos!

[*She injects a hypo.*]

KILROY: I am no guinea pig!

GIPSY: Don't kid yourself. We're all of us guinea pigs in the laboratory of God. Humanity is just a work in progress.

KILROY: I don't make it out.

GIPSY: Who does? The Camino Real is a funny paper read backwards!

[*There is weird piping outside. Kilroy shifts on his seat. The Gipsy grins.*]

Tired? The altitude makes you sleepy?

KILROY: It makes me nervous.

GIPSY: I'll show you how to take a slug of tequila! It dilates the capillaries. First you sprinkle salt on the back of your hand.

Then lick it off with your tongue. Now then you toss the shot down! [*She demonstrates.*] – And then you bite into the lemon. That way it goes down easy, but what a bang! – You're next.

KILROY: No, thanks, I'm on the wagon.

GIPSY: There's an old Chinese proverb that says, 'When your goose is cooked you might as well have it cooked with plenty of gravy.'

[*She laughs.*]

Get up, baby. Let's have a look at yuh! – You're not a bad-looking boy. Sometimes working for the Yankee dollar isn't a painful profession. Have you ever been attracted by older women?

KILROY: Frankly, no, ma'am.

GIPSY: Well, there's a first time for everything.

KILROY: That is a subject I cannot agree with you on.

GIPSY: You think I'm an old bag?

[*Kilroy laughs awkwardly. The Gipsy slaps his face.*]

Will you take the cards or the crystal?

KILROY: It's immaterial.

GIPSY: All right, we'll begin with the cards.

[*She shuffles and deals.*]

Ask me a question.

KILROY: Has my luck run out?

GIPSY: Baby, your luck ran out the day you were born. Another question.

KILROY: Ought I to leave this town?

GIPSY: It don't look to me like you've got much choice in the matter. . . . Take a card.

[*Kilroy takes one.*]

204

GIPSY: Ace?

KILROY: Yes, ma'am.

GIPSY: What colour?

KILROY: Black.

GIPSY: Oh, oh – That does it. How big is your heart?

KILROY: As big as the head of a baby.

GIPSY: It's going to break.

KILROY: That's what I was afraid of.

GIPSY: The Streetcleaners are waiting for you outside the door.

KILROY: Which door, the front one? I'll slip out the back!

GIPSY: Leave us face it frankly, your number is up! You must've known a long time that the name of Kilroy was on the Streetcleaners' list.

KILROY: Sure. But not on top of it!

GIPSY: It's always a bit of a shock. Wait a minute! Here's good news. The Queen of Hearts has turned up in proper position.

KILROY: What's that mean?

GIPSY: Love, Baby!

KILROY: Love?

GIPSY: The Booby Prize! – Esmeralda!

[*She rises and hits a gong. A divan is carried out. The Gipsy's Daughter is seated in a reclining position, like an odalisque, on this low divan. A spangled veil covers her face. From this veil to the girdle below her navel, that supports her diaphanous bifurcated skirt, she is nude except for a pair of glittering emerald snakes coiled over her breasts. Kilroy's head moves in a dizzy circle and a canary warbles inside it.*]

KILROY: WHAT'S – WHAT'S *HER* SPECIALITY? – Tea-leaves?

[*The Gipsy wags a finger.*]

GIPSY: You know what curiosity did to the tom cat! – Nursie, give me my glamour wig and my forty-five. I'm hitting the street! I gotta go down to Walgreen's for change.

KILROY: What change?

GIPSY: The change from that ten-spot you're about to give me.

NURSIE: Don't argue with her. She has a will of iron.

KILROY: I'm not arguing!

[*He reluctantly produces the money.*]

But let's be *fair* about this! I hocked my golden gloves for this sawbuck!

NURSIE: All of them Yankee bastids want something for nothing!

KILROY: I want a receipt for this bill.

NURSIE: No one is gypped at the Gipsy's!

KILROY: That's wonderful! How do I know it?

GIPSY: It's in the cards, it's in the crystal ball, it's in the tea-leaves! Absolutely no one is gypped at the Gipsy's!

[*She snatches the bill. The wind howls.*]

Such changeable weather! I'll slip on my summer furs! Nursie, break out my summer furs!

NURSIE [*leering grotesquely*]: Mink or sable?

GIPSY: *Ha ha, that's a doll!* Here! Clock him!

[*Nursie tosses her a greasy blanket, and the Gipsy tosses Nursie an alarm clock. The Gipsy rushes through the beaded string curtains.*]

Adios! Ha ha!!

[*She is hardly offstage when two shots ring out. Kilroy starts.*]

ESMERALDA [*plaintively*]: Mother has such an awful time on the street.

KILROY: You mean that she is insulted on the street?

ESMERALDA: By strangers.

KILROY [*to the audience*]: I shouldn't think acquaintances would do it.

[*She curls up on the low divan. Kilroy licks his lips.*]

– You seem very different from – this afternoon. . . .

ESMERALDA: This afternoon?

KILROY: Yes, in the plaza when I was being roughed up by them gorillas and you was being dragged in the house by your Mama!

[*Esmeralda stares at him blankly.*]

You don't remember?

ESMERALDA: I never remember what happened before the moonrise makes me a virgin.

KILROY: – That – comes as a shock to you, huh?

ESMERALDA: Yes. It comes as a shock.

KILROY [*smiling*]: You have a little temporary amnesia they call it!

ESMERALDA: Yankee . . .

KILROY: Huh?

ESMERALDA: I'm glad I chose you. I'm glad that you were chosen.

[*Her voice trails off.*]

I'm glad. I'm very glad . . .

NURSIE: Doll!

ESMERALDA: – What is it, Nursie?

NURSIE: How are things progressing?

ESMERALDA: Slowly, Nursie –

[*Nursie comes lumbering in.*]

NURSIE: I want some light reading matter.

ESMERALDA: He's sitting on *Screen Secrets*.

KILROY [*jumping up*]: Aw. Here.

[He hands her the fan magazine. She lumbers back out coyly.]

– I – I feel – self-conscious. . . .

[He suddenly jerks out a silver-framed photo.]

– D'you – like pictures?

ESMERALDA: Moving pictures?

KILROY: No, a – motionless – snapshot!

ESMERALDA: Of you?

KILROY: Of my – real – true woman. . . . She was a platinum blonde the same as Jean Harlow. Do you remember Jean Harlow? No, you wouldn't remember Jean Harlow. It shows you are getting old when you remember Jean Harlow.

[He puts the snapshot away.]

. . . They say that Jean Harlow's ashes are kept in a little private cathedral in Forest Lawn. . . . Wouldn't it be wonderful if you could sprinkle them ashes over the ground like seeds, and out of each one would spring another Jean Harlow? And when spring comes you could just walk out and pick them off the bush! . . . You don't talk much.

ESMERALDA: You want me to *talk*?

KILROY: Well, that's the way we do things in the States. A little vino, some records on the victrola, some quiet conversation – and then if both parties are in a mood for romance . . . Romance –

ESMERALDA: Music!

[She rises and pours some wine from a slender crystal decanter as music is heard.]

They say that the monetary system has got to be stabilized all over the world.

KILROY *[taking the glass]*: Repeat that, please. My radar was not wide open.

ESMERALDA: I said that *they* said that – uh, skip it! But we couldn't care less as long as we keep on getting the Yankee dollar . . . plus federal tax!

KILROY: That's for surely!

ESMERALDA: How do you feel about the class struggle? Do you take sides in that?

KILROY: Not that I –

ESMERALDA: Neither do we because of the dialectics.

KILROY: Who! Which?

ESMERALDA: Languages with accents, I suppose. But Mama don't care as long as they don't bring the Pope over here and put him in the White House.

KILROY: Who would do that?

ESMERALDA: Oh, the Bolsheviskies, those nasty old things with whiskers! *Whiskers scratch!* But little moustaches tickle. . . .

[*She giggles.*]

KILROY: I always got a smooth shave. . . .

ESMERALDA: And how do you feel about the Mumbo Jumbo? Do you think they've got the Old Man in the bag yet?

KILROY: The Old Man?

ESMERALDA: God. We don't think so. We think there has been so much of the Mumbo Jumbo it's put Him to sleep!

[*Kilroy jumps up impatiently.*]

KILROY: This is not what I mean by a quiet conversation. I mean this is nowhere! *Nowhere!*

ESMERALDA: What sort of talk do you want?

KILROY: Something more – intimate sort of! You know, like –

ESMERALDA: – Where did you get those eyes?

KILROY: *PERSONAL! Yeah.* . . .

ESMERALDA: Well, – where did you get those eyes?

KILROY: Out of a dead cod-fish!

NURSIE [*shouting offstage*]: DOLL!

[*Kilroy springs up, pounding his left palm with his right fist.*]

ESMERALDA: What?

NURSIE: Fifteen minutes!

KILROY: I'm no hot-rod mechanic.

[*To the audience:*]

I bet she's out there holding a stop watch to see that I don't overstay my time in this place!

ESMERALDA [*calling through the string curtains*]: Nursie, go to bed, Nursie!

KILROY [*in a fierce whisper*]: That's right, go to bed, Nursie!!

[*There is a loud crash offstage.*]

ESMERALDA: – Nursie has gone to bed. . . .

[*She drops the string curtains and returns to the alcove.*]

KILROY [*with vast relief*]: – Ahhhhhhhhhh. . . .

ESMERALDA: What've you got your eyes on?

KILROY: Those green snakes on you – what do you wear them for?

ESMERALDA: Supposedly for protection, but really for fun.

[*He crosses to the divan.*]

What are you going to do?

KILROY: I'm about to establish a beach-head on that sofa.

[*He sits down.*]

How about – lifting your veil?

ESMERALDA: I can't lift it.

KILROY: Why not?

ESMERALDA: I promised Mother I wouldn't.

KILROY: I thought your mother was the broadminded type.

ESMERALDA: Oh, she is, but you know how mothers are. You can lift it for me, if you say pretty please.

KILROY: Aww –

ESMERALDA: Go on, say it! Say pretty please!

KILROY: No!

ESMERALDA: Why not?

KILROY: It's silly.

ESMERALDA: Then you can't lift my veil!

KILROY: Oh, all right. Pretty please.

ESMERALDA: Say it again!

KILROY: Pretty please.

ESMERALDA: Now say it once more like you meant it.

[*He jumps up. She grabs his hand.*]

Don't go away.

KILROY: You're making a fool out of me.

ESMERALDA: I was just teasing a little. Because you're so cute. Sit down again, please – *pretty* please!

[*He falls on the couch.*]

KILROY: What is that wonderful perfume you've got on?

ESMERALDA: Guess!

KILROY: Chanel! Number Five?

ESMERALDA: No.

KILROY: Tabu?

ESMERALDA: No.

KILROY: I give up.

ESMERALDA: It's *Noche en Acapulco*! I'm just dying to go to Acapulco. I wish that you would take me to Acapulco.

[*He sits up.*]

What's the matter?

KILROY: You gipsies' daughters are invariably reminded of something without which you cannot do – just when it looks like everything has been fixed.

ESMERALDA: That isn't nice at all. I'm not the gold-digger type. Some girls see themselves in silver foxes. I only see myself in Acapulco!

KILROY: At Todd's Place?

ESMERALDA: Oh, no, at the Mirador! Watching those pretty boys dive off the Quebrada!

KILROY: Look again, Baby. Maybe you'll see yourself in Paramount Pictures or having a Singapore Sling at a Statler bar!

ESMERALDA: You're being sarcastic?

KILROY: Nope. Just realistic. All of you gipsies' daughters have hearts of stone, and I'm not whistling 'Dixie'! But just the same, the night before a man dies, he says, 'Pretty please – will you let me lift your veil?' – while the Streetcleaners wait for him right outside the door! – Because to be warm for a little longer is life. And love? – that's a four-letter word which is sometimes no better than one you see printed on fences by kids playing hooky from school! – well – what's the use of complaining? You gipsies' daughters have ears that only catch sounds like the snap of a gold cigarette case! Or, pretty please, Baby – we're going to Acapulco!

ESMERALDA: *Are* we?

KILROY: See what I mean?

[*To the audience:*]

Didn't I tell you?!

[*To Esmeralda:*]

Yes! In the morning!

ESMERALDA: Ohhhh I'm dizzy with joy! My little heart is going pitty-pat!

KILROY: My big heart is going boom-boom! Can I lift your veil now?

ESMERALDA: If you will be gentle.

KILROY: I would not hurt a fly unless it had on leather mittens.

[*He touches a corner of her spangled veil.*]

ESMERALDA: Ohhh . . .
KILROY: What?
ESMERALDA: Ohhhhhh!!
KILROY: Why! What's the matter?
ESMERALDA: You are not being gentle!
KILROY: I *am* being gentle.
ESMERALDA: You *are* not being gentle.
KILROY: What was I being, then?
ESMERALDA: Rough!
KILROY: I am *not* being rough.
ESMERALDA: Yes, you *are* being rough. You have to be gentle
  with me because you're the first.
KILROY: Are you kidding?
ESMERALDA: No.
KILROY: How about all of those other fiestas you've been to?
ESMERALDA: Each one's the first one. That is the wonderful
  thing about gipsies' daughters!
KILROY: You can say that again!
ESMERALDA: I don't like you when you're like that.
KILROY: Like what?
ESMERALDA: Cynical and sarcastic.
KILROY: I am sincere.
ESMERALDA: Lots of boys aren't sincere.
KILROY: Maybe they aren't but I am.
ESMERALDA: Everyone says he's sincere, but everyone isn't
  sincere. If everyone was sincere who says he's sincere there
  wouldn't be half so many insincere ones in the world and
  there would be lots, lots, lots more really sincere ones!
KILROY: I think you have got something there. But how about
  gipsies' daughters?
ESMERALDA: Huh!
KILROY: Are they one hundred per cent in the really sincere
  category?

213

ESMERALDA: Well, yes, and no, mostly no! But some of them are for a while if their sweethearts are gentle.

KILROY: Would you believe I am sincere and gentle?

ESMERALDA: I would believe that you believe that you are.... For a while. . . .

KILROY: Everything's for a while. For a while is the stuff that dreams are made of, Baby! Now? – Now?

ESMERALDA: Yes, now, but be gentle! – *gentle*. . . .

[*He delicately lifts a corner of her veil. She utters a soft cry. He lifts it further. She cries out again. A bit further. . . . He turns the spangled veil all the way up from her face.*]

KILROY: I am sincere.

ESMERALDA: I am sincere.

KILROY: I am sincere.

ESMERALDA: I am sincere.

KILROY: I am sincere.

ESMERALDA: I am sincere.

KILROY: I am sincere.

ESMERALDA: I am sincere.

[*Kilroy leans back, removing his hand from her veil. She opens her eyes.*]

Is that all?

KILROY: I am tired.

ESMERALDA: – Already?

[*He rises and goes down the steps from the alcove.*]

KILROY: I am tired, and full of regret. . . .

ESMERALDA: Oh!

KILROY: It wasn't much to give my golden gloves for.

ESMERALDA: You pity yourself?

KILROY: That's right, I pity myself and everybody that goes to the Gipsy's daughter. I pity the world and I pity the God who made it.

[*He sits down.*]

ESMERALDA: It's always like that as soon as the veil is lifted. They're all so ashamed of having degraded themselves, and their hearts have more regret than a heart can hold!

KILROY: Even a heart that's as big as the head of a baby!

ESMERALDA: You don't even notice how pretty my face is, do you?

KILROY: You look like all gipsies' daughters, no better, no worse. But as long as you get to go to Acapulco, your cup runneth over with ordinary contentment.

ESMERALDA: – I've never been so insulted in all my life!

KILROY: Oh, yes, you have, Baby. And you'll be insulted worse if you stay in this racket. You'll be insulted so much that it will get to be like water off *a duck's back!*

[*The door slams. Curtains are drawn apart on the Gipsy. Esmeralda lowers her veil hastily. Kilroy pretends not to notice the Gipsy's entrance. She picks up a little bell and rings it over his head.*]

Okay, Mamacita! I am aware of your presence!

GIPSY: Ha–ha! I was followed three blocks by some awful man!

KILROY: Then you caught him.

GIPSY: Naw, he ducked into a subway! I waited fifteen minutes outside the men's room and he never came out!

KILROY: Then you went in?

GIPSY: No! I got myself a sailor! – The streets are brilliant! . . . Have you all been good children?

[*Esmeralda makes a whimpering sound.*]

The pussy will play while the old mother cat is away?

KILROY: Your sense of humour is wonderful, but how about my change, Mamacita?

GIPSY: What change are you talking about?

KILROY: Are you boxed out of your mind? The change from that ten-spot you trotted over to Walgreen's?

GIPSY: Ohhhhh –

KILROY: *Oh, what?*

GIPSY [*counting on her fingers*]: Five for the works, one dollar luxury tax, two for the house percentage and two more pour la service! – makes ten! Didn't I tell you?

KILROY: – What kind of a deal is this?

GIPSY [*whipping out a revolver*]: A rugged one, Baby!

ESMERALDA: Mama, don't be unkind!

GIPSY: Honey, the gentleman's friends are waiting outside the door and it wouldn't be nice to detain him! Come on – Get going – Vamoose!

KILROY: Okay, Mamacita! Me voy!

[*He crosses to the beaded string curtains: turns to look back at the Gipsy and Her Daughter. The piping of the Streetcleaners is heard outside.*]

Sincere? – Sure! That's the wonderful thing about gipsies' daughters!

[*He goes out. Esmeralda raises a wondering fingertip to one eye. Then she cries out.*]

ESMERALDA: Look, Mama! Look, Mama! A tear!

GIPSY: You have been watching television too much. . . .

[*She gathers the cards and turns off the crystal ball as –
Light fades out on the phony paradise of the Gipsy's.*]

GUTMAN: Block Thirteen on the Camino Real.

[*He exits.*]

*In the blackout the Streetcleaners place a barrel in the centre and then
hide in the Pit.*

> [*Kilroy, who enters from the right, is followed by a spotlight. He
> sees the barrel and the menacing Streetcleaners and then runs
> to the closed door of the Siete Mares and rings the bell. No one
> answers. He backs up so he can see the balcony and calls.*]

KILROY: Mr Gutman! Just gimme a cot in the lobby. I'll do
odd jobs in the morning. I'll be the Patsy again. I'll light my
nose sixty times a minute. I'll take prat-falls and assume the
position for anybody that drops a dime on the street. . . .
Have a heart! Have just a LITTLE heart. Please!

> [*There is no response from Gutman's balcony. Jacques enters.
> He pounds his cane once on the pavement.*]

JACQUES: Gutman! Open the door! – GUTMAN! GUT-
MAN!

> [*Eva, a beautiful woman, apparently nude, appears on the
> balcony.*]

GUTMAN [*from inside*]: Eva darling, you're exposing yourself!

> [*He appears on the balcony with a portmanteau.*]

JACQUES: What aré you doing with my portmanteau?
GUTMAN: Haven't you come for your luggage?
JACQUES: Certainly not! I haven't checked out of here!
GUTMAN: Very few do . . . but residences are frequently
terminated.
JACQUES: Open the door!
GUTMAN: Open the letter with the remittance cheque in it!

JACQUES: In the morning!
GUTMAN: To-night!
JACQUES: Upstairs in my room!
GUTMAN: Downstairs at the entrance!
JACQUES: I won't be intimidated!
GUTMAN [*raising the portmanteau over his head*]: What?!
JACQUES: Wait! –

[*He takes the letter out of his pocket.*]

Give me some light.

[*Kilroy strikes a match and holds it over Jacques' shoulder.*]

Thank you. What does it say?
GUTMAN: – Remittances?
KILROY [*reading the letter over Jacques' shoulder*]: – *discontinued* . . .

[*Gutman raises the portmanteau again.*]

JACQUES: Careful, I have –

[*The portmanteau lands with a crash.*
    The Bum comes to the window at the crash. A. Ratt comes out to his doorway at the same time.]

– fragile – mementoes. . . .

[*He crosses slowly down to the portmanteau and kneels as* . . .
    Gutman laughs and slams the balcony door. Jacques turns to Kilroy. He smiles at the young adventurer.]

– 'And so at last it has come, the distinguished thing!'

[*A. Ratt speaks as Jacques touches the portmanteau.*]

A. RATT: Hey, Dad – Vacancy here! A bed at the 'Ritz Men Only'. A little white ship to sail the dangerous night in.
JACQUES: Single or double?
A. RATT: There's only singles in this pad.

JACQUES [*to Kilroy*]: Match you for it.

KILROY: What the hell, we're buddies, we can sleep spoons! If we can't sleep, we'll push the wash stand against the door and sing old popular songs till the crack of dawn! . . . 'Heart of my heart, I love that melody!' . . . You bet your life I do.

[*Jacques takes out a pocket handkerchief and starts to grasp the portmanteau handle.*]

– It looks to me like you could use a Redcap and my rates are non-union!

[*He picks up the portmanteau and starts to cross towards the 'Ritz Men Only'. He stops at right centre.*]

Sorry, buddy. Can't make it! The altitude on this block has affected my ticker! And in the distance which is nearer than farther, I hear – the Streetcleaners' – piping!

[*Piping is heard.*]

JACQUES: COME ALONG!

[*He lifts the portmanteau and starts on.*]

KILROY: NO. To-night! I prefer! To sleep! Out! Under! The stars!

JACQUES [*gently*]: I understand, Brother!

KILROY [*to Jacques as he continues toward the 'Ritz Men Only'*]: Bon Voyage! I hope that you sail the dangerous night to the sweet golden port of morning!

JACQUES [*exiting*]: Thanks, Brother!

KILROY: Excuse the *corn*! I'm sincere!

BUM: Show me the way to go home! . . .

GUTMAN [*appearing on the balcony with white parakeet*]: Block Fourteen on the Camino Real.

At opening, the Bum is still at the window.

> [*The Streetcleaners' piping continues a little louder. Kilroy climbs breathing heavily, to the top of the stairs and stands looking out at Terra Incognita as . . .*
>
> *Marguerite enters the plaza through alleyway at right. She is accompanied by a silent Young Man who wears a domino.*]

MARGUERITE: Don't come any farther with me. I'll have to wake the night porter. Thank you for giving me safe conduct through the Medina.

> [*She has offered her hand. He grips it with a tightness that makes her wince.*]

Ohhhh. . . . I'm not sure which is more provocative in you, your ominous silence or your glittering smile or –

> [*He's looking at her purse.*]

What do you want? . . . Oh!

> [*She starts to open her purse. He snatches it. She gasps as he suddenly strips her cloak off her. Then he snatches off her pearl necklace. With each successive despoilment, she gasps and retreats but makes no resistance. Her eyes are closed. He continues to smile. Finally, he rips her dress and runs his hands over her body as if to see if she had anything else of value concealed on her.*]

– What else do I have that you want?

THE YOUNG MAN [*contemptuously*]: Nothing.

[*The Young Man exits through the cantina, examining his loot.
The Bum leans out his window, draws a deep breath and
says:*]

BUM: Lonely.
MARGUERITE [*to herself*]: Lonely . . .
KILROY [*on the steps*]: Lonely . . .

[*The Streetcleaners' piping is heard.
Marguerite runs to the Siete Mares and rings the bell. Nobody
answers. She crosses to the terrace. Kilroy, meanwhile, has
descended the stairs.*]

MARGUERITE: Jacques!

[*Piping is heard.*]

KILROY: Lady?
MARGUERITE: What?
KILROY: – I'm – safe. . . .
MARGUERITE: I wasn't expecting that music to-night, were
you?

[*Piping.*]

KILROY: It's them Streetcleaners.
MARGUERITE: I know.

[*Piping.*]

KILROY: You better go on in, Lady.
MARGUERITE: No.
KILROY: GO ON IN!
MARGUERITE: NO! I want to stay out here and I do what I
want to do!

[*Kilroy looks at her for the first time.*]

Sit down with me please.
KILROY: They're coming for me. The Gipsy told me I'm on
top of their list. Thanks for . . . Taking my . . . Hand.

221

[*Piping is heard.*]

MARGUERITE: Thanks for taking mine.

[*Piping.*]

KILROY: Do me one more favour. Take out of my pocket a picture. My fingers are . . . Stiff.

MARGUERITE: This one?

KILROY: My one. True. Woman.

MARGUERITE: A silver-framed photo! Was she really so fair?

KILROY: She was so fair and much fairer than they could tint that picture!

MARGUERITE: Then you have been on the street when the street was royal.

KILROY: Yeah . . . when the street was royal!

[*Piping is heard. Kilroy rises.*]

MARGUERITE: Don't get up, don't leave me!

KILROY: I want to be on my feet when the Streetcleaners come for me!

MARGUERITE: Sit back down again and tell me about your girl.

[*He sits.*]

KILROY: Y'know what it is you miss most? When you're separated. From someone. You lived. With. And loved? It's waking up in the night! With that – warmness beside you!

MARGUERITE: Yes, that *warmness* beside you!

KILROY: Once you get used to that. *Warmness!* It's a hell of a lonely feeling to wake up without it! Specially in some dollar-a-night hotel room on Skid! A hot-water bottle won't do. And a stranger. Won't do. It has to be some one you're used to. And that you. KNOW LOVES you!

[*Piping is heard.*]

Can you see them?

MARGUERITE: I see no one but you.

KILROY: I looked at my wife one night when she was sleeping and that was the night that the medics wouldn't okay me for no more fights. . . . Well. . . . My wife was sleeping with a smile like a child's. I kissed her. She didn't wake up. I took a pencil and paper. I wrote her. Good-bye!

MARGUERITE: That was the night she would have loved you the most!

KILROY: Yeah, *that* night, but what about *after* that night? Oh, Lady . . . Why should a beautiful girl tie up with a broken-down champ? – The earth still turning and her obliged to turn with it, not out – of dark into light but out of light into dark? Naw, naw, naw, naw! – Washed up! – Finished!

[*Piping.*]

. . . that ain't a word that a man can't look at. . . . There ain't no word in the language a man can't look at . . . and know just what they mean. And be. And act. And *go*!

[*He turns to the waiting Streetcleaners.*]

Come on! . . . Come on! . . . COME ON, YOU SONS OF BITCHES! KILROY IS HERE! HE'S READY!

[*A gong sounds.*

Kilroy swings at the Streetcleaners. They circle about him out of reach, turning him by each of their movements. The swings grow wilder like a boxer's. He falls to his knees still swinging and finally collapses flat on his face.

The Streetcleaners pounce but La Madrecita throws herself protectingly over the body and covers it with her shawl.

Blackout.

MARGUERITE: Jacques!

GUTMAN [*on balcony*]: Block Fifteen on the Camino Real.

La Madrecita is seated: across her knees is the body of Kilroy. Up centre, a low table on wheels bears a sheeted figure. Beside the table stands a Medical Instructor addressing Students and Nurses, all in white surgical outfits.

INSTRUCTOR: This is the body of an unidentified vagrant.

LA MADRECITA: This was thy son, America – and now mine.

INSTRUCTOR: He was found in an alley along the Camino Real.

LA MADRECITA: Think of him, now, as he was before his luck failed him. Remember his time of greatness, when he was not faded, not frightened.

INSTRUCTOR: More light, please!

LA MADRECITA: More light!

INSTRUCTOR: Can everyone see clearly!

LA MADRECITA: Everyone must see clearly!

INSTRUCTOR: There is no external evidence of disease.

LA MADRECITA: He had clear eyes and the body of a champion boxer.

INSTRUCTOR: There are no marks of violence on the body.

LA MADRECITA: He had the soft voice of the South and a pair of golden gloves.

INSTRUCTOR: His death was apparently due to natural causes.

[*The Students make notes. There are keening voices.*]

LA MADRECITA: Yes, blow wind where night thins! He had many admirers!

INSTRUCTOR: There are no legal claimants.

LA MADRECITA: He stood as a planet among the moons of their longing, haughty with youth, a champion of the prize-ring!

INSTRUCTOR: No friend or relatives having identified him –

LA MADRECITA: You should have seen the lovely mono-
grammed robe in which he strode the aisles of the Colos-
seums!

INSTRUCTOR: After the elapse of a certain number of days, his
body becomes the property of the State –

LA MADRECITA: Yes, blow wind where night thins – for laurel
is not everlasting. . . .

INSTRUCTOR: And now is transferred to our hands for the
nominal sum of five dollars.

LA MADRECITA: This was thy son, – and now mine. . . .

INSTRUCTOR: We will now proceed with the dissection.
Knife, please!

LA MADRECITA: Blow wind!

[*Keening is heard offstage.*]

Yes, blow wind where night thins! You are his passing bell
and his lamentation.

[*More keening is heard.*]

Keen for him, all maimed creatures, deformed and muti-
lated – his homeless ghost is your own!

INSTRUCTOR: First we will open the chest cavity and
examine the heart for evidence of coronary occlusion.

LA MADRECITA: His heart was pure gold and as big as the
head of a baby.

INSTRUCTOR: We will make an incision along the vertical
line.

LA MADRECITA: Rise, ghost! Go! Go bird! 'Humankind cannot bear very much reality.'

[*At the touch of her flowers, Kilroy stirs and pushes himself up
slowly from her lap. On his feet again, he rubs his eyes and looks
around him.*]

VOICES [*crying offstage*]: Olé! Olé! Olé!

KILROY: Hey! Hey, somebody! Where am I?

[*He notices the dissection room and approaches.*]

INSTRUCTOR [*removing a glittering sphere from a dummy corpse*]: Look at this heart. It's as big as the head of a baby.

KILROY: My heart!

INSTRUCTOR: Wash it off so we can look for the pathological lesions.

KILROY: Yes, siree, that's my heart!

GUTMAN: Block Sixteen!

[*Kilroy pauses just outside the dissection area as a Student takes the heart and dips it into a basin on the stand beside the table. The Student suddenly cries out and holds aloft a glittering gold sphere.*]

INSTRUCTOR: Look! This heart's solid gold!

BLOCK SIXTEEN

KILROY [*rushing forward*]: That's mine, you bastards!

[*He snatches the golden sphere from the Medical Instructor. The autopsy proceeds as if nothing had happened as the spot of light on the table fades out, but for Kilroy a ghostly chase commences, a dreamlike re-enactment of the chase that occurred at the end of Block Six. Gutman shouts from his balcony.*]

GUTMAN: Stop, thief, stop, corpse! That gold heart is the property of the State! Catch him, catch the golden-heart robber!

[*Kilroy dashes offstage into an aisle of the theatre. There is the wail of a siren: the air is filled with calls and whistles, roar of motors, screeching brakes, pistol-shots, thundering footsteps. The dimness of the auditorium is transected by searching rays of light – but there are no visible pursuers.*]

KILROY [*as he runs panting up the aisle*]: This is my heart! It don't belong to no State, not even the U.S.A. Which way is out? Where's the Greyhound depot? Nobody's going to put my heart in a bottle in a museum and charge admission to support the rotten police! Where are they? Which way are they going? Or coming? Hey, somebody, help me get out of here! Which way do I – which way – which way do I – go! go! go! go! go!

[*He has now arrived in the balcony.*]

Gee, I'm lost! I don't know where I am! I'm all turned around, I'm *confused*, I don't understand – what's – happened, it's like a – dream, it's – just like a – dream. . . . *Mary! Oh, Mary! Mary!*

[*He has entered the box from which he leapt in Block One. A clear shaft of light falls on him. He looks up into it, crying:*]

Mary, help a Christian!! Help a Christian, Mary! – It's like a dream. . . .

[*Esmeralda appears in a childish nightgown beside her gauze-tented bed on the Gipsy's roof. Her Mother appears with a cup of some sedative drink, cooing. . . .*]

GIPSY: Beddy-bye, beddy-bye, darling. It's sleepy-time down South and up North, too, and also East and West!
KILROY [*softly*]: Yes, it's – like a – *dream*. . . .

[*He leans panting over the ledge of the box, holding his heart like a football, watching Esmeralda.*]

GIPSY: Drink your Ovaltine, Ducks, and the sandman will come on tip-toe with a bag full of dreams. . . .

ESMERALDA: I want to dream of the Chosen Hero, Mummy.

GIPSY: Which one, the one that's coming or the one that is gone?

ESMERALDA: The *only* one, *Kilroy*! He was *sincere*!

KILROY: That's *right*! *I was*, for a while!

GIPSY: How do you know that Kilroy was sincere?

ESMERALDA: He said so.

KILROY: That's the truth, I *was*!

GIPSY: When did he say that?

ESMERALDA: When he lifted my veil.

GIPSY: Baby, they're always sincere when they lift your veil; it's one of those natural reflexes that don't mean a thing.

KILROY [*aside*]: What a cynical old bitch that Gipsy mama is!

GIPSY: And there's going to be lots of other fiestas for you, baby doll, and lots of other chosen heroes to lift your little veil when Mamacita and Nursie are out of the room.

ESMERALDA: No, Mummy, never, I mean it!

KILROY: I *believe* she means it!

GIPSY: Finish your Ovaltine and say your Now-I-Lay-Me.

[*Esmeralda sips the drink and hands her the cup.*]

KILROY [*with a catch in his voice*]: I had one true woman, which I can't go back to, but now I've found another.

[*He leaps on to the stage from the box.*]

ESMERALDA [*dropping to her knees*]: Now I lay me down to sleep, I pray the Lord my soul to keep. If I should die before I wake, I pray the Lord my soul to take.

GIPSY: God bless Mummy!

ESMERALDA: And the crystal ball and the tea-leaves.

KILROY: *Pssst!*

ESMERALDA: What's that?

GIPSY: A tom-cat in the plaza.

ESMERALDA: God bless all cats without pads in the plaza to-night.

KILROY: Amen!

[*He falls to his knees in the empty plaza.*]

ESMERALDA: God bless all con men and hustlers and pitchmen who hawk their hearts on the street, all two-time losers who're likely to lose once more, the courtesan who made the mistake of love, the greatest of lovers crowned with the longest horns, the poet who wandered far from his heart's green country and possibly will and possibly won't be able to find his way back, look down with a smile to-night on the last cavaliers, the ones with the rusty armour and soiled white plumes, and visit with understanding and something that's almost tender those fading legends that come and go in this plaza like songs not clearly remembered, oh, sometime and somewhere, let there be something to mean the word *honour* again!

QUIXOTE [*hoarsely and loudly, stirring slightly among his verminous rags*]: Amen!

KILROY: Amen. . . .

GIPSY [*disturbed*]: – That will do, now.

ESMERALDA: *And, oh, God, let me dream to-night of the Chosen Hero!*

GIPSY: Now, sleep. Fly away on the magic carpet of dreams!

[*Esmeralda crawls into the gauze-tented cot. The Gipsy descends from the roof.*]

KILROY: *Esmeralda! My little Gipsy sweetheart!*

ESMERALDA [*sleepily*]: Go away, cat.

[*The light behind the gauze is gradually dimming.*]

KILROY: This is no cat. This is the chosen hero of the big fiesta. Kilroy, the champion of the golden gloves with his gold heart cut from his chest and in his hands to give you!

ESMERALDA: Go away. Let me dream of the Chosen Hero.

KILROY: What a hassle! Mistook for a cat! What can I do to convince this doll I'm real?

[*Three brass balls wink brilliantly.*]

– Another transaction seems to be indicated!

[*He rushes to the Loan Shark's. The entrance immediately lights up.*]

My heart is gold! What will you give me for it?

[*Jewels, furs, sequined gowns, etc., are tossed to his feet. He throws his heart like a basketball to the Loan Shark, snatches up the loot and rushes back to the Gipsy's.*]
Doll!! Behold this loot! I gave my golden heart for it!

ESMERALDA: Go away, cat. . . .

[*She falls asleep. Kilroy bangs his forehead with his fist, then rushes to the Gipsy's door, pounds it with both fists. The door is thrown open and the sordid contents of a large jar are thrown at him. He falls back gasping, spluttering, retching. He retreats and finally assumes an exaggerated attitude of despair.*]

KILROY: Had for a button! Stewed, screwed, and tattooed on the Camino Real! Baptized, finally, with the contents of a slop-jar! – Did anybody say the deal was rugged?!

[*Quixote stirs against the wall of Skid Row. He hawks and spits and staggers to his feet.*]

GUTMAN: Why, the old knight's awake, his dream is over!

QUIXOTE [*to Kilroy*]: Hello! Is that a fountain?

KILROY: – Yeah, but –

QUIXOTE: I've got a mouthful of old chicken feathers. . . .

[*He approaches the fountain. It begins to flow. Kilroy falls back in amazement as the Old Knight rinses his mouth and drinks and*] *removes his jacket to bathe, handing the tattered garment to Kilroy.*]

QUIXOTE [*as he bathes*]: Qué pasa, mi amigo?
KILROY: The deal is rugged. D'you know what I mean?
QUIXOTE: Who knows better than I what a rugged deal is!

[*He produces a toothbrush and brushes his teeth.*]

– Will you take some advice?
KILROY: Brother, at this point on the Camino I will take anything which is offered!
QUIXOTE: *Don't! Pity! Your! Self!*

[*He takes out a pocket mirror and grooms his beard and moustache.*]

The wounds of the vanity, the many offences our egos have to endure, being housed in bodies that age and hearts that grow tired, are better accepted with a tolerant smile – like *this*! – You *see*?

[*He cracks his face in two with an enormous grin.*]

GUTMAN: Follow-spot on the face of the ancient knight!
QUIXOTE: Otherwise what you become is a bag full of curdled cream – *leche mala*, we call it! – attractive to nobody, least of all to yourself!

[*He passes the comb and pocket mirror to Kilroy.*]

Have you got any plans?
KILROY [*a bit uncertainly, wistfully*]: Well, I was thinking of – going *on* from – here!
QUIXOTE: Good! Come with me.
KILROY [*to the audience*]: Crazy old bastard.

[*Then to the Knight:*]

Donde?

QUIXOTE [*starting for the stairs*]: Quien sabe!

[*The fountain is now flowing loudly and sweetly. The Street People are moving toward it with murmurs of wonder. Marguerite comes out upon the terrace.*]

KILROY: Hey, there's – !
QUIXOTE: Shhh! Listen!

[*They pause on the stairs.*]

MARGUERITE: Abdullah!

[*Gutman has descended to the terrace.*]

GUTMAN: Mademoiselle, allow me to deliver the message for you. It would be in bad form if I didn't take some final part in the pageant.

[*He crosses the plaza to the opposite façade and shouts 'Casanova!' under the window of the 'Ritz Men Only'.*
    Meanwhile Kilroy scratches out the verb 'is' and prints the correction 'was' in the inscription on the ancient wall.]

Casanova! Great lover and King of Cuckolds on the Camino Real! The last of your ladies has guaranteed your tabs and is expecting you for breakfast on the terrace!

[*Casanova looks first out of the practical window of the flophouse, then emerges from its scabrous doorway, haggard, unshaven, crumpled in dress but bearing himself as erectly as ever. He blinks and glares fiercely into the brilliant morning light.*
    Marguerite cannot return his look, she averts her face with a look for which anguish would not be too strong a term, but at the same time she extends a pleading hand toward him. After some hesitation, he begins to move toward her, striking the pavement in measured cadence with his cane, glancing once, as he crosses, out at the audience with a wry smile that makes admissions that would be embarrassing to a vainer man than Casanova now is. When he reaches Marguerite she gropes for his hand, seizes it

232

with a low cry and presses it spasmodically to her lips while he draws her into his arms and looks above her sobbing, dyed-golden head with the serene, clouded gaze of someone mortally ill as the mercy of a narcotic laps over his pain.

Quixote raises his lance in a formal gesture and cries out hoarsely, powerfully from the stairs.]

QUIXOTE: *The violets in the mountains have broken the rocks!*

[*Quixote goes through the arch with Kilroy.*]

GUTMAN [*to the audience*]: The Curtain Line has been spoken!

[*To the wings:*]

Bring it down!

[*He bows with a fat man's grace as –*]

THE CURTAIN FALLS

ORPHEUS DESCENDING

FOR MARION BLACK VACCARD

Grateful acknowledgement is made to the
New York *Times* in which the article 'The
Past, the Present, and the Perhaps' first
appeared

THE PAST, THE PRESENT, AND THE PERHAPS

ONE icy bright winter morning in the last week of 1940, my brave representative, Audrey Wood, and I were crossing the Common in Boston, from an undistinguished hotel on one side to the grandeur of the Ritz-Carlton on the other. We had just read the morning notices of *Battle of Angels*, which had opened at the Wilbur the evening before. As we crossed the Common there was a series of loud reports like gunfire from the street that we were approaching, and one of us said, 'My God, they're shooting at us!'

We were still laughing, a bit hysterically, as we entered the Ritz-Carlton suite in which the big brass of the Theatre Guild and director Margaret Webster were waiting for us with that special air of gentle gravity that hangs over the demise of a play so much like the atmosphere that hangs over a home from which a living soul has been snatched by the Reaper.

Not present was little Miriam Hopkins, who was understandably shattered and cloistered after the events of the evening before, in which a simulated on-stage fire had erupted clouds of smoke so realistically over both stage and auditorium that a lot of Theatre Guild first-nighters had fled choking from the Wilbur before the choking star took her bows, which were about the quickest and most distracted that I have seen in a theatre.

It was not that morning that I was informed that the show must close. That morning I was only told that the play must be cut to the bone. I came with a rewrite of the final scene and I remember saying, heroically, 'I will crawl on my belly through brimstone if you will substitute this!' The response was gently evasive. It was a few mornings later that I received the *coup de grâce*, the announcement that the play would close at the completion of its run in Boston. On that occasion I made an equally dramatic statement, on a note of anguish. 'You don't seem to see that I put my heart into this play!'

It was Miss Webster who answered with a remark I have never forgotten and yet never heeded. She said, 'You must never wear your heart on your sleeve for daws to peck at!' Someone else said, 'At least you are not out of pocket.' I don't think I had any answer for that one, any more than I had anything in my pocket to be out of.

Well, in the end, when the Boston run was finished, I was given a cheque for $200 and told to get off somewhere and rewrite the play. I squandered half of this subsidy on the first of four operations performed on a cataracted left eye, and the other half took me to Key West for the rewrite. It was a long rewrite. In fact, it is still going on, though the two hundred bucks are long gone.

Why have I stuck so stubbornly to this play? For seventeen years, in fact? Well, nothing is more precious to anybody than the emotional record of his youth, and you will find the trail of my sleeve-worn heart in this completed play that I now call *Orpheus Descending*. On its surface it was and still is the tale of a wild-spirited boy who wanders into a conventional community of the South and creates the commotion of a fox in a chicken coop.

But beneath that now familiar surface it is a play about unanswered questions that haunt the hearts of people and the difference between continuing to ask them, a difference represented by the four major protagonists of the play, and the acceptance of prescribed answers that are not answers at all, but expedient adaptations or surrender to a state of quandary.

Battle was actually my fifth long play, but the first to be given a professional production. Two of the others, *Candles to the Sun* and *Fugitive Kind*, were produced by a brilliant, but semiprofessional group called The Mummers of St Louis. A third one, called *Spring Storm*, was written for the late Prof. E. C. Mabie's seminar in playwriting at the University of Iowa, and I read it aloud, appropriately in the spring.

When I had finished reading, the good professor's eyes had a glassy look as though he had drifted into a state of trance. There was a long and all but unendurable silence. Everyone seemed more or less embarrassed. At last the professor pushed back his chair, thus dismissing the seminar, and remarked casually and kindly, 'Well, we all have to paint our nudes!' And this is the only reference that I can remember anyone making to the play. That is, in the playwriting class, but I do remember that the late Lemuel Ayers, who was a graduate student at Iowa that year, read it and gave me sufficient praise for its dialogue and atmosphere to reverse my decision to give up the theatre in favour of my other occupation of waiting on tables, or more precisely, handing out trays in the cafeteria of the State Hospital.

Then there was Chicago for a while and a desperate effort to get on the W.P.A. Writers' Project, which didn't succeed, for my work lacked 'social content' or 'protest' and I couldn't prove that my family were destitute and I still had, in those days, a touch of refinement in my social behaviour which made me seem frivolous and decadent to the conscientiously rough-hewn pillars of the Chicago Project.

And so I drifted back to St Louis, again, and wrote my fourth long play which was the best of the lot. It was called *Not About Nightingales* and it concerned prison life, and I have never written anything since then that could compete with it in violence and horror, for it was based on something that actually occurred along about that time, the literal roasting-alive of a group of intransigent convicts sent for correction to a hot room called 'The Klondike'.

I submitted it to The Mummers of St Louis and they were eager to perform it but they had come to the end of their economic tether and had to disband at this point.

Then there was New Orleans and another effort, while waiting on tables in a restaurant where meals cost only two-bits, to get on a Writers' Project or the Theatre Project, again unsuccessful.

And then there was a wild and wonderful trip to California with a young clarinet player. We ran out of gas in El Paso, also out of cash, and it seemed for days that we would never go farther, but my grandmother was an 'easy touch' and I got a letter with a $10 bill stitched neatly to one of the pages, and we continued westward.

In the Los Angeles area, in the summer of 1939, I worked for a while at Clark's Bootery in Culver City, within sight of the M-G-M studio, and I lived on a pigeon ranch, and I rode between the two, a distance of ten miles, on a secondhand bicycle that I bought for $5.

Then a most wonderful thing happened. While in New Orleans I had heard about a play contest being conducted by the Group Theatre of New York. I submitted all four of the long plays I have mentioned that preceded *Battle of Angels*, plus a group of one-acts called *American Blues*. One fine day I received, when I returned to the ranch on my bike, a telegram saying that I had won a special award of $100 for the one-acts, and it was signed by Harold Clurman, Molly Day Thatcher, who is the present Mrs Elia Kazan, and that fine writer, Irwin Shaw, the judges of the contest.

I retired from Clark's Bootery and from picking squabs at the pigeon ranch. And the clarinet player and I hopped on our bicycles and rode all the way down to Tiajuana and back as far as Laguna Beach, where we obtained, rent free, a small cabin on a small ranch in return for taking care of the poultry.

We lived all that summer on the $100 from the Group Theatre and I think it was the happiest summer of my life. All the days were pure gold, the nights were starry, and I looked so young, or carefree, that they would sometimes refuse to sell me a drink because I did not appear to have reached twenty-one. But towards the end of the summer, maybe only because it was the end of the summer as well as the end of the $100, the clarinet player became very moody and disappeared without warning into the San Bernardino Mountains to commune with his soul in solitude, and there was nothing left in the cabin in the canyon but a bag of dried peas.

I lived on stolen eggs and avocados and dried peas for a week, and also on a faint hope stirred by a letter from a lady in New York whose name was Audrey Wood, who had taken hold of all those plays that I had submitted to the Group Theatre contest, and told me that it might be possible to get me one of the Rockefeller Fellowships, or grants, of $1,000 which were being passed out to gifted young writers at that time. And I began to write *Battle of Angels*, a lyrical play about memories and the loneliness of them. Although my beloved grandmother was living on the pension of a retired minister (I believe it was only $85 a month in those days), and her meagre earnings as a piano instructor, she once again stitched some bills to a page of a letter, and I took a bus to St Louis. *Battle of Angels* was finished late that fall and sent to Miss Wood.

One day the phone rang and, in a terrified tone, my mother told me that it was long distance, for me. The voice was Audrey Wood's. Mother waited, shakily, in the doorway. When I hung up I said, quietly, 'Rockefeller has given me a $1,000 grant and they want me to come to New York.' For the first time since I had known her, my mother burst into tears. 'I am so happy,' she said. It was all she could say.

And so you see it is a very old play that *Orpheus Descending* has come out of, but a play is never an old one until you quit working on it and I have never quit working on this one, not even now. It never went into the trunk, it always stayed on the work bench, and I am not presenting it now because I have run out of ideas or material for completely new work. I am offering it this season because I honestly believe that it is finally finished. About 75 per cent of it is new writing, but, what is much more important, I believe that I have now finally managed to say in it what I wanted to say, and I feel that it now has in it a sort of emotional bridge between those early years described in this article and my present state of existence as a playwright.

So much for the past and present. The future is called 'perhaps', which is the only possible thing to call the future. And the important thing is not to allow that to scare you.

TENNESSEE WILLIAMS

ORPHEUS DESCENDING

Orpheus Descending was presented at the Martin Beck Theatre in New York on 21 March 1957, by the Producers Theatre. It was directed by Harold Clurman; the stage set was designed by Boris Aronson, the costumes by Lucinda Ballard, and the lighting by Feder.

The cast was as follows:

DOLLY HAMMA	*Elizabeth Eustis*
BEULAH BINNINGS	*Jane Rose*
PEE WEE BINNINGS	*Warren Kemmerling*
DOG HAMMA	*David Clarke*
CAROL CUTRERE	*Lois Smith*
EVA TEMPLE	*Nell Harrison*
SISTER TEMPLE	*Mary Farrell*
UNCLE PLEASANT	*John Marriott*
VAL XAVIER	*Cliff Robertson*
VEE TALBOTT	*Joanna Roos*
LADY TORRANCE	*Maureen Stapleton*
JABE TORRANCE	*Crahan Denton*
SHERIFF TALBOTT	*R. G. Armstrong*
MR DUBINSKY	*Beau Tilden*
WOMAN	*Janice Mars*
DAVID CUTRERE	*Robert Webber*
NURSE PORTER	*Virgilia Chew*
FIRST MAN	*Albert Henderson*
SECOND MAN	*Charles Tyner*

ACT ONE

PROLOGUE

The set represents in nonrealistic fashion a general drygoods store and part of a connecting 'confectionery' in a small Southern town. The ceiling is high and the upper walls are dark, as if streaked with moisture and cobwebbed. A great dusty window upstage offers a view of disturbing emptiness that fades into late dusk. The action of the play occurs during a rainy season, late winter and early spring, and sometimes the window turns opaque but glistening silver with sheets of rain. 'TORRANCE MERCANTILE STORE' is lettered on the window in gilt of old-fashioned design.

Merchandise is represented very sparsely and it is not realistic. Bolts of pepperel and percale stand upright on large spools, the black skeleton of a dressmaker's dummy stands meaninglessly against a thin white column, and there is a motionless ceiling fan with strips of flypaper hanging from it.

There are stairs that lead to a landing and disappear above it, and on the landing there is a sinister-looking artificial palm tree in a greenish-brown jardinière.

But the confectionery, which is seen partly through a wide arched door, is shadowy and poetic as some inner dimension of the play.

Another, much smaller, playing area is a tiny bedroom alcove which is usually masked by an Oriental drapery which is worn dim but bears the formal design of a gold tree with scarlet fruit and fantastic birds.

[*At the rise of the curtain two youngish middle-aged women,* DOLLY *and* BEULAH, *are laying out a buffet supper on a pair of pink-and-grey-veined marble-topped tables with gracefully curved black-iron legs, brought into the main area from the confectionery. They are wives of small planters and tastelessly overdressed in a somewhat bizarre fashion.*

A train whistles in the distance and dogs bark in response from various points and distances. The women pause in their occupations at the tables and rush to the archway, crying out harshly.]

DOLLY: Pee Wee!

BEULAH: Dawg!

DOLLY: Cannonball is comin' into th' depot!

BEULAH: You all git down to th' depot an' meet that train!

[*Their husbands slouch through, heavy, red-faced men in clothes that are too tight for them or too loose, and mud-stained boots.*]

PEE WEE: I fed that one-armed bandit a hunnerd nickels an' it coughed up five.

DOG: Must have hed indigestion.

PEE WEE: I'm gonna speak to Jabe about them slots. [*They go out and a motor starts and pauses.*]

DOLLY: I guess Jabe Torrance has got more to worry about than the slot machines and pinball games in that confectionery.

BEULAH: You're not tellin' a lie. I wint to see Dr Johnny about Dawg's condition. Dawg's got sugar in his urine again, an' as I was leavin' I ast him what was the facks about Jabe Torrance's operation in Memphis. Well –

DOLLY: What'd he tell you, Beulah?

BEULAH: He said the worse thing a doctor ever can say.

DOLLY: What's that, Beulah?

BEULAH: Nothin' a-tall, not a spoken word did he utter! He just looked at me with those big dark eyes of his and shook his haid like this!

DOLLY [*with doleful satisfaction*]: I guess he signed Jabe Torrance's death warrant with just that single silent motion of his haid.

BEULAH: That's exactly what passed through my mind. I understand that they cut him open – [*Pauses to taste something on the table.*]

DOLLY: – An' sewed him right back up! – that's what I
heard. . . .

BEULAH: I didn't know these olives had seeds in them!

DOLLY: You thought they was stuffed?

BEULAH: Uh-huh. Where's the Temple sisters?

DOLLY: Where d'you think?

BEULAH: Snoopin' aroun' upstairs. If Lady catches 'em at it
she'll give those two old maids a touch of her tongue! She's
not a Dago for nothin'!

DOLLY: Ha, ha, no! You spoke a true word, honey. . . . [*Looks
out door as car passes.*] Well, I was surprised when I wint up
myself!

BEULAH: You wint up you'self?

DOLLY: I did and so did you because I seen you, Beulah.

BEULAH: I never said that I didn't. Curiosity is a human
instinct.

DOLLY: They got two separate bedrooms which are not even
connectin'. At opposite ends of the hall, and everything is
so dingy an' dark up there. Y'know what it seemed like to
me? A county jail! I swear to goodness it didn't seem to me
like a place for white people to live in! – that's the truth. . . .

BEULAH [*darkly*]: Well, I wasn't surprised. Jabe Torrance
bought that woman.

DOLLY: Bought her?

BEULAH: Yais, he bought her, when she was a girl of eighteen!
He bought her and bought her cheap because she'd been
thrown over and her heart was broken by that – [*jerks head
towards a passing car, then continues*] – that Cutrere boy. . . .
Oh, what a – *Mmmm*, what a – *beautiful* thing he was. . . .
And those two met like you struck two stones together and
made a fire! – yes – fire . . .

DOLLY: What?

BEULAH: *Fire!* – Ha . . . [*Strikes another match and lights one of
the candelabra. Mandolin begins to fade in. The following monologue should be treated frankly as exposition, spoken to audience,*

247

almost directly, with a force that commands attention. DOLLY *does not remain in the playing area, and after the first few sentences, there is no longer any pretence of a duologue.*]

Well, that was a long time ago, before you and Dog moved into Two River County. Although you must have heard of it. Lady's father was a Wop from the old country and when he first come here with a mandolin and a monkey that wore a little green velvet suit, ha ha.

He picked up dimes and quarters in the saloons – this was before Prohibition . . .

People just called him The Wop, nobody knew his name, just called him 'The Wop', ha ha ha. . . .

DOLLY [*off, vaguely*]: Anh-hannnh. . . .

[BEULAH *switches in the chair and fixes the audience with her eyes, leaning slightly forward to compel their attention. Her voice is rich with nostalgia, and at a sign of restlessness, she rises and comes straight out to the proscenium, like a pitchman. This monologue should set the nonrealistic key for the whole production.*]

BEULAH: Oh, my law, well, that was Lady's daddy! Then come prohibition an' first thing ennyone knew, The Wop had took to bootleggin' like a duck to water! He picked up a piece of land cheap, it was on the no'th shore of Moon Lake which used to be the old channel of the river and people thought some day the river might swing back that way, and so he got it cheap. . . . [*Moves her chair up closer to proscenium.*] He planted an orchard on it; he covered the whole no'th shore of the lake with grapevines and fruit trees, and then he built little arbours, little white wooden arbours with tables and benches to drink in and carry on in, ha ha! And in the spring and the summer, young couples would come out there, like me and Pee Wee, we used to go out there, an' court up a storm, ha ha, just court up a – storm! Ha ha! – The county was dry in those days, I don't mean

dry like now, why, now you just walk a couple of feet off
the highway and whistle three times like a jaybird and a
nigger pops out of a bush with a bottle of corn!

DOLLY: Ain't that the truth? Ha ha.

BEULAH: But in those days the county was dry for true, I
mean bone dry except for The Wop's wine garden. So we'd
go out to The Wop's an' drink that Dago red wine an' cut
up an' carry on an' raise such Cain in those arbours! Why,
I remember one Sunday old Doctor Tooker, Methodist
minister then, he bust a blood vessel denouncing The Wop
in the pulpit!

DOLLY: Lawd have mercy!

BEULAH: Yes, ma'am! – Each of those white wooden arbours
had a lamp in it, and one by one, here and there, the lamps
would go out as the couples began to make love . . .

DOLLY: *Oh* – oh . . .

BEULAH: What strange noises you could hear if you listened,
calls, cries, whispers, moans – giggles. . . . [*Her voice is soft
with recollection*] – And then, one by one, the lamps would
be lighted again, and The Wop and his daughter would
sing and play Dago songs. . . . [*Bring up mandolin: voice
under* 'Dicitencello Vuoi'.] But sometimes The Wop would
look around for his daughter, and all of a sudden Lady
wouldn't be there!

DOLLY: Where would she be?

BEULAH: She'd be with David Cutrere.

DOLLY: Awwwwww – ha ha . . .

BEULAH: Carol Cutrere's big brother, Lady and him would
disappear in the orchard and old Papa Romano, The Wop,
would holler, 'Lady, Lady!' – no answer whatsoever, no
matter how long he called and no matter how loud. . . .

DOLLY: Well, I guess it's hard to shout back, 'Here I am,
Papa', when where you are is in the arms of your lover!

BEULAH: Well, that spring, no, it was late that summer . . .
[DOLLY *retires again from the playing area.*] – Papa Romano

made a bad mistake. He sold liquor to niggers. The Mystic Crew took action. – They rode out there, one night, with gallons of coal oil – it was a real dry summer – and set that place on fire! – They burned the whole thing up, vines, arbours, fruit trees. – Pee Wee and me, we stood on the dance pavilion across the lake and watched that fire spring up. Inside of tin minutes the whole nawth shore of the lake was a mass of flames, a regular sea of flames, and all the way over the lake we could hear Lady's papa shouting, 'Fire, fire, fire!' – as if it was necessary to let people know, and the whole sky lit up with it, as red as Guinea red wine! – Ha ha ha ha . . . Not a fire engine, not a single engine pulled out of a station that night in Two River County! – The poor old fellow, The Wop, he took a blanket and run up into the orchard to fight the fire singlehanded – *and* burned *alive*. . . . Uh-huh! *burned alive*. . . .

[*Mandolin stops short.* DOLLY *has returned to the table to have her coffee.*]

You know what I sometimes wonder?

DOLLY: No. What do you wonder?

BEULAH: I wonder sometimes if Lady has any suspicion that her husband, Jabe Torrance, was the leader of the Mystic Crew the night they burned up her father in his wine garden on Moon Lake?

DOLLY: Beulah Binnings, you make my blood run cold with such a thought! How could she live in marriage twenty years with a man if she knew he'd burned her father up in his wine garden?

[*Dog bays in distance.*]

BEULAH: She could live with him in hate. People can live together in hate for a long time, Dolly. Notice their passion for money. I've always noticed when couples don't love each other they develop a passion for money. Haven't you seen that happen? Of course you have. Now there's not many couples that stay devoted for ever. Why, some git so they just barely tolerate each other's existence. Isn't that true?

DOLLY: You couldn't of spoken a truer word if you read it out loud from the Bible!

BEULAH: Barely tolerate each other's existence, and some don't even do that. You know, Dolly Hamma, I don't think half as many married min have committed suicide in this county as the Coroner says has done so!

DOLLY [*with voluptuous appreciation of Beulah's wit*]: You think it's their wives that give them the deep six, honey?

BEULAH: I don't think so, I know so. Why there's couples that loathe and despise the sight, smell, and sound of each other before that round-trip honeymoon ticket is punched at both ends, Dolly.

DOLLY: I hate to admit it but I can't deny it.

BEULAH: But they hang on together.

DOLLY: Yes, they hang on together.

BEULAH: Year after year after year, accumulating property and money, building up wealth and respect and position in the towns they live in and the counties and cities and the churches they go to, belonging to the clubs and so on and so forth and not a soul but them knowin' they have to go wash their hands after touching something the other one just put down! ha ha ha ha ha! –

DOLLY: Beulah, that's an evil laugh of yours, that laugh of yours is evil!

BEULAH [*louder*]: Ha ha ha ha ha! – But you know it's the truth.

DOLLY: Yes, she's tellin' the truth! [*Nods to audience.*]

BEULAH: Then one of them – gits – *cincer* or has a – *stroke* or somethin'? – The other one –

DOLLY: – Hauls in the loot?

BEULAH: That's right, hauls in the loot! Oh, my, then you

should see how him or her blossoms out. New house, new car, new clothes. Some of 'em even change to a different church! – If it's a widow, she goes with a younger man, and if it's a widower, he starts courtin' some chick, ha ha ha ha ha!

And so I said, I said to Lady this morning before she left for Memphis to bring Jabe home, I said, 'Lady, I don't suppose you're going to reopen the confectionery till Jabe is completely recovered from his operation.' She said, 'It can't wait for anything that might take that much time.' Those are her exact words. It can't wait for anything that might take that much time. Too much is invested in it. It's going to be done over, redecorated, and opened on schedule the Saturday before Easter this spring! – Why? – Because – she knows Jabe is dying and she wants to clean up quick!

DOLLY: An awful thought. But a true one. Most awful thoughts are.

[*They are startled by sudden light laughter from the dim upstage area. The light changes on the stage to mark a division.*]

SCENE ONE

[*The women turn to see* CAROL CUTRERE *in the archway between the store and the confectionery. She is past thirty and, lacking prettiness, she has an odd, fugitive beauty which is stressed, almost to the point of fantasy, by a style of makeup with which a dancer named Valli has lately made such an impression in the bohemian centres of France and Italy, the face and lips powdered white and the eyes outlined and exaggerated with black pencil and the lids tinted blue. Her family name is the oldest and most distinguished in the country.*]

BEULAH: Somebody don't seem to know that the store is closed.

DOLLY: Beulah?

BEULAH: What?

DOLLY: Can you understand how anybody would deliberately make themselves look fantastic as that?

BEULAH: Some people have to show off, it's a passion with them, anything on earth to get attention.

DOLLY: I sure wouldn't care for that kind of attention. Not me. I wouldn't desire it. . . .

[*During these lines, just loud enough for her to hear them,* CAROL *has crossed to the pay-phone and deposited a coin.*]

CAROL: I want Tulane 0370 in New Orleans. What? Oh. Hold on a minute.

[EVA TEMPLE *is descending the stairs, slowly, as if awed by Carol's appearance.* CAROL *rings open the cashbox and removes some coins; returns to deposit coins in phone.*]

BEULAH: She helped herself to money out of the cashbox.

[EVE *passes Carol like a timid child skirting a lion cage.*]

CAROL: Hello, Sister.

EVA: I'm Eva.

CAROL: Hello, Eva.

EVA: Hello . . . [*Then in a loud whisper to Beulah and Dolly*] She took money out of the cashbox.

DOLLY: Oh, she can do as she pleases, she's a Cutrere!

BEULAH: Shoot . . .

EVA: What is she doin' barefooted?

BEULAH: The last time she was arrested on the highway, they say that she was naked under her coat.

CAROL [*to operator*]: I'm waiting. [*Then to women*] – I caught the heel of my slipper in that rotten boardwalk out there and it broke right off. [*Raises slippers in hand.*] They say if you break the heel of your slipper in the morning it means you'll meet the love of your life before dark. But it was already dark when I broke the heel of my slipper. Maybe that means I'll meet the love of my life before daybreak. [*The quality of her voice is curiously clear and childlike.* SISTER TEMPLE *appears on stair landing bearing an old waffle iron.*]

SISTER: Wasn't that them?

EVA: No, it was Carol Cutrere!

CAROL [*at phone*]: Just keep on ringing, please, he's probably drunk.

[SISTER *crosses by her as Eva did.*]

Sometimes it takes quite a while to get through the living-room furniture. . . .

SISTER: – She a *sight*?

EVA: Uh-huh!

CAROL: Bertie? – Carol! – Hi, doll! Did you trip over something? I heard a crash. Well, I'm leaving right now, I'm already on the highway and everything's fixed, I've got my allowance back on condition that I remain for ever away from Two River County! I had to blackmail them a little. I came to dinner with my eyes made up and my little black sequin jacket and Betsy Boo, my brother's wife, said, 'Carol, you going out to a fancy dress ball?' I said, 'Oh, no, I'm just going jooking tonight up and down the Dixie Highway between here and Memphis like I used to when I lived here.' Why, honey, she flew so fast you couldn't see her passing and came back in with the ink still wet on the cheque! And this will be done once a month as long as I stay away from Two River County. . . . [*Laughs gaily.*] – How's Jackie? Bless his heart, give him a sweet kiss for me! Oh, honey, I'm driving straight through, not even stopping for pickups unless you need one! I'll meet you in the Starlite Lounge before it closes, or if I'm irresistibly delayed, I'll certainly join you for coffee at the Morning Call before the all-night places have closed for the day . . . – I – Bertie? Bertie? [*Laughs uncertainly and hangs up.*] – let's see, now. . . . [*Removes a revolver from her trench-coat pocket and crosses to fill it with cartridges back of counter.*]

EVA: What she looking for?

SISTER: Ask her.

EVA [*advancing*]: What're you looking for, Carol?

CAROL: Cartridges for my revolver.

DOLLY: She don't have a licence to carry a pistol.

BEULAH: She don't have a licence to drive a car.

CAROL: When I stop for someone I want to be sure it's someone I want to stop for.

DOLLY: Sheriff Talbott ought to know about this when he gits back from the depot.

CAROL: Tell him, ladies, I've already given him notice that if he ever attempts to stop me again on the highway, I'll shoot it out with him. . . .

BEULAH: When anybody has trouble with the law –

[*Her sentence is interrupted by a panicky scream from* EVA *immediately repeated by* SISTER. *The* TEMPLE SISTERS *scramble upstairs to the landing.* DOLLY *also cries out and turns, covering her face. A Negro* CONJURE MAN *has entered the store. His tattered garments are fantastically bedizened with many talismans and good-luck charms of shell and bone and feather. His blue-black skin is daubed with cryptic signs in white paint.*]

DOLLY: Git him out, git him out, he's going to mark my baby!

BEULAH: Oh, shoot, Dolly. . . .

[DOLLY *has now fled after the Temple Sisters, to the landing of the stairs. The* CONJURE MAN *advances with a soft, rapid, toothless mumble of words that sound like wind in dry grass. He is holding out something in his shaking hand.*]

It's just that old crazy conjure man from Blue Mountain. He cain't mark your baby.

[*Phrase of primitive music or percussion as* NEGRO *moves into light.* BEULAH *follows Dolly to landing.*]

CAROL [*very high and clear voice*]: Come here, Uncle, and let me see what you've got there. Oh, it's a bone of some kind. No, I don't want to touch it, it isn't clean yet, there's still some flesh clinging to it.

[*Women make sounds of revulsion.*]

Yes, I know it's the breastbone of a bird but it's still tainted with corruption. Leave it a long time on a bare rock in the rain and the sun till every sign of corruption is burned and washed away from it, and then it will be a good charm, a white charm, but now it's a black charm, Uncle. So take it away and do what I told you with it. . . .

[*The* NEGRO *makes a ducking obeisance and shuffles slowly back to the door.*]

Hey, Uncle Pleasant, give us the Choctaw cry.

[NEGRO *stops in confectionery.*]

He's part Choctaw, he knows the Choctaw cry.
SISTER TEMPLE: Don't let him holler in *here*!
CAROL: Come on, Uncle Pleasant, *you* know it!

[*She takes off her coat and sits on the R. window sill. She starts the cry herself. The* NEGRO *throws back his head and completes it: a series of barking sounds that rise to a high sustained note of wild intensity. The women on the landing retreat further upstairs. Just then, as though the cry had brought him,* VAL *enters the store. He is a young man, about thirty, who has a kind of wild beauty about him that the cry would suggest. He does not wear Levi's or a T-shirt, he has on a pair of dark serge pants, glazed from long wear and not excessively tight-fitting. His remarkable garment is a snakeskin jacket, mottled white, black, and grey. He carries a guitar which is covered with inscriptions.*]

CAROL [*looking at the young man*]: Thanks, Uncle ...

BEULAH: *Hey, old man, you! Choctaw! Conjure man! Nigguh! Will you go out-a this sto'? So we can come back down stairs?*

[CAROL *hands Negro a dollar; he goes out R. cackling.* VAL *holds the door open for* VEE TALBOTT, *a heavy, vague woman in her forties. She does primitive oil paintings and carries one into the store.*]

VEE: I got m'skirt caught in th' door of the Chevrolet an' I'm afraid I tore it.

[*The women descend into store: laconic greetings, interest focused on* VAL.]

Is it dark in here or am I losin' my eyesight? I been painting all day, finished a picture in a ten-hour stretch, just stopped a few minutes fo' coffee and went back to it again while I had a clear vision. I think I got it this time. But I'm so exhausted I could drop in my tracks. There's nothing more exhausting than that kind of work on earth, it's not so much that it tires your body out, but it leaves you drained inside. Y'know what I mean? Inside? Like you was burned out by something? Well! Still! – You feel you've accomplished something when you're through with it, sometimes you feel – *elevated!* How are you, Dolly?

DOLLY: All right, Mrs Talbott.

VEE: That's good. How are *you*, Beulah?

BEULAH: Oh, I'm all right, I reckon.

VEE: Still can't make out much. Who is that there? [*Indicates*

Carol's figure by the window. A significant silence greets this question. Suddenly] *Oh!* I thought her folks had got her out of the county . . .

[CAROL *utters a very light slightly rueful laugh, her eyes drifting back to Val as she moves back into confectionery.*]

Jabe and Lady back yet?

DOLLY: Pee Wee an' Dawg have gone to the depot to meet 'em.

VEE: Aw. Well, I'm just in time. I brought my new picture with me, the paint isn't dry on it yet. I thought that Lady might want to hang it up in Jabe's room while he's convalescin' from the operation, cause after a close shave with death, people like to be reminded of spiritual things. Huh? Yes! This is the Holy Ghost ascending. . . .

DOLLY [*looking at canvas*]: You didn't put a head on it.

VEE: The head was a blaze of light, that's all I saw in my vision.

DOLLY: Who's the young man with yuh?

VEE: Aw, excuse me, I'm too worn out to have manners. This is Mr Valentine Xavier, Mrs Hamma and Mrs – I'm sorry, Beulah. I never *can* get y' last *name*!

BEULAH: I fo'give you. My name is Beulah Binnings.

VAL: What shall I do with this here?

VEE: Oh, that bowl of sherbet. I thought that Jabe might need something light an' digestible so I brought a bowl of sherbet.

DOLLY: What flavour is it?

VEE: Pineapple.

DOLLY: Oh, goody, I love pineapple. Better put it in the ice-box before it starts to melt.

BEULAH [*looking under napkin that covers bowl*]: I'm afraid you're lockin' th' stable after the horse is gone.

DOLLY: Aw, is it melted already?

BEULAH: Reduced to juice.

VEE: Aw, shoot. Well, put it on ice anyhow, it might thicken up.

[*Women are still watching Val.*]

Where's the icebox?

BEULAH: In the confectionery.

VEE: I thought that Lady had closed the confectionery.

BEULAH: Yes, but the Frigidaire's still there.

[VAL *goes out R. through confectionery.*]

VEE: Mr Xavier is a stranger in our midst. His car broke down in that storm last night and I let him sleep in the lockup. He's lookin' for work and I thought I'd introduce him to Lady an' Jabe because if Jabe can't work they're going to need somebody to help out in th' store.

BEULAH: That's a good idea.

DOLLY: Uh-huh.

BEULAH: Well, come on in, you all, it don't look like they're comin' straight home from the depot anyhow.

DOLLY: Maybe that wasn't the Cannonball Express.

BEULAH: Or maybe they stopped off fo' Pee Wee to buy some liquor.

DOLLY: Yeah . . . at Ruby Lightfoot's.

[*They move past Carol and out of sight.* CAROL *has risen. Now she crosses into the main store area, watching Val with the candid curiosity of one child observing another. He pays no attention but concentrates on his belt buckle which he is repairing with a pocketknife.*]

CAROL: What're you fixing?

VAL: Belt buckle.

CAROL: Boys like you are always fixing something. Could you fix my slipper?

VAL: What's wrong with your slipper?

CAROL: Why are you pretending not to remember me?

VAL: It's hard to remember someone you never met.

CAROL: Then why'd you look so startled when you saw me?

VAL: Did I?

CAROL: I thought for a moment you'd run back out the door.

VAL: The sight of a woman can make me walk in a hurry but I don't think it's ever made me run. – You're standing in my light.

CAROL [*moving aside slightly*]: Oh, excuse me. Better?

VAL: Thanks. . . .

CAROL: Are you afraid I'll snitch?

VAL: Do what?

CAROL: Snitch? I wouldn't; I'm not a snitch. But I can prove that I know you if I have to. It was New Year's Eve in New Orleans.

VAL: I need a small pair of pliers. . . .

CAROL: You had on that jacket and a snake ring with a ruby eye.

VAL: I never had a snake ring with a ruby eye.

CAROL: A snake ring with an emerald eye?

VAL: I never had a snake ring with any kind of an eye. . . .

[*Begins to whistle softly, his face averted.*]

CAROL [*smiling gently*]: Then maybe it was a dragon ring with an emerald eye or a diamond or a ruby eye. You told us that it was a gift from a lady osteopath that you'd met somewhere in your travels and that any time you were broke you'd wire this lady osteopath collect, and no matter how far you were or how long it was since you'd seen her, she'd send you a money order for twenty-five dollars with the same sweet message each time. 'I love you. When will you come back?' And to prove the story, not that it was difficult to believe it, you took the latest of these sweet messages from your wallet for us to see. . . . [*She throws back her head with soft laughter. He looks away still further and busies himself with the belt buckle.*] – We followed you through five places before we made contact with you and I was the one that made contact. I went up to the bar where you were standing and touched your jacket and said, 'What stuff is this made of?' and when you said it was snakeskin, I said, 'I wish you'd told me before I touched it.' And you said something not nice. You said, 'Maybe that will learn you to hold back your hands.' I was drunk by that time which was after midnight. Do you remember what I said to you? I said, 'What on earth can you do on this earth but catch at whatever comes near you, with both your hands, until your fingers are broken?' I'd never said that before, or even consciously thought it, but afterwards it seemed like the truest thing that my lips had ever spoken, what on earth can you do but catch at whatever comes near you with both your hands until your fingers are broken. . . . You gave me a quick, sober look. I think you nodded slightly, and then you picked up your guitar and began to sing. After singing you passed the kitty. Whenever paper money was dropped in the kitty you blew a whistle. My cousin Bertie and I dropped in five dollars, you blew the whistle five times and then sat down at our table for a drink, Schenley's with Seven Up. You showed us all those signatures on your guitar. . . . Any correction so far?

VAL: Why are you so anxious to prove I know you?

CAROL: Because I want to know you better and better! I'd like to go out jooking with you tonight.

VAL: What's jooking?

CAROL: Oh, don't you know what that is? That's where you get in a car and drink a little and drive a little and stop and dance a little to a juke box and then you drink a little more and drive a little more and stop and dance a little more to a juke box and then you stop dancing and you just drink and drive and then you stop driving and just drink, and then, finally, you stop drinking.

VAL: What do you do, then?

CAROL: That depends on the weather and who you're jooking with. If it's a clear night you spread a blanket among the memorial stones on Cypress Hill, which is the local bone orchard, but if it's not a fair night, and this one certainly isn't, why, usually then you go to the Idlewild cabins between here and Sunset on the Dixie Highway. . . .

VAL: That's about what I figured. But I don't go that route. Heavy drinking and smoking the weed and shacking with strangers is okay for kids in their twenties but this is my thirtieth birthday and I'm all through with that route. [*Looks up with dark eyes.*] I'm not young any more.

CAROL: You're young at thirty – I hope so! I'm twenty-nine!

VAL: Naw, you're not young at thirty if you've been on a goddam party since you were fifteen!

[*Picks up his guitar and sings and plays 'Heavenly Grass'. CAROL has taken a pint of bourbon from her trench-coat pocket and she passes it to him.*]

CAROL: Thanks. That's lovely. Many happy returns of your birthday, Snakeskin.

[*She is very close to him. VEE enters.*]

VEE [*sharply*]: Mr Xavier don't drink.

CAROL: Oh, ex-cuse *me*!

VEE: And if you behaved yourself better your father would not be paralysed in bed!

[*Sound of car out front. Women come running with various cries. LADY enters, nodding to the women, and holding the door open for her husband and the men following him. She greets the women in almost toneless murmurs, as if too tired to speak. She could be any age between thirty-five and forty-five, in appearance, but her figure is youthful. Her face taut. She is a woman who met with emotional disaster in her girlhood; verges on hysteria under strain. Her voice is often shrill and her body tense. But when in repose, a girlish softness emerges again and she looks ten years younger.*]

LADY: Come in, Jabe. We've got a reception committee here to meet us. They've set up a buffet supper.

[JABE *enters. A gaunt, wolfish man, grey and yellow. The women chatter idiotically.*]

BEULAH: Well, look who's here!

DOLLY: Well, *Jabe*!

BEULAH: I don't think he's been sick. I think he's been to Miami. Look at that wonderful colour in his face!

DOLLY: I never seen him look better in my life!

BEULAH: Who does he think he's foolin'? Ha ha ha! – not *me*!

JABE: Whew, Jesus – I'm mighty – tired. . . .

[*An uncomfortable silence, everyone greedily staring at the dying man with his tense, wolfish smile and nervous cough.*]

PEE WEE: Well, Jabe, we been feedin' lots of nickels to those one-arm bandits in there.

DOG: An' that pinball machine is hotter'n a pistol.

PEE WEE: Ha ha.

[EVA TEMPLE *appears on stairs and screams for her sister.*]

EVA: Sistuh! Sistuh! Sistuh! Cousin Jabe's here!

[*A loud clatter upstairs and shrieks.*]

JABE: Jesus. . . .

[EVA *rushing at him – stops short and bursts into tears.*]

LADY: Oh, cut that out, Eva Temple! – What were you doin' upstairs?

EVA: I can't help it, it's so good to see him, it's so wonderful to see our cousin again, oh, Jabe, *blessed*!

SISTER: Where's Jabe, where's precious Jabe? Where's our precious cousin?

EVA: Right here, Sister!

SISTER: Well, bless your old sweet life, and lookit the colour he's got in his face, will you?

BEULAH: I just told him he looks like he's been to Miami and got a Florida suntan, ha ha ha!

[*The preceding speeches are very rapid, all overlapping.*]

JABE: I ain't been out in no sun an' if you all will excuse me I'm gonna do my celebratin' upstairs in bed because I'm kind of – worn out. [*Goes creakily to foot of steps while* EVA *and* SISTER *sob into their handkerchiefs behind him.*] – I see they's been some changes made here. Uh-huh. Uh-huh. How come the shoe department's back here now? [*Instant hostility as if habitual between them.*]

LADY: We always had a problem with light in this store.

JABE: So you put the shoe department further away from the window? That's sensible. A very intelligent solution to the problem, Lady.

LADY: Jabe, you know I told you we got a fluorescent tube coming to put back here.

JABE: Uh-huh. Uh-huh. Well. Tomorrow I'll get me some niggers to help me move the shoe department back front.

LADY: You do whatever you want to, it's your store.

JABE: Uh-huh. Uh-huh. I'm glad you reminded me of it.

[LADY *turns sharply away. He starts up stairs.* PEE WEE *and* DOG *follow him up. The women huddle and whisper in the store.* LADY *sinks wearily into chair at table.*]

BEULAH: That man will never come down those stairs again!

DOLLY: Never in this world, honey.

BEULAH: He has th' death sweat on him! Did you notice that death sweat on him?

DOLLY: An' yellow as butter, just as yellow as –

[SISTER *sobs.*]

EVA: Sister, Sister!

BEULAH [*crossing to Lady*]: Lady, I don't suppose you feel much like talking about it right now but Dog and me are so worried.

DOLLY: Pee Wee and me are worried sick about it.

LADY: – About what?

BEULAH: Jabe's operation in Memphis. Was it successful?

DOLLY: Wasn't it successful?

[LADY *stares at them blindly. The women, except Carol, close avidly about her, tense with morbid interest.*]

SISTER: Was it too late for surgical interference?

EVA: Wasn't it successful?

[*A loud, measured knock begins on the floor above.*]

BEULAH: Somebody told us it had gone past the knife.

DOLLY: We do hope it ain't hopeless.

EVA: We hope and pray it ain't hopeless.

[*All their faces wear faint, unconscious smiles.* LADY *looks from face to face; then utters a slight, startled laugh and springs up from the table and crosses to the stairs.*]

LADY [*as if in flight*]: Excuse me, I have to go up, Jabe's knocking for me. [LADY *goes upstairs. The women gaze after her.*]

CAROL [*suddenly and clearly, in the silence*]: Speaking of knocks, I have a knock in my engine. It goes knock, knock, and I say who's there. I don't know whether I'm in communication with some dead ancestor or the motor's about to drop out and leave me stranded in the dead of night on the Dixie Highway. Do you have any knowledge of mechanics? I'm sure you do. Would you be sweet and take a short drive with me? So you could hear that knock?

VAL: I don't have time.

CAROL: What have you got to do?

VAL: I'm waiting to see about a job in this store.

CAROL: I'm offering you a job.

VAL: I want a job that pays.

CAROL: I expect to pay you.

[*Women whisper loudly in the background.*]

VAL: Maybe sometime tomorrow.

CAROL: I can't stay here overnight; I'm not allowed to stay overnight in this county.

[*Whispers rise. The word 'corrupt' is distinguished.*]

[*Without turning, smiling very brightly*] What are they saying about me? Can you hear what those women are saying about me?

VAL: – Play it cool. . . .

CAROL: I don't like playing it cool! What are they saying about me? That I'm corrupt?

VAL: If you don't want to be talked about, why do you make up like that, why do you –

CAROL: *To show off!*

VAL: What?

CAROL: *I'm an exhibitionist!* I want to be noticed, seen, heard, felt! I want them to know I'm alive! Don't you want them to know you're alive?

VAL: I want to live and I don't care if they know I'm alive or not.

CAROL: Then why do you play a guitar?

VAL: Why do you make a goddam show of yourself?

CAROL: That's right, for the same reason.

VAL: We don't go the same route. . . .

[*He keeps moving away from her; she continually follows him. Her speech is compulsive.*]

CAROL: I used to be what they call a Christ-bitten reformer. You know what that is? – A kind of benign exhibitionist. . . . I delivered stump speeches, wrote letters of protest about the gradual massacre of the coloured majority in the county. I thought it was wrong for pellagra and slow starvation to cut them down when the cotton crop failed from army worm or boll weevil or too much rain in summer. I wanted to, tried to, put up free clinics. I squandered the money my mother left me on it. And when that Willie McGee thing came along – he was sent to the chair for having improper relations with a white whore – [*Her voice is like a passionate incantation.*] I made a fuss about it. I put on a potato sack and set out for the Capitol on foot. This was in winter. I walked barefoot in this burlap sack to deliver a personal protest to the Governor of the State. Oh, I suppose it was partly exhibitionism on my part, but it wasn't completely exhibitionism; there was something else in it, too. You know how far I got? Six miles out of town – hooted, jeered at, even spit on! – every step of the way – and then arrested! Guess what for? Lewd vagrancy! Uh-huh, that was the charge, 'lewd vagrancy', because they said that potato sack I had on was not a respectable garment. . . . Well, all that was a pretty long time ago, and now I'm not a reformer any more. I'm just a 'lewd vagrant'. And I'm showing the 'S.O.B.s' how lewd a 'lewd vagrant' can be if she puts her whole heart in it like I do mine! All right. I've told you my story, the story of an exhibitionist. Now I want you to do something for me. Take me out to Cypress Hill in my car. And we'll hear the dead people talk. They do talk there. They chatter together like birds on Cypress Hill, but all they say is one word and that one word is 'live', they say 'Live, live, live, live, live!' It's all they've learned, it's the only advice they can give. – Just live. . . . [*She opens the door.*] Simple! – a very simple instruction. . . .

[*Goes out. Women's voices rise from the steady, indistinct murmur, like hissing geese.*]

WOMEN'S VOICES: – No, not liquor! Dope!

– Something not normal all right!

– Her father and mother were warned by the Vigilantes to keep her out of this county.

– She's absolutely degraded!

– Yes, corrupt!

– Corrupt! [Etc., etc.]

[*As if repelled by their hissing voices,* VAL *suddenly picks up his guitar and goes out of the store as* VEE TALBOTT *appears on the landing and calls down to him.*]

VEE: Mr Xavier! Where is Mr Xavier?

BEULAH: Gone, honey.

DOLLY: You might as well face it, Vee. This is one candidate for salvation that you have lost to the opposition.

BEULAH: He's gone off to Cypress Hill with the Cutrere girl.

VEE [*descending*]: – If some of you older women in Two River County would set a better example there'd be more decent young people!

BEULAH: What was that remark?

VEE: I mean that people who give drinkin' parties an' get so drunk they don't know which is their husband and which is somebody else's and people who serve on the altar guild and still play cards on Sundays –

BEULAH: Just stop right there! Now I've discovered the source of that dirty gossip!

VEE: I'm only repeating what I've been told by others. I never been to these parties!

BEULAH: No, and you never will! You're a public kill-joy, a professional hypocrite!

VEE: I try to build up characters! You and your drinkin' parties are only concerned with tearin' characters down! I'm goin' upstairs, I'm goin' back upstairs! [*Rushes upstairs.*]

BEULAH: Well, I'm glad I said what I said to that woman. I've got no earthly patience with that sort of hypocriticism.

268

Dolly, let's put this perishable stuff in the Frigidaire and leave here. I've never been so thoroughly disgusted!

DOLLY: Oh, my Lawd. [*Pauses at stairs and shouts*]: PEE WEE! [*Goes off with the dishes.*]

SISTER: Both of those wimmen are as common as dirt.

EVA: Dolly's folks in Blue Mountain are nothin' at all but the poorest kind of white trash. Why, Lollie Tucker told me the old man sits on the porch with his shoes off drinkin' beer out of a bucket! – Let's take these flowers with us to put on the altar.

SISTER: Yes, we can give Jabe credit in the parish notes.

EVA: I'm going to take these olive-nut sandwiches, too. They'll come in handy for the Bishop Adjutant's tea.

[DOLLY *and* BEULAH *cross through.*]

DOLLY: We still have time to make the second show.

BEULAH [*shouting*]: Dog!

DOLLY: Pee Wee!

[*They rush out of store.*]

EVA: Sits on the porch with his shoes off?

SISTER: Drinkin' beer out of a bucket!

[*They go out with umbrellas, etc. Men descend stairs.*]

SHERIFF TALBOTT: Well, it looks to me like Jabe will more than likely go under before the cotton comes up.

PEE WEE: He never looked good.

DOG: Naw, but now he looks worse.

[*They cross to door.*]

SHERIFF: Vee!

VEE [*from landing*]: Hush that bawling. I had to speak to Lady about that boy and I couldn't speak to her in front of Jabe because he thinks he's gonna be able to go back to work himself.

SHERIFF: Well, move along, quit foolin'.

VEE: I think I ought to wait till that boy gits back.

SHERIFF: I'm sick of you making a goddam fool of yourself over every stray bastard that wanders into this county.

[*Car horn honks loudly.* VEE *follows her husband out. Sound of cars driving off. Dogs bay in distance as lights dim to indicate short passage of time.*]

SCENE TWO

[*A couple of hours later that night. Through the great window the landscape is faintly luminous under a scudding moonlit sky. Outside a girl's laughter,* CAROL'S, *rings out high and clear and is followed by the sound of a motor, rapidly going off.*
VAL *enters the store before the car sound quite fades out and while a dog is still barking at it somewhere along the highway. He says 'Christ' under his breath, goes to the buffet table and scrubs lipstick stain off his mouth and face with a paper napkin, picks up his guitar which he had left on a counter.*
Footsteps descending: LADY *appears on the landing in a flannel robe, shivering in the cold air; she snaps her fingers impatiently for the old dog, Bella, who comes limping down beside her. She doesn't see Val, seated on the shadowy counter, and she goes directly to the phone near the stairs. Her manner is desperate, her voice harsh and shrill.*]

LADY: Ge' me the drugstore, will you? I know the drugstore's closed, this is Mrs Torrance, my store's closed, too, but I got a sick man here, just back from the hospital, yeah, yeah, an emergency, wake up Mr Dubinsky, keep ringing till he answers, it's an emergency! [*Pause: she mutters under her breath*] – *Porca la miseria!* – I wish I was dead, dead, dead. . . .

VAL [*quietly*]: No, you don't, Lady.

[*She gasps, turning and seeing him, without leaving the phone, she rings the cashbox open and snatches out something.*]

LADY: What're you doin' here? You know this store is closed!

VAL: I seen a light was still on and the door was open so I come back to –

LADY: You see what I got in my hand? [*Raises revolver above level of counter.*]

VAL: You going to shoot me?

LADY: You better believe it if you don't get out of here, mister!

VAL: That's all right, Lady, I just come back to pick up my guitar.

LADY: To pick up your guitar?

[*He lifts it gravely.*]

– Huh. . . .

VAL: Miss Talbott brought me here. I was here when you got back from Memphis, don't you remember?

LADY: – Aw. Aw, yeah. . . . You been here all this time?

VAL: No. I went out and come back.

LADY [*into the phone*]: I told you to keep ringing till he answers! Go on, keep ringing, keep ringing! [*Then to Val*] You went out and come back?

VAL: Yeah.

LADY: What for?

VAL: You know that girl that was here?

LADY: Carol Cutrere?

VAL: She said she had car trouble and could I fix it.

LADY: – Did you fix it?

VAL: She didn't have no car trouble, that wasn't her trouble, oh, she had trouble, all right, but *that* wasn't it. . . .

LADY: What was her trouble?

VAL: She made a mistake about me.

LADY: What mistake?

VAL: She thought I had a sign 'Male at Stud' hung on me.

LADY: She thought you – ? [*Into phone suddenly*] Oh, Mr Dubinsky, I'm sorry to wake you up but I just brought my husband back from the Memphis hospital and I left my box of luminal tablets in the – I got to have some! I ain't slep' for three nights, I'm going to pieces, you hear me, I'm going to pieces, I ain't slept in three nights, I got to have some tonight. Now you look here, if you want to keep my trade, you send me over some tablets. Then bring them yourself, God damn it, excuse my French! Because I'm going to pieces right this minute! [*Hangs up violently.*] – *Mannage la miseria!* – Christ. . . . I'm shivering! – It's cold as a goddam ice-plant in this store, I don't know why, it never seems to hold heat, the ceiling's too high or something, it don't hold heat at all. – Now what do you want? I got to go upstairs.

VAL: Here. Put this on you.

[*He removes his jacket and hands it to her. She doesn't take it at once, stares at him questioningly, and then slowly takes the jacket in her hands and examines it, running her fingers curiously over the snakeskin.*]

LADY: What is this stuff this thing's made of? It looks like it was snakeskin.

VAL: Yeah, well, that's what it is.

LADY: What're you doing with a snakeskin jacket?

VAL: It's a sort of a trademark; people call me Snakeskin.

LADY: Who calls you Snakeskin?

VAL: Oh, in the bars, the sort of places I work in – but I've quit that. I'm through with that stuff now. . . .

LADY: You're a – entertainer?

VAL: I sing and play the guitar.

LADY: – Aw? [*She puts the jacket on as if to explore it.*] It feels warm all right.

VAL: It's warm from my body, I guess. . . .

LADY: You must be a warm-blooded boy. . . .

VAL: That's right. . . .

LADY: Well, what in God's name are you lookin' for around here?

VAL: Work.

LADY: Boys like you don't work.

VAL: What d'you mean by boys like me?

LADY: Ones that play th' guitar and go around talkin' about how warm they are. . . .

VAL: That happens t' be the truth. My temperature's always a couple degrees above normal the same as a dog's, it's normal for me the same as it is for a dog, that's the truth. . . .

LADY: – Huh!

VAL: You don't believe me?

LADY: I have no reason to doubt you, but what about it?

VAL: Why – nothing. . . .

[LADY *laughs softly and suddenly;* VAL *smiles slowly and warmly.*]

LADY: You're a peculiar somebody all right, you sure are! How did you get around here?

VAL: I was driving through here last night and an axle broke on my car, that stopped me here, and I went to the county jail for a place to sleep out of the rain. Miss Talbott took me in and give me a cot in the lockup and said if I hung around till you got back that you might give me a job in the store to help out since your husband was tooken sick.

LADY: – Uh-huh. Well – she was wrong about that. . . . If I took on help here it would have to be local help, I couldn't hire no stranger with a – snakeskin jacket and a guitar . . . and that runs a temperature as high as a dog's! [*Throws back her head in another soft, sudden laugh and starts to take off the jacket.*]

VAL: Keep it on.

LADY: No, I got to go up now and you had better be going. . . .

VAL: I got nowhere to go.

LADY: Well, everyone's got a problem and that's yours.

VAL: What nationality are you?

LADY: Why do you ask me that?

VAL: You seem to be like a foreigner.

LADY: I'm the daughter of a Wop bootlegger burned to death in his orchard! – Take your jacket. . . .

VAL: What was that you said about your father?

LADY: Why?

VAL: – A 'Wop bootlegger'?

LADY: – They burned him to death in his orchard! What about it? The story's well known around here.

[JABE knocks on ceiling.]

I got to go up, I'm being called for.

[She turns out light over counter and at the same moment he begins to sing softly with his guitar: 'Heavenly Grass'. He suddenly stops short.]

VAL [abruptly]: I do electric repairs.

[LADY stares at him softly.]

I can do all kinds of odd jobs. Lady, I'm thirty today and I'm through with the life that I've been leading. [Pause. Dog bays in distance.] I lived in corruption but I'm not corrupted. Here is why. [Picks up his guitar.] My life's companion! It washes me clean like water when anything unclean has touched me. . . . [Plays softly, with a slow smile.]

LADY: What's all that writing on it?

VAL: Autographs of musicians I run into here and there.

LADY: Can I see it?

VAL: Turn on that light above you.

[She turns on green-shaded bulb over counter. VAL holds the

274

instrument tenderly between them as if it were a child; his voice is soft, intimate, tender.]

See this name? Leadbelly?

LADY: Leadbelly?

VAL: Greatest man ever lived on the twelve-string guitar! Played it so good he broke the stone heart of a Texas governor with it and won himself a pardon out of jail. . . . And see this name? Oliver? King Oliver? That name is immortal, Lady. Greatest man since Gabriel on a horn. . . .

LADY: What's this name?

VAL: Oh. That name? That name is also immortal. The name Bessie Smith is written in the stars! – Jim Crow killed her, John Barleycorn and Jim Crow killed Bessie Smith but that's another story. . . . See this name here? That's another immortal!

LADY: Fats Waller? Is his name written in the stars, too?

VAL: Yes, his name is written in the stars, too. . . .

[*Her voice is also intimate and soft: a spell of softness between them, their bodies almost touching, only divided by the guitar.*]

LADY: You had any sales experience?

VAL: All my life I been selling something to someone.

LADY: So's everybody. You got any character reference on you?

VAL: I have this – letter.

[*Removes a worn, folded letter from a wallet, dropping a lot of snapshots and cards of various kinds on the floor. He passes the letter to her gravely and crouches to collect the dropped articles while she peruses the character reference.*]

LADY [*reading slowly aloud*]: 'This boy worked for me three months in my auto repair shop and is a real hard worker and is good and honest but is a peculiar talker and that is the reason I got to let him go but would like to – [*Holds*

275

letter closer to light.] – would like to – keep him. Yours
truly.'

[VAL *stares at her gravely, blinking a little.*]

Huh! – Some reference!

VAL: – Is that what it says?

LADY: Didn't you know what it said?

VAL: No – The man sealed the envelope on it.

LADY: Well, that's not the sort of character reference that will
do you much good, boy.

VAL: Naw. I guess it ain't.

LADY: – However . . .

VAL: – What?

LADY: What people say about you don't mean much. Can
you read shoe sizes?

VAL: I guess so.

LADY: What does 75 David mean?

[VAL *stares at her, shakes head slowly.*]

75 means seven and one half long and David means 'D'
wide. You know how to make change?

VAL: Yeah, I could make change in a store.

LADY: Change for better or worse? Ha ha! – Well – [*Pause.*]
Well – you see that other room there, through that arch
there? That's the confectionery; it's closed now but it's
going to be reopened in a short while and I'm going to
compete for the night life in this county, the after-the-
movies trade. I'm going to serve setups in there and I'm
going to redecorate. I got it all planned. [*She is talking
eagerly now, as if to herself.*] Artificial branches of fruit trees
in flower on the walls and ceilings! – It's going to be like
an orchard in the spring! – My father, he had an orchard on
Moon Lake. He made a wine garden of it. We had fifteen
little white arbours with tables in them and they were
covered with – grapevines and – we sold Dago red wine

an' bootleg whisky and beer. – They burned it up! My father was burned up in it. . . .

[JABE *knocks above more loudly and a hoarse voice shouts 'Lady!' Figure appears at the door and calls: 'Mrs Torrance?'*]

Oh, that's the sandman with my sleeping tablets. [*Crosses to door.*] Thanks, Mr Dubinsky, sorry I had to disturb you, sorry I –

[*Man mutters something and goes. She closes the door.*]

Well, go to hell, then, old bastard. . . . [*Returns with package.*] – You ever have trouble sleeping?

VAL: I can sleep or not sleep as long or short as I want to.

LADY: Is that right?

VAL: I can sleep on a concrete floor or go without sleeping, without even feeling sleepy, for forty-eight hours. And I can hold my breath three minutes without blacking out; I made ten dollars betting I could do it and I did it! And I can go a whole day without passing water.

LADY [*startled*]: Is that a fact?

VAL [*very simply as if he'd made an ordinary remark*]: That's a fact. I served time on a chain gang for vagrancy once and they tied me to a post all day and I stood there all day without passing water to show the sons of bitches that I could do it.

LADY: – I see what that auto repair man was talking about when he said this boy is a peculiar talker! Well – what else can you do? Tell me some more about your self-control!

VAL [*grinning*]: Well, they say that a woman can burn a man down. But I can burn down a woman.

LADY: Which woman?

VAL: Any two-footed woman.

LADY [*throws back her head in sudden friendly laughter as he grins at her with the simple candour of a child*]: – Well, there's lots

277

of two-footed women round here that might be willin' to test the truth of that statement.

VAL: I'm saying I could. I'm not saying I would.

LADY: Don't worry, boy. I'm one two-footed woman that you don't have to convince of your perfect controls.

VAL: No, I'm done with all that.

LADY: What's the matter? Have they tired you out?

VAL: I'm not tired. I'm disgusted.

LADY: Aw, you're disgusted, huh?

VAL: I'm telling you, Lady, there's people bought and sold in this world like carcasses of hogs in butcher shops!

LADY: You ain't tellin' me nothin' I don't know.

VAL: You might think there's many and many kinds of people in this world but, Lady, there's just two kinds of people, the ones that are bought and the buyers! No! – there's one other kind . . .

LADY: What kind's that?

VAL: The kind that's never been branded.

LADY: You will be, man.

VAL: They got to catch me first.

LADY: Well, then, you better not settle down in this county.

VAL: You know they's a kind of bird that don't have legs so it can't light on nothing but has to stay all its life on its wings in the sky? That's true. I seen one once, it had died and fallen to earth and it was light-blue coloured and its body was tiny as your little finger, that's the truth, it had a body as tiny as your little finger and so light on the palm of your hand it didn't weigh more than a feather, but its wings spread out this wide but they were transparent, the colour of the sky and you could see through them. That's what they call protection colouring. Camouflage, they call it. You can't tell those birds from the sky and that's why the hawks don't catch them, don't see them up there in the high blue sky near the sun!

LADY: How about in grey weather?

VAL: They fly so high in grey weather the goddam hawks would get dizzy. But those little birds, they don't have no legs at all and they live their whole lives on the wing, and they sleep on the wind, that's how they sleep at night, they just spread their wings and go to sleep on the wind like other birds fold their wings and go to sleep on a tree. . . . [*Music fades in.*] – They sleep on the wind and . . . [*His eyes grow soft and vague and he lifts his guitar and accompanies the very faint music.*] – never light on this earth but one time when they die.

LADY: – I'd like to be one of those birds.

VAL: So'd I like to be one of those birds; they's lots of people would like to be one of those birds and never be – corrupted!

LADY: If one of those birds ever dies and falls on the ground and you happen to find it, I wish you would show it to me because I think maybe you just imagine there is a bird of that kind of existence. Because I don't think nothing living has ever been that free, not even nearly. Show me one of them birds and I'll say, Yes, God's made one perfect creature! – I sure would give this mercantile store and every bit of stock in it to be that tiny bird the colour of the sky . . . for one night to sleep on the wind and – float! – around under th' – stars . . .

  [JABE *knocks on floor.* LADY'S *eyes return to Val.*]

– Because I sleep with a son of a bitch who bought me at a fire sale, not in fifteen years have I had a single good dream, not one – oh! – *Shit* . . . I don't know why I'm – telling a stranger – this. . . . [*She rings the cashbox open.*] Take this dollar and go eat at the Al-Nite on the highway and come back here in the morning and I'll put you to work. I'll break you in clerking here and when the new confectionery opens, well, maybe I can use you in there. – That door locks when you close it! – But let's get one thing straight.

VAL: What thing?

LADY: I'm not interested in your perfect functions, in fact you don't interest me no more than the air that you stand in. If that's understood we'll have a good working relation, but otherwise trouble! – Of course I know you're crazy, but they's lots of crazier people than you are still running loose and some of them in high positions, too. Just remember. No monkey business with me. Now go. Go eat, you're hungry.

VAL: Mind if I leave this here? My life's companion? [*He means his guitar.*]

LADY: Leave it here if you want to.

VAL: Thanks, Lady.

LADY: Don't mention it.

[*He crosses towards the door as a dog barks with passionate clarity in the distance. He turns to smile back at her.*]

VAL: I don't know nothing about you except you're nice but you are just about the nicest person that I have ever run into! And I'm going to be steady and honest and hard-working to please you and any time you have any more trouble sleeping, I know how to fix that for you. A lady osteopath taught me how to make little adjustments in the neck and spine that give you sound, natural sleep. Well, g'night, now.

[*He goes out. Count five. Then she throws back her head and laughs as lightly and gaily as a young girl. Then she turns and wonderingly picks up and runs her hands tenderly over his guitar as the curtain falls.*]

ACT TWO

SCENE ONE

[*The store, afternoon, a few weeks later. The table and chair are back in the confectionery.* LADY *is hanging up the phone.* VAL *is standing just outside the door. He turns and enters. Outside on the highway a mule team is labouring to pull a big truck back on the icy pavement. A Negro's voice shouts:* 'Hyyyyyyyyy-up.']

VAL [*moving to R. window*]: One a them big Diamond T trucks an' trailers gone off the highway last night and a six mule team is tryin' t' pull it back on. . . . [*He looks out window.*]

LADY [*coming from behind to R. of counter*]: Mister, we just now gotten a big fat complaint about you from a woman that says if she wasn't a widow her husband would come in here and beat the tar out of you.

VAL [*taking a step toward her*]: Yeah? – Is this a small pink-headed woman!

LADY: *Pin*-headed woman did you say?

VAL: Naw, I said, 'Pink!' – A little pink-haired woman, in a checkered coat with pearl buttons this big on it.

LADY: I talked to her on the phone. She didn't go into such details about her appearance but she did say you got familiar. I said, 'How? by his talk or behaviour?' And she said, 'Both!' – Now I was afraid of this when I warned you last week, 'No monkey business here, boy!'

VAL: This little pink-headed woman bought a valentine from me and all I said is my *name* is Valentine to her. Few minutes later a small coloured boy came in and delivered the valentine to me with something wrote on it an' I believe I still got it. . . . [*Finds and shows it to Lady, who goes to*

281

him. LADY *reads it, and tears it fiercely to pieces. He lights a cigarette.*]

LADY: Signed it with a lipstick kiss? You didn't show up for this date?

VAL: No, ma'am. That's why she complained. [*Throws match on floor.*]

LADY: Pick that match up off the floor.

VAL: Are you bucking for sergeant, or something?

[*He throws match out the door with elaborate care. Her eyes follow his back.* VAL *returns lazily towards her.*]

LADY: Did you walk around in front of her that way?

VAL [*at counter*]: What way?

LADY: Slew-foot, slew-foot!

[*He regards her closely with good-humoured perplexity.*]

Did you stand in front of her like that? That close? In that, that – *position*?

VAL: What position?

LADY: Ev'rything you do is suggestive!

VAL: Suggestive of what?

LADY: Of what you said you was through with – somethin' – Oh, shoot, you know what I mean – Why'd 'ya think I give you a plain, dark business suit to work in?

VAL [*sadly*]: Un-hun. . . . [*Sighs and removes his blue jacket.*]

LADY: Now what're you takin' that off for?

VAL: I'm giving the suit back to you. I'll change my pants in the closet. [*Gives her the jacket and crosses into alcove.*]

LADY: Hey! I'm sorry! You hear me? I didn't sleep well last night. Hey! I said I'm sorry! You hear me? [*She enters alcove and returns immediately with Val's guitar and crosses to D.R. He follows.*]

VAL: Le' me have my guitar, Lady. You find too many faults with me and I tried to do good.

LADY: I told you I'm sorry. You want me to go down and lick the dust off your shoes?

VAL: Just give me back my guitar.

LADY: I ain't dissatisfied with you. I'm pleased with you, sincerely!

VAL: You sure don't show it.

LADY: My nerves are all shot to pieces. [*Extends hand to him.*] Shake.

VAL: You mean I ain't fired, so I don't have to quit?

[*They shake hands like two men. She hands him guitar – then silence falls between them.*]

LADY: You see, we don't know each other, we're, we're – just gettin' – acquainted.

VAL: That's right, like a couple of animals sniffin' around each other. . . .

[*The image embarrasses her. He crosses to counter, leans over, and puts guitar behind it.*]

LADY: Well, not exactly like that, but – !

VAL: We don't know each other. How do people get to know each other? I used to think they did it by touch.

LADY: By what?

VAL: By touch, by touchin' each other.

LADY [*moving up and sitting on shoe fitting chair which has been moved to R. window*]: Oh, you mean by close – contact!

VAL: But later it seemed like that made them more strangers than ever, uhh, huh, more strangers than ever. . . .

LADY: Then how d'you think they get to know each other?

VAL [*sitting on counter*]: Well, in answer to your last question, I would say this: Nobody ever gets to know *no body*! We're all of us sentenced to solitary confinement inside our own skins, for life! You understand me, Lady? – I'm tellin' you it's the truth, we got to face it, we're under a life-long sentence to solitary confinement inside our own lonely skins for as long as we live on this earth!

LADY [*rising and crossing to him*]: Oh, no, I'm not a big optimist but I cannot agree with something as sad as that statement!

[*They are sweetly grave as two children; the store is somewhat dusky. She sits in chair R. of counter.*]

VAL: *Listen!* – When I was a kid on Witches Bayou. After my folks all scattered away like loose chicken's feathers blown around by the wind – I stayed there alone on the bayou, hunted and trapped out of season and hid from the law! – *Listen!* – All that time, all that lonely time, I felt I was – waiting for something!

LADY: What for?

VAL: What does anyone wait for? For something to happen, for anything to happen, to make things make more sense.... It's hard to remember what that feeling was like because I've lost it now, but I was waiting for something like if you ask a question you wait for someone to answer, but you ask the wrong question or you ask the wrong person and the answer don't come.

Does everything stop because you don't get the answer? No, it goes right on as if the answer was given, day comes after day and night comes after night, and you're still waiting for someone to answer the question and going right on as if the question was answered. And then – well – then . . .

LADY: Then what?

VAL: You get the make-believe answer.

LADY: What answer is that?

VAL: Don't pretend you don't know because you do!

LADY: – Love?

VAL [*placing hand on her shoulder*]: That's the make-believe

284

answer. It's fooled many a fool besides you an' me, that's the God's truth, Lady, and you had better believe it.

[LADY *looks reflectively at Val and he goes on speaking and sits on stool below counter.*]

– I met a girl on the bayou when I was fourteen. I'd had a feeling that day that if I just kept poling the boat down the bayou a little bit further I would come bang into whatever it was I'd been so long expecting!

LADY: Was she the answer, this girl that you met on the bayou?

VAL: She made me think that she was.

LADY: How did she do that?

VAL: By coming out on the dogtrot of a cabin as naked as I was in that flat-bottom boat! She stood there a while with the daylight burning around her as bright as heaven as far as I could see. You seen the inside of a shell, how white that is, pearly white? Her naked skin was like that. – Oh, God, I remember a bird flown out of the moss and its wings made a shadow on her, and then it sung a single, high clear note, and as if she was waiting for that as a kind of a signal to catch me, she turned and smiled, and walked on back in the cabin. . . .

LADY: You followed?

VAL: Yes, I followed, I followed, like a bird's tail follows a bird, I followed!

I thought that she give me the answer to the question I'd been waiting for, but afterwards I wasn't sure that was it, but from that time the question wasn't much plainer than the answer and –

LADY: – What?

VAL: At fifteen I left Witches Bayou. When the dog died I sold my boat and the gun. . . . I went to New Orleans in this snakeskin jacket. . . . It didn't take long for me to learn the score.

LADY: What did you learn?

VAL: I learned that I had something to sell besides snakeskins and other wild things' skins I caught on the bayou. I was corrupted! That's the answer. . . .

LADY: Naw, that ain't the answer!

VAL: Okay, *you* tell me the answer!

LADY: I don't know the answer. I just know corruption ain't the answer. I know that much. If I thought that was the answer I'd take Jabe's pistol or his morphine tablets and –

[*A woman bursts into store.*]

WOMAN: I got to use your pay-phone!

LADY: Go ahead. Help yourself.

[*Woman crosses to phone, deposits coin.* LADY *crosses to confectionery.*]

[*To Val*] Get me a coke from the cooler.

[VAL *crosses and goes out R. During the intense activity among the choral women,* LADY *and* VAL *seem bemused as if they were thinking back over their talk before. For the past minute or two a car horn has been heard blowing repeatedly in the near distance.*]

WOMAN [*at phone*]: Cutrere place, get me the Cutrere place, will yuh? David Cutrere or his wife, whichever comes to the phone!

[BEULAH *rushes in from the street to R.C.*]

BEULAH: Lady, Lady, where's Lady! Carol Cutrere is – !

WOMAN: Quiet, please! I am callin' her brother about her!

[LADY *sits at table in confectionery.*]

[*At phone*] Who's this I'm talking to? Good! I'm calling about your sister, Carol Cutrere. She is blowing her car horn at the Red Crown station, she is blowing and blowing her car horn at the Red Crown station because my husband give the station attendants instructions not to service her car, and she is blowing and blowing and blowing on her horn, drawing a big crowd there and, Mr Cutrere, I thought that you and your father had agreed to keep that girl out of Two River County for good, that's what we all understood around here.

[*Car horn.*]

BEULAH [*listening with excited approval*]: Good! Good! Tell him that if –

[DOLLY *enters.*]

DOLLY: She's gotten out of the car and –
BEULAH: *Shhh!*
WOMAN: Well, I just wanted to let you know she's back here in town makin' another disturbance and my husband's on the phone now at the Red Crown station –

[DOLLY *goes outside and looks off.*]

trying to get the Sheriff, so if she gits picked up again by th' law, you can't say I didn't warn you, Mr Cutrere.

[*Car horn.*]

DOLLY [*coming back in*]: Oh, good! Good!
BEULAH: Where is she, where's she gone now?
WOMAN: You better be quick about it. Yes, I do, I sympathize with you and your father and with Mrs Cutrere, but Carol cannot demand service at our station, we just refuse to wait on her, she's not – Hello? Hello? [*She jiggles phone violently.*]
BEULAH: What's he doin'? Comin' to pick her up?
DOLLY: Call the Sheriff's office!

[BEULAH *goes outside again.* VAL *comes back with a bottle of Coca-Cola – hands it to Lady and leans on juke box.*]

[*Going out to Beulah*] What's goin' on now?

BEULAH [*outside*]: Look, look, they're pushing her out of the station driveway.

[*They forget Lady in this new excitement. Ad libs continual. The short woman from the station charges back out of the store.*]

DOLLY: Where is Carol?

BEULAH: Going into the White Star Pharmacy!

[DOLLY *rushes back in to the phone.*]

BEULAH [*crossing to Lady*]: Lady, I want you to give me your word that if that Cutrere girl comes in here, you won't wait on her! You hear me?

LADY: No.

BEULAH: – What? Will you refuse to wait on her?

LADY: I can't refuse to wait on anyone in this store.

BEULAH: Well, I'd like to know why you can't.

DOLLY: Shhh! I'm on the phone!

BEULAH: Who you phonin', Dolly?

DOLLY: That White Star Pharmacy! I want to make sure that Mr Dubinsky refuses to wait on that girl! [*Having found and deposited coin*] I want the White Far Starmacy. I mean the – [*stamps foot*] – White Star Pharmacy! – I'm so upset my tongue's twisted!

[LADY *hands coke to Val.* BEULAH *is at the window.*]

I'm getting a busy signal. Has she come out yet?

BEULAH: No, she's still in the White Star!

DOLLY: Maybe they're not waiting on her.

BEULAH: Dubinsky'd wait on a purple-bottom baboon if it put a dime on th' counter an' pointed at something!

DOLLY: I know she sat at a table in the Blue Bird Café half'n hour last time she was here and the waitresses never came near her!

BEULAH: That's different. They're not foreigners there!

[DOLLY *crosses to counter.*]

You can't ostracize a person out of this county unless everybody cooperates. Lady just told me that she was going to wait on her if she comes here.

DOLLY: Lady wouldn't do that.

BEULAH: *Ask* her! She told *me* she would!

LADY [*rising and turning at once to the women and shouting at them*]: Oh, for God's sake, no! I'm not going to refuse to wait on her because you all don't like her! Besides I'm delighted that wild girl is givin' her brother so much trouble! [*After this outburst she goes back of the counter.*]

DOLLY [*at phone*]: Hush! Mr Dubinsky! This is Dolly Hamma, Mr 'Dog' Hamma's wife!

[CAROL *quietly enters the front door.*]

I want to ask you, is Carol Cutrere in your drugstore?

BEULAH [*warningly*]: Dolly!

CAROL: No. She isn't.

DOLLY: – What?

CAROL: She's here.

[BEULAH *goes into confectionery.* CAROL *moves towards Val to D.R.C.*]

DOLLY: – Aw! – Never mind, Mr Dubinsky, I – [*Hangs up furiously and crosses to door.*]

[*A silence in which they all stare at the girl from various positions about the store. She has been on the road all night in an open car: her hair is blown wild, her face flushed and eyes bright with fever. Her manner in the scene is that of a wild animal at bay, desperate but fearless.*]

LADY [*finally and quietly*]: Hello, Carol.

CAROL: Hello, Lady.

LADY [*defiantly cordial*]: I thought that you were in New Orleans, Carol.

CAROL: Yes, I was. Last night.

LADY: Well, you got back fast.

CAROL: I drove all night.

LADY: In that storm?

CAROL: The wind took the top off my car but I didn't stop.

[*She watches Val steadily; he steadily ignores her; turns away and puts bottles of Coca-Cola on a table.*]

LADY [*with growing impatience*]: Is something wrong at home, is someone sick?

CAROL [*absently*]: No. No, not that I know of, I wouldn't know if there was, they – may I sit down?

LADY: Why, sure.

CAROL [*crossing to chair at counter and sitting*]: – They pay me to stay away so I wouldn't know. . . .

[*Silence.* VAL *walks deliberately past her and goes into alcove.*]

– I think I have a fever. I feel like I'm catching pneumonia, everything's so far away. . . .

[*Silence again except for the faint, hissing whispers of* BEULAH *and* DOLLY *at the back of the store.*]

LADY [*with a touch of exasperation*]: Is there something you want?

CAROL: Everything seems miles away. . . .

LADY: Carol, I said is there anything you want here?

CAROL: Excuse me! – yes. . . .

LADY: Yes, what?

CAROL: Don't bother now. I'll wait.

[VAL *comes out of alcove with the blue jacket on.*]

LADY: Wait for what, what are you waiting for? You don't

have to wait for nothing, just say what you want and if I got it in stock I'll give it to you!

[*Phone rings once.*]

CAROL [*vaguely*]: – Thank you – no. . . .
LADY [*to Val*]: Get that phone, Val.

[DOLLY *crosses and hisses something inaudible to Beulah.*]

BEULAH [*rising*]: I just want to wait here to see if she does or she don't.
DOLLY: She just said she would!
BEULAH: Just the same, I'm gonna wait!!
VAL [*at phone*]: Yes, sir, she is. – I'll tell her. [*Hangs up and speaks to Lady*] Her brother's heard she's here and he's coming to pick her up.
LADY: *David Cutrere is not coming in this store!*
DOLLY: Aw-aw!
BEULAH: David Cutrere used to be her lover.
DOLLY: I remember you told me.
LADY [*wheels about suddenly toward the women*]: Beulah! Dolly! Why're you back there hissing together like geese? [*Coming from behind counter to R.C.*] Why don't you go to th' – Blue Bird and – have some hot coffee – talk there!
BEULAH: It looks like we're getting what they call the bum's rush.
DOLLY: I never stay where I'm not wanted and when I'm not wanted somewhere I never come back!

[*They cross out and slam door.*]

LADY [*after a pause*]: What did you come here for?
CAROL: To deliver a message.
LADY: To me?
CAROL: No.
LADY: Then who?

[CAROL *stares at Lady gravely a moment, then turns slowly to look at Val.*]

– Him? – Him?

[CAROL *nods slowly and slightly.*]

O.K., then, give him the message, deliver the message to him.

CAROL: It's a private message. Could I speak to him alone, please?

[LADY *gets a shawl from a hook.*]

LADY: Oh, for God's sake! Your brother's plantation is ten minutes from here in that sky-blue Cadillac his rich wife give him. Now look, he's on his way here but I won't let him come in, I don't even want his hand to touch the door-handle. I know your message, this boy knows your message, there's nothing private about it. But I tell you, that this boy's not for sale in my store! – Now – I'm going out to watch for the sky-blue Cadillac on the highway. When I see it, I'm going to throw this door open and holler and when I holler, I want you out of this door like a shot from a pistol! – that fast! Understand?

[NOTE: *Above scene is overextended. This can be remedied by a very lively performance. It might also help to indicate a division between the Lady-Val scene and the group scene that follows.*]

[LADY *slams door behind her. The loud noise of the door-slam increases the silence that follows.* VAL's *oblivious attitude is not exactly hostile, but deliberate. There's a kind of purity in it; also a kind of refusal to concern himself with a problem that isn't his own. He holds his guitar with a specially tender concentration, and strikes a soft chord on it. The girl stares at Val; he whistles a note and tightens a guitar string to the pitch of the*

292

whistle, not looking at the girl. Since this scene is followed by the emotional scene between Lady and David, it should be keyed somewhat lower than written; it's important that Val should not seem brutal in his attitude towards Carol; there should be an air between them of two lonely children.]

VAL [*in a soft, preoccupied tone*]: You told the lady I work for that you had a message for me. Is that right, Miss? Have you got a message for me?

CAROL [*rises, moves a few steps towards him, hesitantly.* VAL *whistles, plucks guitar string, changes pitch*]: You've spilt some ashes on your new blue suit.

VAL: Is that the message?

CAROL [*moves away a step*]: No. No, that was just an excuse to touch you. The message is –

VAL: What?

[*Music fades in – guitar.*]

CAROL: – I'd love to hold something the way you hold your guitar, that's how I'd love to hold something, with such – *tender protection!* I'd love to hold *you* that way, with that same – *tender protection!* [*Her hand has fallen on to his knee, which he has drawn up to rest a foot on the counter stool.*] – *Because you hang the moon for me!*

VAL [*speaks to her, not roughly but in a tone that holds a long history that began with a romantic acceptance of such declarations as she has just made to him, and that turned gradually to his present distrust. He puts guitar down and goes to her*]: Who're you tryin' t' fool beside you'self? You couldn't stand the weight of a man's body on you. [*He casually picks up her wrist and pushes the sleeve back from it.*] What's this here? A human wrist with a bone? It feels like a twig I could snap with two fingers. . . . [*Gently, negligently, pushes collar of her trench coat back from her bare throat and shoulders. Runs a finger along her neck tracing a vein.*] Little girl, you're transparent,

I can see the veins in you. A man's weight on you would break you like a bundle of sticks. . . .

[*Music fades out.*]

CAROL [*gazes at him, startled by his perception*]: Isn't it funny! You've hit on the truth about me. The act of love-making is almost unbearably painful, and yet, of course, I do bear it, because to be not alone, even for a few moments, is worth the pain and the danger. It's dangerous for me because I'm not built for child-bearing.

VAL: Well, then, fly away, little bird, fly away before you – get broke. [*He turns back to his guitar.*]

CAROL: Why do you dislike me?

VAL [*turning back*]: I never dislike nobody till they interfere with me.

CAROL: How have I interfered with you? Did I snitch when I saw my cousin's watch on you?

VAL [*beginning to remove his watch*]: – You won't take my word for a true thing I told you. I'm thirty years old and I'm done with the crowd you run with and the places you run to. The Club Rendezvous, the Starlite Lounge, the Music Bar, and all the night places. Here – [*offers watch*] – take this Rolex Chronometer that tells the time of the day and the day of the week and the month and all the crazy moon's phases. I never stole nothing before. When I stole that I known it was time for me to get off the party, so take it back, now, to Bertie. . . . [*He takes her hand and tries to force the watch into her fist. There is a little struggle, he can't open her fist. She is crying, but staring fiercely into his eyes. He draws a hissing breath and hurls watch violently across the floor.*] – That's my message to you and the pack you run with!

CAROL [*flinging coat away*]: I RUN WITH NOBODY! – I hoped I could run with you. . . . [*Music stops short.*] You're in danger here, Snakeskin. You've taken off the jacket that said: 'I'm wild, I'm alone!' and put on the nice blue uniform of a convict!... Last night I woke up thinking about you again. I drove all night to bring you this warning of danger.... [*Her trembling hand covers her lips.*] – The message I came here to give you was a warning of danger! I hoped you'd hear me and let me take you away before it's – too late.

[*Door bursts open.* LADY *rushes inside, crying out.*]

LADY: *Your brother's coming, go out! He can't come in!*

[CAROL *picks up coat and goes into confectionery, sobbing.* VAL *crosses toward door.*]

Lock that door! Don't let him come in my store!

[CAROL *sinks sobbing at table.* LADY *runs up to the landing of the stairs as* DAVID CUTRERE *enters the store. He is a tall man in hunter's clothes. He is hardly less handsome now than he was in his youth but something has gone: his power is that of a captive who rules over other captives. His face, his eyes, have something of the same desperate, unnatural hardness that Lady meets the world with.*]

DAVID: Carol?
VAL: She's in there. [*He nods toward the dim confectionery into which the girl has retreated.*]
DAVID [*crossing*]: Carol!

[*She rises and advances a few steps into the lighted area of the stage.*]

You broke the agreement.

[CAROL *nods slightly, staring at Val.*]

[*Harshly:*] All right. I'll drive you back. Where's your coat?

[CAROL *murmurs something inaudible, staring at* VAL.]

Where is her coat, where is my sister's coat?

[VAL *crosses below and picks up the coat that Carol has dropped on the floor and hands it to David. He throws it roughly about Carol's shoulders and propels her forcefully toward the store entrance.* VAL *moves away to D.R.*]

LADY [*suddenly and sharply*]: Wait, please!

[DAVID *looks up at the landing; stands frozen as* LADY *rushes down the stairs.*]

DAVID [*softly, hoarsely*]: How – are you, Lady?
LADY [*turning to Val*]: Val, go out.
DAVID [*to Carol*]: Carol, will you wait for me in my car?

[*He opens the door for his sister; she glances back at Val with desolation in her eyes.* VAL *crosses quickly through the confectionery. Sound of door closing in there.* CAROL *nods slightly as if in sad response to some painful question and goes out of the store. Pause.*]

LADY: I told you once to never come in this store.
DAVID: I came for my sister. . . . [*He turns as if to go.*]
LADY: No, wait!
DAVID: I don't dare leave my sister alone on the road.
LADY: I have something to tell you I never told you before.

[*She crosses to him.* DAVID *turns back to her, then moves away to D.R.C.*]

– I – carried your child in my body the summer you quit me.

[*Silence.*]

DAVID: – I – didn't know.
LADY: No, no, I didn't write you no letter about it; I was proud then; I had pride. But I had your child in my body the summer you quit me, that summer they burned my father in his wine garden, and you, you washed your hands clean of any connection with a Dago bootlegger's daughter

296

and – [*Her breathless voice momentarily falters and she makes a fierce gesture as she struggles to speak.*] – took that – society girl that – restored your homeplace and give you such – [*Catches breath.*] – wellborn children. . . .

DAVID: – I – didn't know.

LADY: Well, now you do know, you know now I carried your child in my body the summer you quit me but I had it cut out of my body, and they cut my heart out with it!

DAVID: – I – didn't know.

LADY: I wanted death after that, but death don't come when you *want* it, it comes when you don't want it! I wanted death, then, but I took the next best thing. *You* sold *yourself*. *I* sold *my* self. *You* was bought. *I* was bought. You made whores of us both!

DAVID: – I – didn't know. . . .

[*Mandolin, barely audible, 'Dicitincello Vuoi'.*]

LADY: But that's all a long time ago. Some reason I drove by there a few nights ago; the shore of the lake where my father had his wine garden? You remember? You remember the wine garden of my father?

[DAVID *stares at her. She turns away.*]

No, you don't? You don't remember it even?

DAVID: – Lady, I don't – remember – anything else. . . .

LADY: The mandolin of my father, the songs that I sang with my father and my father's wine garden?

DAVID: Yes, I don't remember anything else. . . .

LADY: *Core Ingrata! Come Le Rose!* And we disappeared and he would call, '*Lady? Lady?*' [*Turns to him.*] *How could I answer him with two tongues in my mouth!* [*A sharp hissing intake of breath, eyes opened wide, hand clapped over her mouth as if what she said was unendurable to her. He turns instantly, sharply away.*]

297

[*Music stops short.* JABE *begins to knock for her on the floor above. She crosses to stairs, stops, turns.*]

I hold hard feelings! – Don't ever come here again. If your wild sister comes here, send somebody else for her, not you, not you. Because I hope never to feel this knife again in me.

[*Her hand is on her chest; she breathes with difficulty. He turns away from her; starts toward the door. She takes a step toward him.*]

And don't pity me either. I haven't gone down so terribly far in the world. I got a going concern in this mercantile store, in there's the confectionery which'll reopen this spring, it's being done over to make it the place that all the young people will come to, it's going to be like –

[*He touches the door, pauses with his back to her.*]

– the wine garden of my father, those wine-drinking nights when you had something better than anything you've had since!

DAVID: Lady – *That's* –

LADY: – *What?*

DAVID: *True!* [*Opens door.*]

LADY: Go now. I just wanted to tell you my life ain't over.

[*He goes out as* JABE *continues knocking. She stands, stunned, motionless till* VAL *quietly re-enters the store. She becomes aware of his return rather slowly; then she murmurs*]

I made a fool of myself. . . .

VAL: What?

[*She crosses to stairs.*]

LADY: *I made a fool of myself!*

[*She goes up the stairs with effort as the lights change slowly to mark a division of scenes.*]

SCENE TWO

[Sunset of that day. VAL *is alone in the store, as if preparing to go. The sunset is fiery. A large woman opens the door and stands there looking dazed. It is* VEE TALBOTT.*]*

VAL *[turning]*: Hello, Mrs Talbott.

VEE: Something's gone wrong with my eyes. I can't see nothing.

VAL *[going to her]*: Here, let me help you. You probably drove up here with that setting sun in your face. *[Leading her to shoe-fitting chair at R. window.]* There now. Set down right here.

VEE: Thank you – so – much. . . .

VAL: I haven't seen you since that night you brought me here to ask for this job.

VEE: Has the minister called on you yet? Reverend Tooker? I made him promise he would. I told him you were new around here and weren't affiliated to any church yet. I want you to go to ours.

VAL: – That's – mighty kind of you.

VEE: The Church of the Resurrection, it's Episcopal.

VAL: Uh, huh.

VEE: Unwrap that picture, please.

VAL: Sure. *[He tears paper off canvas.]*

VEE: It's the Church of the Resurrection. I give it a sort of imaginative treatment. You know, Jabe and Lady have never darkened a church door. I thought it ought to be hung where Jabe could look at it, it might help to bring that poor dying man to Jesus. . . .

*[*VAL *places it against chair R. of counter and crouches before*

the canvas, studying it long and seriously. VEE coughs nervously, gets up, bends to look at the canvas, sits uncertainly back down. VAL smiles at her warmly, then back to the canvas.]

VAL [*at last*]: What's this here in the picture?

VEE: The steeple.

VAL: Aw. – Is the church steeple red?

VEE: Why – no, but –

VAL: Why'd you paint it red, then?

VEE: Oh, well, you see, I – [*laughs nervously, childlike in her growing excitement*] – I just *felt* it that way! I paint a thing how I feel it instead of always the way it actually is. Appearances are misleading, nothing is what it looks like to the eyes. You got to have – *vision* – to see!

VAL: – Yes. Vision. Vision! – to see.... [*Rises, nodding gravely, emphatically.*]

VEE: I paint from vision. They call me a visionary.

VAL: Oh.

VEE [*with shy pride*]: That's what the New Orleans and Memphis newspaper people admire so much in my work. They call it a primitive style, the work of a visionary. One of my pictures is hung on the exhibition in Audubon Park museum and they have asked for others. I can't turn them out fast enough! – I have to wait for – visions, no, I – I can't paint without visions.... I couldn't *live* without visions!

VAL: Have you always had visions?

VEE: No, just since I was born, I – [*Stops short, startled by the absurdity of her answer. Both laugh suddenly, then she rushes on, her great bosom heaving with curious excitement, twisting in her chair, gesturing with clenched hands.*] I was born, I was born with a caul! A sort of thing like a veil, a thin, thin sort of a web over my eyes. They call that a caul. It's a sign that you're going to have visions, and I did, I had them! [*Pauses for breath; light fades.*] – When I was little my baby sister

300

died. Just one day old, she died. They had to baptize her at midnight to save her soul.

VAL: Uh-huh. [*He sits opposite her, smiling, attentive.*]

VEE: The minister came at midnight, and after the baptism service, he handed the bowl of holy water to me and told me, 'Be sure to empty this out on the ground!' – I didn't. I was scared to go out at midnight with, with – death! in the – house and – I sneaked into the kitchen; I emptied the holy water into the kitchen sink – thunder struck! – the kitchen sink turned black, the kitchen sink turned absolutely black!

[SHERIFF TALBOTT *enters the front door.*]

TALBOTT: Mama! What're you doin'?

VEE: Talkin'.

TALBOTT: I'm gonna see Jabe a minute, you go out and wait in th' car. [*He goes up. She rises slowly, picks up canvas, and moves to counter.*]

VEE: – Oh, I – tell you! – since I got into this painting, my whole outlook is different. I can't explain how it is, the difference to me.

VAL: You don't have to explain. I know what you mean. Before you started to paint, it didn't make sense.

VEE: – What – what didn't?

VAL: Existence!

VEE [*slowly and softly*]: No – no, it didn't. . . . existence didn't make sense. . . . [*She places canvas on guitar on counter and sits in chair.*]

VAL [*rising and crossing to her*]: You lived in Two River County, the wife of the county Sheriff. You saw awful things take place.

VEE: Awful! Things!

VAL: Beatings!

VEE: Yes!

VAL: Lynchings!

VEE: Yes!

VAL: Runaway convicts torn to pieces by hounds!

[*This is the first time she could express this horror.*]

VEE: *Chain-gang dogs!*

VAL: Yeah?

VEE: Tear fugitives!

VAL: Yeah?

VEE: – *to pieces. . . .*

> [*She had half risen: now sinks back faintly.* VAL *looks beyond her in the dim store, his light eyes have a dark gaze. It may be that his speech is too articulate: counteract this effect by groping, hesitations.*]

VAL [*moving away a step*]: But violence ain't quick always. Sometimes it's slow. Some tornadoes are slow. Corruption – rots men's hearts and – rot is slow. . . .

VEE: – How do you – ?

VAL: Know? I been a witness, I know!

VEE: *I* been a witness! *I* know!

VAL: We seen these things from seats down front at the show. [*He crouches before her and touches her hands in her lap. Her breath shudders.*] And so you begun to paint your visions. Without no plan, no training, you started to paint as if God touched your fingers. [*He lifts her hands slowly, gently from her soft lap.*] You made some beauty out of this dark country with these two, soft, woman hands. . . .

[TALBOTT *appears on the stair landing, looks down, silent.*]

Yeah, you made some beauty! [*Strangely, gently, he lifts her hands to his mouth. She gasps.* TALBOTT *calls out.*]

TALBOTT: *Hey!*

[VEE *springs up, gasping.*]

[*Descending*] Cut this crap!

[VAL *moves away to R.C.*]

[*To Vee*] Go out. Wait in the car.

[*He stares at Val till* VEE *lumbers out as if dazed. After a while*]:

Jabe Torrance told me to take a good look at you. [*Crosses to Val.*] Well, now, I've taken that look. [*Nods shortly. Goes out of store. The store is now very dim. As door closes on Talbott,* VAL *picks up painting; he goes behind counter and places it on a shelf, then picks up his guitar and sits on counter. Lights go down to mark a division as he sings and plays 'Heavenly Grass'.*]

SCENE THREE

[*As* VAL *finishes the song,* LADY *descends the stair. He rises and turns on a green-shaded light bulb.*]

VAL [*to Lady*]: You been up there a long time.
LADY: – I gave him morphine. He must be out of his mind. He says such awful things to me. He says I want him to die.
VAL: You sure you don't?
LADY: I don't want no one to die. Death's terrible, Val.

[*Pause. She wanders to the front window R. He takes his guitar and crosses to the door.*]

You gotta go now?
VAL: I'm late.
LADY: Late for what? You got a date with somebody?
VAL: – No. . . .
LADY: Then stay a while. Play something. I'm all unstrung. . . .

303

[*He crosses back and leans against counter; the guitar is barely audible, under the speeches.*]

I made a terrible fool of myself down here today with –

VAL: – That girl's brother?

LADY: Yes, I – threw away – pride. . . .

VAL: His sister said she'd come here to give me a warning. I wonder what of?

LADY [*sitting in shoe-fitting chair*]: – I said things to him I should of been too proud to say. . . .

[*Both are pursuing their own reflections; guitar continues softly.*]

VAL: Once or twice lately I've woke up with a fast heart, shouting something, and had to pick up my guitar to calm myself down. . . . Somehow or other I can't get used to this place, I don't feel safe in this place, but I – want to stay. . . .

[*Stops short; sound of wild baying.*]

LADY: The chain-gang dogs are chasing some runaway convict. . . .

VAL: *Run boy! Run fast, brother! If they catch you, you never will run again! That's* – [*He has thrust his guitar under his arm on this line and crossed to the door.*] – for sure. . . . [*The baying of the dogs changes, becomes almost a single savage note.*] – Uh-huh – the dogs've got him. . . . [*Pause.*] They're tearing him to pieces! [*Pause. Baying continues. A shot is fired. The baying dies out. He stops with his hand on the door; glances back at her; nods; draws the door open. The wind sings loud in the dusk.*]

LADY: *Wait!*

VAL: – Huh?

LADY: – Where do you stay?

VAL: – When?

LADY: Nights.

VAL: I stay at the Wildwood cabins on the highway.

LADY: You like it there?

VAL: Uh-huh.

LADY: – Why?

VAL: I got a comfortable bed, a two-burner stove, a shower, and ice-box there.

LADY: You want to save money?

VAL: I never could in my life.

LADY: You could if you stayed on the place.

VAL: What place?

LADY: This place.

VAL: Whereabouts on this place?

LADY [pointing to alcove]: Back of that curtain.

VAL: – Where they try on clothes?

LADY: There's a cot there. A nurse slept on it when Jabe had his first operation, and there's a washroom down here and I'll get a plumber to put in a hot an' cold shower! I'll – fix it up nice for you. . . . [She rises, crosses to foot of stairs. Pause. He lets the door shut, staring at her.]

VAL [moving D.C.]: – I – don't like to be – obligated.

LADY: There wouldn't be no obligation, you'd do me a favour. I'd feel safer at night with somebody on the place. I would; it would cost you nothing! And you could save up that money you spend on the cabin. How much? Ten a week? Why, two or three months from now you'd – save enough money to – [Makes a wide gesture with a short laugh as if startled.] Go on! Take a look at it! See if it don't suit you! – All right. . . .

[But he doesn't move; he appears reflective.]

LADY [shivering, hugging herself]: Where does heat go in this building?

VAL [reflectively]: – Heat rises. . . .

LADY: You with your dog's temperature, don't feel cold, do you? I do! I turn blue with it!

VAL: – Yeah. . . .

[*The wait is unendurable to Lady.*]

LADY: *Well, aren't you going to look at it, the room back there, and see if it suits you or not?!*

VAL: – I'll go and take a look at it. . . .

[*He crosses to the alcove and disappears behind the curtain. A light goes on behind it, making its bizarre pattern translucent: a gold tree with scarlet fruit and white birds in it, formally designed. Truck roars; lights sweep the frosted window.* LADY *gasps aloud; takes out a pint bottle and a glass from under the counter, setting them down with a crash that makes her utter a startled exclamation: then a startled laugh. She pours a drink and sits in chair R. of counter. The lights turn off behind the alcove curtain and* VAL *comes back out. She sits stiffly without looking at him as he crosses back lazily, goes behind counter, puts guitar down. His manner is gently sad as if he had met with a familiar, expected disappointment. He sits down quietly on edge of counter and takes the pint bottle and pours himself a shot of the liquor with a reflective sigh. Boards creak loudly, contracting with the cold.* LADY'S *voice is harsh and sudden, demanding.*]

LADY: *Well, is it okay or – what?*

VAL: I never been in a position where I could turn down something I got for nothing in my life. I like that picture in there. That's a famous picture, that 'September Morn' picture you got on the wall in there. Ha ha! I might have trouble sleeping in a room with that picture. I might keep turning the light on to take another look at it! The way she's cold in that water and sort of crouched over in it, holding her body like that, that – might – ha ha! – sort of keep me awake. . . .

LADY: Aw, you with your dog's temperature and your control of all functions, it would take more than a picture to keep you awake!

VAL: I was just kidding.

LADY: I was just kidding, too.

VAL: But you know how a single man is. He don't come home every night with just his shadow.

[*Pause. She takes a drink.*]

LADY: You bring girls home nights to the Wildwood cabins, do you?

VAL: I ain't so far. But I would like to feel free to. That old life is what I'm used to. I always worked nights in cities and if you work nights in cities you live in a different city from those that work days.

LADY: Yes, I know, I – imagine. . . .

VAL: The ones that work days in cities and the ones that work nights in cities, they live in different cities. The cities have the same name but they are different cities. As different as night and day. There's something wild in the country that only the night people know. . . .

LADY: Yeah, I know!

VAL: I'm thirty years old! – but sudden changes don't work, it takes –

LADY: – Time – yes. . . .

[*Slight pause which she finds disconcerting. He slides off counter and moves around below it.*]

VAL: You been good to me, Lady. – Why d'you want me to stay here?

LADY [*defensively*]: I told you why.

VAL: For company nights?

LADY: Yeah to, to – *guard the store*, nights!

VAL: To be a night watchman?

LADY: Yeah, to be a night *watchman*.

VAL: You feel nervous alone here?

LADY: Naturally now! – Jabe sleeps with a pistol next to him but if somebody broke in the store, he couldn't git up and all I could do is holler! – Who'd *hear* me? They got a telephone girl on the night shift with – sleepin' sickness, I think! Anyhow, why're you so suspicious? You look at me like you thought I was *plottin'*. – Kind people *exist*: even me! [*She sits up rigid in chair, lips and eyes tight closed, drawing in a loud breath which comes from a tension both personal and vicarious.*]

VAL: I understand, Lady, but. . . . Why're you sitting up so stiff in that chair?

LADY: Ha! [*Sharp laugh; she leans back in chair.*]

VAL: You're still unrelaxed.

LADY: I know.

VAL: Relax. [*Moving around close to her.*] I'm going to show you some tricks I learned from a lady osteopath that took me in, too.

LADY: What tricks?

VAL: How to manipulate joints and bones in a way that makes you feel like a loose piece of string. [*Moves behind her chair. She watches him.*] Do you trust me or don't you?

LADY: Yeah, I trust you completely, but –

VAL: Well, then, lean forward a little and raise your arms up and turn sideways in the chair.

[*She follows these instructions.*]

Drop your head. [*He manipulates her head and neck.*] Now the spine, Lady. [*He places his knee against the small of her backbone and she utters a sharp, startled laugh as he draws her backbone hard against his kneecap.*]

LADY: Ha, ha! – That makes a sound like, like, like! – boards contracting with cold in the building, ha, ha!

[*He relaxes.*]

VAL: Better?

LADY: Oh, yes! – much . . . thanks. . . .

VAL [*stroking her neck*]: Your skin is like silk. You're light-skinned to be Italian.

LADY: Most people in this country think Italian people are dark. Some are but not all are! Some of them are fair . . . very fair. . . . My father's people were dark but my mother's people were fair. Ha ha!

[*The laughter is senseless. He smiles understandingly at her as she chatters to cover confusion. He turns away, then goes above, and sits on counter close to her.*]

My mother's mother's sister – come here from Monte Cassino, to die, with relations! – but I think people always die alone . . . with or without relations. I was a little girl then and I remember it took her such a long, long time to die we almost forgot her. – And she was so quiet . . . in a corner. . . . And I remember asking her one time, Zia Teresa, how does it feel to die? – Only a little girl would ask such a question, ha ha! Oh, and I remember her answer. She said – 'It's a lonely feeling.'

I think she wished she had stayed in Italy and died in a place that she knew. . . . [*Looks at him directly for the first time since mentioning the alcove.*] Well, there is a washroom, and I'll get the plumber to put in a hot and cold shower! Well – [*Rises, retreats awkwardly from the chair. His interest seems to have wandered from her.*] I'll go up and get some clean linen and make up that bed in there.

[*She turns and walks rapidly, almost running, to stairs. He appears lost in some private reflection but as soon as she has disappeared above the landing, he says something under his breath and crosses directly to the cashbox. He coughs loudly to cover the sound of ringing it open; scoops out a fistful of bills and coughs again to cover the sound of slamming drawer shut. Picks up his guitar and goes out the front door of store. LADY returns downstairs, laden with linen. The outer darkness moans*] *through the door left open. She crosses to the door and a little outside it, peering both ways down the dark road. Then she comes in furiously, with an Italian curse, shutting the door with her foot or shoulder, and throws the linen down on counter. She crosses abruptly to cashbox, rings it open, and discovers theft. Slams drawer violently shut.]*

Thief! Thief!

[Turns to phone, lifts receiver. Holds it a moment, then slams it back into place. Wanders desolately back to the door, opens it, and stands staring out into the starless night as the scene dims out. Music: blues – guitar.]

SCENE FOUR

[Late that night. VAL enters the store, a little unsteadily, with his guitar; goes to the cashbox and rings it open. He counts some bills off a big wad and returns them to the cashbox and larger wad to the pocket of his snakeskin jacket. Sudden footsteps above; light spills on to stair landing. He quickly moves away from the cashbox as LADY appears on the landing in a white sateen robe; she carries a flashlight.]

LADY: Who's that?

[Music fades out.]

VAL: – Me.

[She turns the flashlight on his figure.]

LADY: Oh, my God, how you scared me!

VAL: You didn't expect me?

LADY: How'd I know it was you I heard come in?

VAL: I thought you give me a room here.

LADY: You left without letting me know if you took it or not. [*She is descending the stairs into store, flashlight still on him.*]

VAL: Catch me turning down something I get for nothing.

LADY: Well, you might have said something so I'd expect you or not.

VAL: I thought you took it for granted.

LADY: I don't take nothing for granted.

[*He starts back to the alcove.*]

Wait! – I'm coming downstairs. . . . [*She descends with the flashlight beam on his face.*]

VAL: You're blinding me with that flashlight.

[*He laughs. She keeps the flashlight on him. He starts back again toward the alcove.*]

LADY: The bed's not made because I didn't expect you.

VAL: That's all right.

LADY: I brought the linen downstairs and you'd cut out.

VAL: – Yeah, well –

[*She picks up linen on counter.*]

Give me that stuff. I can make up my own rack. Tomorrow you'll have to get yourself a new clerk. [*Takes it from her and goes again towards alcove.*] I had a lucky night. [*Exhibits a wad of bills.*]

LADY: Hey!

[*He stops near the curtain. She goes and turns on green-shaded bulb over cashbox.*]

– *Did you just open this cashbox?*

VAL: – Why you ask that?

LADY: I thought I heard it ring open a minute ago, that's why I come down here.

VAL: – In your – white satin – kimona?

LADY: *Did you just open the cashbox?!*

VAL: – I wonder who did if I didn't. . . .

LADY: Nobody did if you didn't, but somebody did! [*Opens cashbox and hurriedly counts money. She is trembling violently.*]

VAL: How come you didn't lock the cash up in the safe this evening, Lady?

LADY: Sometimes I forget to.

VAL: That's careless.

LADY: – Why'd you open the cashbox when you come in?

VAL: I opened it twice this evening, once before I went out and again when I come back. I borrowed some money and put it back in the box an' got all this left over! [*Shows her the wad of bills.*] I beat a blackjack dealer five times straight. With this much loot I can retire for the season. . . . [*He returns money to pocket.*]

LADY: *Chicken-feed!* – I'm sorry for you.

VAL: You're sorry for me?

LADY: I'm sorry for you because nobody can help you. I was touched by your – strangeness, your strange talk. – That thing about birds with no feet so they have to sleep on the wind? – I said to myself, 'This boy is a bird with no feet so he has to sleep on the wind,' and that softened my fool Dago heart and I wanted to help you. . . . Fool, me! – I got what I should of expected. You robbed me while I was upstairs to get sheets to make up your bed!

[*He starts out toward the door.*]

I guess I'm a fool to even feel disappointed.

VAL [*stopping C. and dropping linen on counter*]: You're disappointed in me. I was disappointed in you.

LADY [*coming from behind counter*]: – How did I disappoint you?

VAL: There wasn't no cot behind that curtain before. You put it back there for a purpose.

312

LADY: It was back there! – folded behind the mirror.

VAL: It wasn't back of no mirror when you told me three times to go and –

LADY [*cutting in*]: I left that money in the cashbox on purpose, to find out if I could trust you.

VAL: You got back th' . . .

LADY: No, no, no, I can't trust you, now I know I can't trust you, I got to trust anybody or I don't want him.

VAL: That's O.K., I don't expect no character reference from you.

LADY: I'll give you a character reference. I'd say this boy's a peculiar talker! But I wouldn't say a real hard worker or honest. I'd say a peculiar slew-footer that sweet talks you while he's got his hand in the cashbox.

VAL: I took out less than you owed me.

LADY: Don't mix up the issue. I see through you, mister!

VAL: I see through you, Lady.

LADY: What d'you see through me?

VAL: You sure you want me to tell?

LADY: I'd love for you to.

VAL: – A not so young and not so satisfied woman, that hired a man off the highway to do double duty without paying overtime for it. . . . I mean a store clerk days and a stud nights, and –

LADY: God, no! You – ! [*She raises her hand as if to strike at him.*] Oh, God no. . . . you cheap little – [*Invectives fail her so she uses her fists, hammering at him with them. He seizes her wrists. She struggles a few moments more, then collapses, in chair, sobbing. He lets go of her gently.*]

VAL: It's natural. You felt – lonely. . . .

[*She sobs brokenly against the counter.*]

LADY: Why did you come back here?

VAL: To put back the money I took so you wouldn't remember me as not honest or grateful – [*He picks up his guitar and starts to the door nodding gravely. She catches her breath; rushes to intercept him, spreading her arms like a crossbar over the door.*]

LADY: NO, NO, DON'T GO . . . I NEED YOU ! ! !

[*He faces her for five beats. The true passion of her outcry touches him then, and he turns about and crosses to the alcove. . . . As he draws the curtain across it he looks back at her.*]

TO LIVE. . . . TO GO ON LIVING ! ! !

[*Music fades in – 'Lady's Love Song' – guitar. He closes the curtain and turns on the light behind it, making it translucent. Through an opening in the alcove entrance, we see him sitting down with his guitar.* LADY *picks up the linen and crosses to the alcove like a spellbound child. Just outside it she stops, frozen with uncertainty, a conflict of feelings, but then he begins to whisper the words of a song so tenderly that she is able to draw the curtain open and enter the alcove. He looks up gravely at her from his guitar. She closes the curtain behind her. Its bizarre design, a gold tree with white birds and scarlet fruit in it, is softly translucent with the bulb lighted behind it. The guitar continues softly for a few moments, stops; the stage darkens till only the curtain of the alcove is clearly visible.*]

CURTAIN

SCENE ONE

[*An early morning. The Saturday before Easter. The sleeping alcove is lighted.* VAL *is smoking, half dressed, on the edge of the cot.* LADY *comes running, panting downstairs, her hair loose, in dressing robe and slippers and calls out in a panicky, shrill whisper.*]

LADY: Val! Val, he's comin' downstairs!

VAL [*hoarse with sleep*]: Who's – what?

LADY: Jabe!

VAL: Jabe?

LADY: I swear he is, he's coming downstairs!

VAL: What of it?

LADY: Jesus, will you get up and put some clothes on? The damned nurse told him that he could come down in the store to check over the stock! You want him to catch you half dressed on that bed there?

VAL: Don't he know I sleep here?

LADY: Nobody knows you sleep here but you and me.

[*Voices above.*]

Oh, God! – they've started.

NURSE: Don't hurry now. Take one step at a time.

[*Footsteps on stairs, slow, shuffling. The professional, nasal cheer of a nurse's voice.*]

LADY [*panicky*]: Get your shirt on! Come out!

NURSE: That's right. One step at a time, one step at a time, lean on my shoulder and take one step at a time.

[VAL *rises, still dazed from sleep.* LADY *gasps and sweeps the*

315

curtain across the alcove just a moment before the descending figures enter the sight-lines on the landing. LADY *breathes like an exhausted runner as she backs away from the alcove and assumes a forced smile.* JABE *and the nurse,* MISS PORTER, *appear on the landing of the stairs and at the same moment scudding clouds expose the sun. A narrow window on the landing admits a brilliant shaft of light upon the pair. They have a bizarre and awful appearance, the tall man, his rusty black suit hanging on him like an empty sack, his eyes burning malignantly from his yellow face, leaning on a stumpy little woman with bright pink or orange hair, clad all in starched white, with a voice that purrs with the faintly contemptuous cheer and sweetness of those hired to care for the dying.*]

NURSE: Aw, now, just look at that, that nice bright sun comin' out.

LADY: Miss Porter? – it's cold down here!

JABE: What's she say?

NURSE: She says it's cold down here.

LADY: The – the – the air's not warm enough yet, the air's not heated!

NURSE: He's determined to come right down, Mrs Torrance.

LADY: I know but –

NURSE: Wild horses couldn't hold him a minute longer.

JABE [*exhausted*]: – Let's – rest here a minute. . . .

LADY [*eagerly*]: Yes! Rest there a minute!

NURSE: Okay. We'll rest here a minute. . . .

[*They sit down side by side on a bench under the artificial palm tree in the shaft of light.* JABE *glares into the light like a fierce dying old beast. There are sounds from the alcove. To cover them up,* LADY *keeps making startled, laughing sounds in her throat, half laughing, half panting, chafing her hands together at the foot of the stairs, and coughing falsely.*]

JABE: Lady, what's wrong? Why are you so excited?

LADY: It seems like a miracle to me.

JABE: What seems like a miracle to you?

LADY: You coming downstairs.

JABE: You never thought I would come downstairs again?

LADY: Not this quick! Not as quick as this, Jabe! Did you think he would pick up as quick as this, Miss Porter?

[JABE *rises*.]

NURSE: Ready?

JABE: Ready.

NURSE: He's doing fine, knock wood.

LADY: Yes, knock wood, knock wood!

[*Drums counter loudly with her knuckles.* VAL *steps silently from behind the alcove curtain as the* NURSE *and* JABE *resume their slow, shuffling descent of the stairs.*]

[*Moving back to D.R.C.*] You got to be careful not to over-do. You don't want another setback. Ain't that right, Miss Porter?

NURSE: Well, it's my policy to mobilize the patient.

LADY [*to Val in a shrill whisper*]: Coffee's boiling, take the goddam coffee pot off the burner! [*She gives Val a panicky signal to go in the alcove.*]

JABE: Who're you talking to, Lady?

LADY: To – to – to Val, the clerk! I told him to – get you a – chair!

JABE: Who's that?

LADY: Val, Val, the clerk, you know Val!

JABE: Not yet. I'm anxious to meet him. Where is he?

LADY: Right here, right here, here's Val!

[VAL *returns from the alcove.*]

JABE: He's here bright and early.

LADY: The early bird catches the worm!

JABE: That's right. Where is the worm?

LADY [*loudly*]: Ha ha!

NURSE: Careful! One step at a time, Mr Torrance.

LADY: Saturday before Easter's our biggest sales-day of the year, I mean second biggest, but sometimes it's even bigger than Christmas Eve! So I told Val to get here a half-hour early.

[JABE *misses his step and stumbles to foot of stairs.* LADY *screams.* NURSE *rushes down to him.* VAL *advances and raises the man to his feet.*]

VAL: Here. Here.

LADY: Oh, my God.

NURSE: Oh, oh!

JABE: I'm all right.

NURSE: Are you sure?

LADY: Are you sure?

JABE: Let me go! [*He staggers to lean against counter, panting, glaring, with a malignant smile.*]

LADY: Oh, my God. Oh, my – God. . . .

JABE: This is the boy that works here?

LADY: Yes, this is the clerk I hired to help us out, Jabe.

JABE: How is he doing?

LADY: Fine, fine.

JABE: He's mighty good-looking. Do women give him much trouble?

LADY: When school lets out the high-school girls are thick as flies in this store!

JABE: How about older women? Don't he attract older women? The older ones are the buyers, they got the money. They sweat it out of their husbands and throw it away! What's your salary, boy, how much do I pay you?

LADY: Twenty-two fifty a week.

JABE: You're getting him cheap.

VAL: I get – commissions.

JABE: Commissions?

VAL: Yes. One per cent of all sales.

JABE: Oh? Oh? I didn't know about that.

LADY: I knew he would bring in trade and he brings it in.

JABE: I bet.

LADY: Val, get Jabe a chair, he ought to sit down.

JABE: No, I don't want to sit down. I want to take a look at the new confectionery.

LADY: Oh, yes, yes! Take a look at it! Val, Val, turn on the lights in the confectionery! I want Jabe to see the way I done it over! I'm – real – *proud*!

[VAL *crosses and switches on lights in confectionery. The bulbs in the arches and the juke box light up.*]

Go in and look at it, Jabe. I am real proud of it!

[*He stares at Lady a moment; then shuffles slowly into the spectral radiance of the confectionery.* LADY *moves D.C. At the same time a calliope becomes faintly audible and slowly but steadily builds.* MISS PORTER *goes with the patient, holding his elbow.*]

VAL [*returning to Lady*]: He looks like death.

LADY [*moving away from him*]: *Hush!*

[VAL *goes up above counter and stands in the shadows.*]

NURSE: Well, isn't this artistic?

JABE: Yeh. Artistic as hell.

NURSE: I never seen anything like it before.

JABE: Nobody else did either.

NURSE [*coming back to U.R.C.*]: Who done these decorations?

LADY [*defiantly*]: I did them, all by myself!

NURSE: What do you know. It sure is something artistic.

[*Calliope is now up loud.*]

JABE [*coming back to D.R.*]: Is there a circus or carnival in the county?

LADY: What?

JABE: That sounds like a circus calliope on the highway.

LADY: That's no circus calliope. It's advertising the gala open-ing of the Torrance Confectionery tonight!

JABE: Doing what did you say?

LADY: It's announcing the opening of our confectionery, it's going all over Glorious Hill this morning and all over Sunset and Lyon this afternoon. Hurry on here so you can see it go by the store. [*She rushes excitedly to open the front door as the ragtime music of the calliope approaches.*]

JABE: I married a live one, Miss Porter. How much does that damn' thing cost me?

LADY: You'll be surprised how little. [*She is talking with a hysterical vivacity now.*] I hired it for a song!

JABE: How much of a song did you hire it for?

LADY [*closing door*]: Next to nothing, seven-fifty an hour! And it covers three towns in Two River County!

[*Calliope fades out.*]

JABE [*with a muted ferocity*]: Miss Porter, I married a live one! Didn't I marry a live one? [*Switches off lights in confectionery.*] Her daddy 'The Wop' was just as much of a live one till he burned up.

[LADY *gasps as if struck.*]

[*With a slow, ugly grin*] He had a wine garden on the north shore of Moon Lake. The new confectionery sort of reminds me of it. But he made a mistake, he made a bad mistake, one time, selling liquor to niggers. We burned him out. We burned him out, house and orchard and vines and 'The Wop' was burned up trying to fight the fire. [*He turns.*] I think I better go up.

LADY: – Did you say 'WE'?

320

JABE: – I have a kind of a cramp. . . .

NURSE [*taking his arm*]: Well, let's go up.

JABE: – Yes, I better go up. . . .

[*They cross to stairs. Calliope fades in.*]

LADY [*almost shouting as she moves D.C.*]: Jabe, did you say 'WE' did it, did you say 'WE' did it?

JABE [*at foot of stairs, stops, turns*]: Yes, I said '*We*' did it. You heard me, Lady.

NURSE: One step at a time, one step at a time, take it easy.

[*They ascend gradually to the landing and above. The calliope passes directly before the store and a clown is seen, or heard, shouting through megaphone.*]

CLOWN: Don't forget tonight, folks, the gala opening of the Torrance Confectionery, free drinks and free favours, don't forget it, the gala opening of the confectionery.

[*Fade.* JABE *and the* NURSE *disappear above the landing. Calliope gradually fades. A hoarse cry above. The* NURSE *runs back downstairs.*]

NURSE: He's bleeding, he's having a hemm'rhage! [*Runs to phone.*] Dr Buchanan's office! [*Turns again to Lady.*] Your husband is having a hemm'rhage!

[*Calliope is loud still.* LADY *appears not to hear.*]

LADY [*to Val*]: Did you hear what he said? He said 'We' did it, 'WE' burned – house – vines – orchard – 'The Wop' burned fighting the fire. . . .

[*The scene dims out; calliope fades out.*]

SCENE TWO

[*Sunset of the same day. At rise* VAL *is alone. He is standing stock-still down centre stage, almost beneath the proscenium, in the tense, frozen attitude of a wild animal listening to something that warns it of danger, his head turned as if he were looking off stage left, out over the house, frowning slightly, attentively. After a moment he mutters something sharply, and his body relaxes; he takes out a cigarette and crosses to the store entrance, opens the door and stands looking out. It has been raining steadily and will rain again in a while, but right now it is clearing: the sun breaks through, suddenly, with great brilliance; and almost at the same instant, at some distance, a woman cries out a great hoarse cry of terror and exaltation; the cry is repeated as she comes running nearer.*

VEE TALBOTT *appears through the window as if blind and demented, stiff, groping gestures, shielding her eyes with one arm as she feels along the store window for the entrance, gasping for breath.* VAL *steps aside, taking hold of her arm to guide her into the store. For a few moments she leans weakly, blindly panting for breath against the oval glass of the door, then calls out.*]

VEE: I'm – *struck blind!*

VAL: You can't see?

VEE: – No! Nothing. . . .

VAL [*assisting her to stool below counter*]: Set down here, Mrs Talbott.

VEE: – Where?

VAL [*pushing her gently*]: Here.

[VEE *sinks moaning on to stool.*]

What hurt your eyes, Mrs Talbott, what happened to your eyes?

VEE [*drawing a long, deep breath*]: The vision I waited and prayed for all my life long!

VAL: You had a vision?

VEE: I saw the eyes of my Saviour! – They struck me blind. [*Leans forward, clasping her eyes in anguish.*] Ohhhh, they burned out my eyes!

VAL: Lean back.

VEE: Eyeballs burn like fire. . . .

VAL [*going off R.*]: I'll get you something cold to put on your eyes.

VEE: I knew a vision was coming, oh, I had many signs!

VAL [*in confectionery*]: It must be a terrible shock to have a vision. . . . [*He speaks gravely, gently, scooping chipped ice from the soft-drink cooler and wrapping it in his handkerchief.*]

VEE [*with the naïveté of a child as* VAL *comes back to her*]: I thought I would see my Saviour on the day of His passion, which was yesterday, Good Friday, that's when I expected to see Him. But I was mistaken, I was – disappointed. Yesterday passed and nothing, nothing much happened but – today –

[VAL *places handkerchief over her eyes.*]

– this afternoon, somehow I pulled myself together and walked outdoors and started to go to pray in the empty church and meditate on the Rising of Christ tomorrow. Along the road as I walked, thinking about the mysteries of Easter, veils! –

[*She makes a long shuddering word out of 'veils'.*]

– seemed to drop off my eyes! Light, oh, light! I never have seen such brilliance! It PRICKED my eyeballs like NEEDLES!

VAL: Light?

VEE: Yes, yes, light. YOU know, you know we live in light and shadow, that's what we *live* in, a world of – *light* and – *shadow*. . . .

VAL: Yes. In light and shadow. [*He nods with complete understanding and agreement. They are like two children who have found life's meaning, simply and quietly, along a country road.*]

VEE: A world of light and shadow is what we live in, and – it's – confusing. . . .

[*A man is peering in at store window.*]

VAL: Yeah, they – *do* get – *mixed*. . . .

VEE: Well, and then – [*hesitates to recapture her vision*] – I heard this clap of thunder! Sky! – Split open! – And there in the split-open sky, I saw, I tell you, I *saw* the TWO HUGE BLAZING EYES OF JESUS CHRIST RISEN! – Not crucified but Risen! I mean Crucified and *then* RISEN! – The blazing eyes of Christ Risen! And then a great – [*Raises both arms and makes a great sweeping motion to describe an apocalyptic disturbance of the atmosphere*] – His hand! – *Invisible!* – I didn't *see* his hand! – But it *touched* me – here! [*She seizes Val's hand and presses it to her great heaving bosom.*]

TALBOTT [*appearing R. in confectionery, furiously*]: VEE!

[*She starts up, throwing the compress from her eyes. Utters a sharp gasp and staggers backward with terror and blasted ecstasy and dismay and belief, all confused in her look.*]

VEE: You!

TALBOTT: VEE!

VEE: *You!*

TALBOTT [*advancing*]: VEE!

VEE [*making two syllables of the word 'eyes'*]: – The Ey – es! [*She collapses, forward, falls to her knees, her arms thrown about Val. He seizes her to lift her. Two or three men are peering in at the store window.*]

TALBOTT [*pushing Val away*]: Let go of her, don't put your

hands on my wife! [*He seizes her roughly and hauls her to the door.* VAL *moves up to help Vee.*] Don't move. [*At door to Val*] I'm coming back.

VAL: I'm not goin' nowhere.

TALBOTT [*to Dog, as he goes off L. with Vee*]: Dog, go in there with that boy.

VOICE [*outside*]: Sheriff caught him messin' with his wife.

[*Repeat:* ANOTHER VOICE *at a distance.* 'DOG' HAMMA *enters and stands silently beside the door while there is a continued murmur of excited voices on the street. The following scene should be underplayed, played almost casually, like the performance of some familiar ritual.*]

VAL: What do you want?

[DOG *says nothing but removes from his pocket and opens a spring-blade knife and moves to D.R.* PEE WEE *enters. Through the open door – voices.*]

VOICES [*outside*]: Son of a low-down bitch foolin' with –
– That's right, ought to be –
– Cut the son of a –

VAL: What do you – ?

[PEE WEE *closes the door and silently stands beside it, opening a spring-blade knife.* VAL *looks from one to the other.*]

– it's six o'clock. Store's closed.

[*Men chuckle like dry leaves rattling.* VAL *crosses toward the door; is confronted by* TALBOTT; *stops short.*]

TALBOTT: Boy, I said stay here.

VAL: I'm not – goin' nowhere. . . .

TALBOTT: Stand back under that light.

VAL: Which light?

TALBOTT: That light.

[*Points.* VAL *goes behind counter.*]

I want to look at you while I run through some photos of men wanted.

VAL: I'm not wanted.

TALBOTT: A good-looking boy like you is always wanted.

[*Men chuckle.* VAL *stands in hot light under green-shaded bulb.* TALBOTT *shuffles through photos he has removed from his pocket.*]

– How tall are you, boy?

VAL: Never measured.

TALBOTT: How much do you weigh?

VAL: Never weighed.

TALBOTT: Got any scars or marks of identification on your face or body?

VAL: No, sir.

TALBOTT: Open your shirt.

VAL: What for? [*He doesn't.*]

TALBOTT: Open his shirt for him, Dog.

[DOG *steps quickly forward and rips shirt open to waist.* VAL *starts forward; men point knives; he draws back.*]

That's right, stay there, boy. What did you do before?

[PEE WEE *sits on stairs.*]

VAL: Before – what?

TALBOTT: Before you come here?

VAL: – Travelled and – played. . . .

TALBOTT: Played?

DOG [*advancing to C.*]: What?

PEE WEE: With wimmen?

[DOG *laughs.*]

VAL: No. Played guitar – and sang. . . .

326

[VAL *touches guitar on counter.*]

TALBOTT: Let me see that guitar.

VAL: Look at it. But don't touch it. I don't let nobody but musicians touch it.

[*Men come close.*]

DOG: What're you smiling for, boy?

PEE WEE: He ain't smiling, his mouth's just twitching like a dead chicken's foot.

[*They laugh.*]

TALBOTT: What is all that writing on the guitar?

VAL: – Names. . . .

TALBOTT: What of?

VAL: Autographs of musicians dead and living.

[*Men read aloud the names printed on the guitar: Bessie Smith, Leadbelly, Woody Guthrie, Jelly Roll Morton, etc. They bend close to it, keeping the open knife blades pointed at Val's body;* DOG *touches neck of the guitar, draws it toward him.* VAL *suddenly springs, with catlike agility, on to the counter. He runs along it, kicking at their hands as they catch at his legs. The* NURSE *runs down to the landing.*]

MISS PORTER: *What's going on?*

TALBOTT [*at the same time*]: *Stop that!*

[JABE *calls hoarsely above.*]

MISS PORTER [*excitedly, all in one breath, as Jabe calls*]:Where's Mrs Torrance? I got a very sick man up there and his wife's disappeared.

[JABE *calls out again.*]

I been on a whole lot of cases but never seen one where a wife showed no concern for a –

327

[JABE *cries out again. Her voice fades out as she returns above.*]

TALBOTT [*overlapping Nurse's speech*]: Dog! Pee Wee! You all stand back from that counter. Dog, why don't you an' Pee Wee go up an' see Jabe. Leave me straighten this boy out, go on, go on up.

PEE WEE: C'mon, Dawg. . . .

[*They go up.* VAL *remains panting on counter.*]

TALBOTT [*sits on shoe chair at R. window. In* TALBOTT'*s manner there is a curious, half-abashed gentleness, when alone with the boy, as if he recognized the purity in him and was, truly, for the moment, ashamed of the sadism implicit in the occurrence*]: Awright, boy. Git on down off th' counter, I ain't gonna touch y'r guitar.

[VAL *jumps off counter.*]

But I'm gonna tell you something. They's a certain county I know of which has a big sign at the county line that says, 'Nigger, don't let the sun go down on you in this county.' That's all it says, it don't threaten nothing, it just says, 'Nigger, don't let the sun go down on you in this county!' [*Chuckles hoarsely. Rises and takes a step towards Val.*] Well, son! You ain't a nigger and this is not that county, but, son, I want you to just imagine that you seen a sign that said to you: 'Boy, don't let the sun rise on you in this county.' I said 'rise', not 'go down' because it's too close to sunset for you to git packed an' move on before that. But I think if you value that instrument in your hands as much as you seem to, you'll simplify my job by not allowing the sun tomorrow to rise on you in this county. 'S that understood, now, boy?

[VAL *stares at him, expressionless, panting.*]

[*Crossing to door*] I hope so. I don't like *violence.*

[*He looks back and nods at Val from the door. Then goes outside in the fiery afterglow of the sunset. Dogs bark in the distance. Music fades in: 'Dog Howl Blues' minor – guitar. Pause in which* VAL *remains motionless, cradling guitar in his arms. Then* VAL's *faraway, troubled look is resolved in a slight, abrupt nod of his head. He sweeps back the alcove curtain and enters the alcove and closes the curtain behind him. Lights dim down to indicate a division of scenes.*]

SCENE THREE

Half an hour later. The lighting is less realistic than in the previous scenes of the play. The interior of the store is so dim that only the vertical lines of the pillar and such selected items as the palm tree on the stair landing and the ghostly paper vineyard of the confectionery are plainly visible. The view through the great front window has virtually become the background of the action. A singing wind sweeps clouds before the moon so that the witchlike country brightens and dims and brightens again. The Marshall's hounds are restless: their baying is heard now and then. A lamp outside the door sometimes catches a figure that moves past with mysterious urgency, calling out softly and raising an arm to beckon, like a shade in the under kingdom.

[*At rise, or when the stage is lighted again, it is empty but footsteps are descending the stairs as* DOLLY *and* BEULAH *rush into the store and call out, in soft shouts.*]

DOLLY: Dawg?

BEULAH: Pee Wee?

EVA TEMPLE [*appearing on landing and calling down softly in the superior tone of a privileged attendant in a sick-chamber*]: Please don't shout! – Mr Binnings and Mr Hamma [*names of the*

two husbands] are upstairs sitting with Jabe. . . . [*She continues her descent. Then* SISTER TEMPLE *appears, sobbing, on landing.*]
– Come down carefully, Sister.

SISTER: Help me, I'm all to pieces. . . .

[EVA *ignores this request and faces the two women.*]

BEULAH: Has the bleedin' quit yit?

EVA: The haemorrhage seems to have stopped. Sister, Sister, pull yourself together, we all have to face these things sometime in life.

DOLLY: Has he sunk into a coma?

EVA: No. Cousin Jabe is conscious. Nurse Porter says his pulse is remarkably strong for a man that lost so much blood. Of course he's had a transfusion.

SISTER: Two of 'em.

EVA [*crossing to Dolly*]: Yais, an' they put him on glucose. His strength came back like magic.

BEULAH: She up there?

EVA: *Who?*

BEULAH: Lady!

EVA: No! When last reported she had just stepped into the Glorious Hill Beauty Parlour.

BEULAH: You don't mean it.

EVA: Ask Sister!

SISTER: She's planning to go ahead with – !

EVA: – the gala opening of the confectionery. Switch on the lights in there, Sister.

[SISTER *crosses and switches on lights and moves off R. The decorated confectionery is lighted.* DOLLY *and* BEULAH *exclaim in awed voices.*]

– Of course it's not normal behaviour; it's downright lunacy, but still that's no excuse for it! And when she called up at five, about one hour ago, it wasn't to ask about Jabe, oh, no, she didn't mention his name. She asked if Ruby Light-foot had delivered a case of Seagram's. Yais, she just shouted that question and hung up the phone, before I could – [*She crosses and goes off R.*]

BEULAH [*going into confectionery*]: *Oh, I understand, now! Now I see what she's up to!* Electric moon, cut-out silver-paper stars, and artificial vines? Why, it's her father's wine garden on Moon Lake she's turned this room into!

DOLLY [*suddenly as she sits in shoe chair*]: *Here she comes, here she comes!*

[*The* TEMPLE SISTERS *retreat from view in confectionery as* LADY *enters the store. She wears a hooded rain-cape and carries a large paper shopping bag and paper carton box.*]

LADY: Go on, ladies, don't stop, my ears are burning!

BEULAH [*coming in to U.R.C.*]: – Lady, oh, Lady, Lady. . . .

LADY: Why d'you speak my name in that pitiful voice? Hanh? [*Throws back hood of cape, her eyes blazing, and places bag and box on counter.*] Val? Val! Where is that boy that works here?

[DOLLY *shakes her head.*]

I guess he's havin' a T-bone steak with French fries and coleslaw fo' ninety-five cents at the Blue Bird. . . .

[*Sounds in confectionery.*]

Who's in the confectionery, is that you, Val?

[TEMPLE SISTERS *emerge and stalk past her.*]

Going, girls?

[*They go out of store.*]

Yes, gone! [*She laughs and throws off rain-cape, on to counter, revealing a low-cut gown, triple strand of pearls, and a purple satin-ribboned corsage.*]

331

BEULAH [*sadly*]: How long have I known you, Lady?

LADY [*going behind counter, unpacks paper hats and whistles*]: A long time, Beulah. I think you remember when my people come here on a banana boat from Palermo, Sicily, by way of Caracas, Venezuela, yes, with a grind-organ and a monkey my papa had bought in Venezuela. I was not much bigger than the monkey, ha ha! You remember the monkey, but he was a liar, it was a very old monkey, it was on its last legs, ha ha ha! But it was a well-dressed monkey. [*Coming around to R. of counter*] It had a green velvet suit and a little red cap that it tipped and a tambourine that it passed around for money, ha ha ha. . . . The grind-organ played and the monkey danced in the sun, ha ha! – '*O Sole Mio, Da Da Da daaa . . . !*' [*Sits in chair at counter*] – One day, the monkey danced too much in the sun and it was a very old monkey and it dropped dead. . . . My Papa, he turned to the people, he made them a bow, and he said, 'The show is over, the monkey is dead.' Ha ha!

[*Slight pause. Then* DOLLY *pipes up venomously.*]

DOLLY: Ain't it wonderful Lady can be so brave?

BEULAH: Yaiss, wonderful! Hanh . . .

LADY: For me the show is not over, the monkey is not dead yet! [*Then suddenly*] Val, is that you, Val?

[*Someone has entered the confectionery door, out of sight, and the draught of air has set the wind-chimes tinkling wildly.* LADY *rushes forward but stops short as* CAROL *appears. She wears a trench coat and a white sailor's cap with a turned-down brim, inscribed with the name of a vessel and a date, past or future, memory or anticipation.*]

DOLLY: Well, here's your first customer, Lady.

LADY [*going behind counter*]: – Carol, that room ain't open.

CAROL: There's a big sign outside that says 'Open Tonite!'

LADY: It ain't open to you.

CAROL: I have to stay here a while. They stopped my car, you see, I don't have a licence; my licence has been revoked and I have to find someone to drive me across the river.

LADY: You can call a taxi.

CAROL: I heard that the boy that works for you is leaving tonight and I –

LADY: *Who said he's leaving?*

CAROL [*crossing to counter*]: Sheriff Talbott. The County Marshal suggested I get him to drive me over the river since he'd be crossing it too.

LADY: You got some mighty wrong information!

CAROL: Where is he? I don't see him?

LADY: Why d'you keep coming back here bothering that boy? He's not interested in you! Why would he be leaving here tonight?

[*Door opens off as she comes from behind counter.*]

Val, is that you, Val?

[CONJURE MAN *enters through confectionery, mumbling rapidly, holding out something.* BEULAH *and* DOLLY *take flight out the door with cries of revulsion.*]

No conjure stuff, go away!

[*He starts to withdraw.*]

CAROL [*crossing to U.R.C.*]: Uncle! The Choctaw cry! I'll give you a dollar for it.

[LADY *turns away with a gasp, with a gesture of refusal. The* NEGRO *nods, then throws back his turkey neck and utters a series of sharp barking sounds that rise to a sustained cry of great intensity and wildness. The cry produces a violent reaction in the building.* BEULAH *and* DOLLY *run out of the store.* LADY *does not move but she catches her breath.* DOG *and* PEE WEE *run down the stairs with ad libs and hustle the* NEGRO

out of the store, ignoring LADY, *as their wives call:* 'PEE
WEE!' *and* 'DAWG!' *outside on the walk.* VAL *sweeps back
the alcove curtain and appears as if the cry were his cue. Above,
in the sick room, hoarse, outraged shouts that subside with
exhaustion.* CAROL *crosses downstage and speaks to the
audience and to herself.*]

CAROL: Something is still wild in the country! This country
used to be wild, the men and women were wild and there
was a wild sort of sweetness in their hearts, for each other,
but now it's sick with neon, it's broken out sick, with neon,
like most other places. . . . I'll wait outside in my car. It's the
fastest thing on wheels in Two River County!

[*She goes out of the store R.* LADY *stares at Val with great
asking eyes, a hand to her throat.*]

LADY [*with false boldness*]: Well, ain't you going with her?
VAL: I'm going with no one I didn't come here with. And I
come here with no one.
LADY: Then get into your white jacket. I need your services
in that room there tonight.

[VAL *regards her steadily for several beats.*]

[*Clapping her hands together twice*] Move, move, stop goofing! The Delta Brilliant lets out in half'n hour and they'll
be driving up here. You got to shave ice for the setups!
VAL [*as if he thought she'd gone crazy*]: 'Shave ice for the setups'? [*He moves up to counter.*]
LADY: Yes, an' call Ruby Lightfoot, tell her I need me a dozen
more half-pints of Seagram's. They all call for Seven-and-
Sevens. You know how t' sell bottle goods under a counter?
It's O.K. We're gonna git paid for protection. [*Gasps, touching her diaphragm.*] But one thing you gotta watch out for is
sellin' to minors. Don't serve liquor to minors. Ask for his
driver's licence if they's any doubt. Anybody born earlier

than – let's see, twenty-one from – oh, I'll figure it later.
Hey! Move! Move! Stop goofing!

VAL [*placing guitar on counter*]: – You're the one that's goofing,
not me, Lady.

LADY: Move, I said, *move!*

VAL: What kick are you on, are you on a benny kick, Lady?
've you washed down a couple of bennies with a pot of
black coffee t' make you come on strong for th' three
o'clock show? [*His mockery is gentle, almost tender, but he has
already made a departure; he is back in the all-night bars with the
B-girls and raffish entertainers. He stands at counter as she rushes
about. As she crosses between the two rooms, he reaches out to
catch hold of her bare arm and he pulls her to him and grips her
arms.*]

LADY: Hey!

VAL: Will you quit thrashin' around like a hooked catfish?

LADY: Go git in y'r white jacket an' –

VAL: Sit down. I want to talk to you.

LADY: I don't have time.

VAL: I got to reason with you.

LADY: It's not possible to.

VAL: You can't open a night-place here this night.

LADY: You bet your sweet life I'm *going* to!

VAL: Not *me*, not *my* sweet life!

LADY: I'm betting *my* life on it! Sweet or *not* sweet, I'm –

VAL: Yours is yours, mine is mine. . . . [*He releases her with a sad
shrug.*]

LADY: You don't get the point, huh? There's a man up there
that set fire to my father's wine garden and I lost my life
in it, yeah, I lost my life in it, *three* lives was lost in it, two
born lives and *one* – *not*. . . . I was made to commit a *murder*
by him up there! [*Has frozen momentarily*] – I want that man
to see the wine garden come open again when he's dying!
I want him to hear it coming open again here tonight!
While he's dying. It's necessary, no power on earth can

stop it. Hell, I don't even want it, it's just necessary, it's just something's got to be done to square things away, to, to, to – be *not defeated! You get me? Just to be not defeated!* Ah, oh, I won't be defeated, not again, in my life! [*Embraces him.*] Thank you for staying here with me! – God bless you for it. . . . Now please go and get in your white jacket. . . .

[VAL *looks at her as if he were trying to decide between a natural sensibility of heart and what his life's taught him since he left Witches' Bayou. Then he sighs again, with the same slight, sad shrug, and crosses into alcove to put on a jacket and remove from under his cot a canvas-wrapped package of his belongings.* LADY *takes paper hats and carnival stuff from counter, crosses into confectionery, and puts them on the tables, then starts back but stops short as she sees* VAL *come out of alcove with his snakeskin jacket and luggage.*]

LADY: That's not your white jacket, that's that snakeskin jacket you had on when you come here.

VAL: I come and I go in this jacket.

LADY: Go, did you say?

VAL: Yes, ma'am, I did, I said go. All that stays to be settled is a little matter of wages.

[*The dreaded thing's happened to her. This is what they call 'the moment of truth' in the bull ring, when the matador goes in over the horns of the bull to plant the mortal sword-thrust.*]

LADY: – So you're – cutting out, are you?

VAL: My gear's all packed. I'm catchin' the southbound bus.

LADY: Uh-huh, in a pig's eye. You're not conning me, mister. She's waiting for you outside in her high-powered car and you're –

[*Sudden footsteps on stairs. They break apart,* VAL *puts suitcase down, drawing back into shadow, as* NURSE PORTER *appears on the stair landing.*]

NURSE PORTER: Mrs Torrance, are you down there?

LADY [crossing to foot of stairs]: Yeah, I'm here. I'm back.

NURSE PORTER: Can I talk to you up here about Mr Torrance?

LADY [shouting to Nurse]: I'll be up in a minute.

[Door closes above. LADY turns to Val.]

O.K. now, mister. You're scared about something, ain't you?

VAL: I been threatened with violence if I stay here.

LADY: I got paid for protection in this county, plenty paid for it, and it covers you too.

VAL: No, ma'am. My time is up here.

LADY: Y' say that like you'd served a sentence in jail.

VAL: I got in deeper than I meant to, Lady.

LADY: Yeah, and how about me?

VAL [going to her]: I would of cut out before you got back to the store, but I wanted to tell you something I never told no one before. [Places hand on her shoulder.] I feel a true love for you, Lady! [He kisses her.] I'll wait for you out of this county, just name the time and the . . .

LADY [moving back]: Oh, don't talk about love, not to me. It's easy to say 'Love, Love!' with fast and free transportation waiting right out the door for you!

VAL: D'you remember some things I told you about me the night we met here?

LADY [crossing to R.C.]: Yeah, many things. Yeah, temperature of a dog. And some bird, oh, yeah, without legs so it had to sleep on the wind!

VAL [through her speech]: Naw, not that; not that.

LADY: And how you could burn down a woman? I said 'Bull!' I take that back. You can! You can burn down a woman and stamp on her ashes to make sure the fire is put out!

VAL: I mean what I said about gettin' away from . . .

337

LADY: How long've you held this first steady job in your life?

VAL: Too long, too long!

LADY: Four months and five days, mister. All right! How much pay have you took?

VAL: I told you to keep out all but –

LADY: Y'r living expenses. I can give you the figures to a dime. Eighty-five bucks, no, ninety! Chicken-feed, mister! Y'know how much you got coming? If you get it? I don't need paper to figure, I got it all in my head. You got five hundred and eighty-six bucks coming to you, not, not chicken-feed, that. But, mister. [*Gasps for breath.*] – If you try to walk out on me, now, tonight, without notice! – You're going to get just nothing! A great big zero. . . .

> [*Sómebody hollers at door off R.: 'Hey! You open?' She rushes toward it shouting,* 'CLOSED! CLOSED! GO AWAY!' – VAL *crosses to the cashbox. She turns back toward him, gasps.*]

Now you watch your next move and I'll watch mine. You open that cashbox and I swear I'll throw open that door and holler, clerk's robbing the store!

VAL: – Lady?

LADY [*fiercely*]: Hanh?

VAL: – Nothing, you've –

LADY: – Hanh?

VAL: Blown your stack. I will go without pay.

LADY [*coming to C.*]: Then you ain't understood me! With or without pay, you're staying!

VAL: I've got my gear. [*Picks up suitcase. She rushes to seize his guitar.*]

LADY: Then I'll go up and git mine! And take this with me, just t'make sure you wait till I'm – [*She moves back to R.C. He puts suitcase down.*]

VAL [*advancing towards her*]: Lady, what're you – ?

LADY [*entreating with guitar raised*]: Don't – !

VAL: – doing with –

338

LADY: – *Don't!*

VAL: – my guitar!

LADY: *Holding it for security while I –*

VAL: Lady, you been a lunatic since this morning!

LADY: Longer, longer than morning! I'm going to keep hold of your 'life companion' while I pack! I am! I am goin' to pack an' go, if you go, where you go!

[*He makes a move toward her. She crosses below and around to counter.*]

You didn't think so, you actually didn't think so! What was I going to do, in your opinion? What, in your opinion, would I be doing? Stay on here in a store full of bottles and boxes while you go far, while you go fast and far, without me having your – forwarding address! – even?

VAL: I'll – give you a forwarding address. . . .

LADY: Thanks, oh, thanks! Would I take your forwarding address back of that curtain? 'Oh, dear forwarding address, hold me, kiss me, be faithful!' [*Utters grotesque, stifled cry; presses fist to mouth.*]

[*He advances cautiously, hand stretched towards the guitar. She retreats above to U.R.C., biting lip, eyes flaring.* JABE *knocks above.*]

Stay back! You want me to smash it!

VAL [*D.C.*]: He's – knocking for you. . . .

LADY: I know! Death's knocking for me! Don't you think I hear him, knock, knock, knock? It sounds like what it is! Bones knocking bones. . . . Ask me how it felt to be coupled with death up there, and I can tell you. My skin crawled when he touched me. But I endured it. I guess my heart knew that somebody must be coming to take me out of this hell! You did. You came. Now look at me! I'm alive once more! [*Convulsive sobbing controlled: continues more calmly and harshly*]

– I won't wither in dark! Got that through your skull? Now.
Listen! Everything in this rotten store is yours, not just your
pay, but everything – Death's scraped together down here!
– but Death has got to die before we can go. . . . You got that
memorized, now? – Then get into your white jacket! –
Tonight is the gala opening – [*Rushes through confectionery.*] –
of the confectionery –

[VAL *runs and seizes her arm holding guitar. She breaks
violently free.*]

*Smash me against a rock and I'll smash your guitar! I will, if
you –*

[*Rapid footsteps on stairs.*]

Oh, Miss Porter!

[*She motions Val back. He retreats into alcove.* LADY *puts
guitar down beside juke-box.* MISS PORTER *is descending the
stairs.*]

NURSE PORTER [*descending watchfully*]: You been out a long
time.

LADY [*moving U.R.C.*]: Yeah, well, I had lots of – [*Her voice
expires breathlessly. She stares fiercely, blindly, into the other's
hard face.*]

NURSE PORTER: – Of what?

LADY: Things to – things to – take care of. . . . [*Draws a deep,
shuddering breath, clenched fist to her bosom.*]

NURSE PORTER: Didn't I hear you shouting to someone just
now?

LADY: – Uh-huh. Some drunk tourist made a fuss because I
wouldn't sell him no – liquor. . . .

NURSE [*crossing to the door*]: Oh, Mr Torrance is sleeping under
medication.

LADY: That's good. [*She sits in shoe-fitting chair.*]

NURSE: I gave him a hypo at five.

LADY: – Don't all that morphine weaken the heart, Miss Porter?

NURSE: Gradually, yes.

LADY: How long does it usually take for them to let go?

NURSE: It varies according to the age of the patient and the condition his heart's in. Why?

LADY: Miss Porter, don't people sort of help them let go?

NURSE: How do you mean, Mrs Torrance?

LADY: Shorten their suffering for them?

NURSE: Oh, I see what you mean. [*Snaps her purse shut.*] – I see what you mean, Mrs Torrance. But killing is killing, regardless of circumstances.

LADY: Nobody said killing.

NURSE: You said 'shorten their suffering'.

LADY: Yes, like merciful people shorten an animal's suffering when he's . . .

NURSE: A human being is not the same as an animal, Mrs Torrance. And I don't hold with what they call –

LADY [*overlapping*]: *Don't give me a sermon,* Miss Porter, I just wanted to know if –

NURSE [*overlapping*]: I'm not giving a sermon. I just answered your question. If you want to get somebody to shorten your husband's life –

LADY [*jumping up; overlapping*]: Why, how dare you say that I –

NURSE: I'll be back at ten-thirty.

LADY: Don't!

NURSE: What?

LADY [*crossing behind counter*]: Don't come back at ten-thirty, don't come back.

NURSE: I'm always discharged by the doctors on my cases.

LADY: This time you're being discharged by the patient's wife.

NURSE: That's something we'll have to discuss with Dr Buchanan.

341

LADY: I'll call him myself about it. I don't like you. I don't think you belong in the nursing profession, you have cold eyes; I think you like to watch pain!

NURSE: I know why you don't like my eyes. [*Snaps purse shut.*] You don't like my eyes because you know they see clear.

LADY: Why are you staring at *me*?

NURSE: I'm not staring at you, I'm staring at the curtain. There's something burning in there, smoke's coming out! [*Starts towards alcove.*] Oh.

LADY: Oh, no, you don't. [*Seizes her arm.*]

NURSE [*pushes her roughly aside and crosses to the curtain.* VAL *rises from cot, opens the curtain, and faces her coolly*]: Oh, excuse me! [*She turns to Lady.*] – The moment I looked at you when I was called on this case last Friday morning I knew that you were pregnant.

[LADY *gasps.*]

I also knew the moment I looked at your husband it wasn't by him.

[*She stalks to the door.* LADY *suddenly cries out.*]

LADY: Thank you for telling me what I hoped for is true.

MISS PORTER: You don't seem to have any shame.

LADY [*exalted*]: No. I don't have shame. I have – *great* – *joy!*

MISS PORTER [*venomously*]: Then why don't you get the calliope and the clown to make the announcement?

LADY: You do it for me, save me the money! Make the announcement, all over!

[NURSE *goes out.* VAL *crosses swiftly to the door and locks it. Then he advances toward her.*]

VAL: Is it true what she said?

[LADY *moves as if stunned to the counter; the stunned look gradually turns to a look of wonder. On the counter is a heap*

*of silver and gold paper hats and trumpets for the gala opening
of the confectionery.*]

VAL [*in a hoarse whisper*]: Is it true or not true, what the woman
told you?

LADY: You sound like a scared little boy.

VAL: She's gone out to tell.

[*Pause.*]

LADY: You gotta go now – it's dangerous for you to stay
here.... Take your pay out of the cashbox, you can go. Go,
go, take the keys to my car, cross the river into some other
county. You've done what you came here to do....

VAL: – It's true then, it's – ?

LADY [*sitting in chair of counter*]: True as God's word! I have
life in my body, this dead tree, my body, has burst in flower!
You've given me life, you can go!

[*He crouches down gravely opposite her, gently takes hold of
her knotted fingers, and draws them to his lips, breathing on
them as if to warm them. She sits bolt upright, tense, blind as a
clairvoyant.*]

VAL: – Why didn't you tell me before?

LADY: – When a woman's been childless as long as I've been
childless, it's hard to believe that you're still able to bear! –
We used to have a little fig tree between the house and the
orchard. It never bore any fruit, they said it was barren.
Time went by it, spring after useless spring, and it almost
started to – die.... Then one day I discovered a small green
fig on the tree they said wouldn't bear! [*She is clasping a gilt
paper horn.*] I ran through the orchard. I ran through the
wine garden shouting, 'Oh, Father, it's going to bear, the
fig tree is going to bear!' – It seemed such a wonderful thing,
after those ten barren springs, for the little fig tree to bear,
it called for a celebration – I ran to a closet, I opened a box

that we kept Christmas ornaments in! – I took them out, glass bells, glass birds, tinsel, icicles, stars. . . . And I hung the little tree with them, I decorated the fig tree with glass bells and glass birds, and silver icicles and stars, because it won the battle and it would bear! [*Rises ecstatic.*] Unpack the box! Unpack the box with the Christmas ornaments in it, put them on me, glass bells and glass birds and stars and tinsel and snow! [*In a sort of delirium she thrusts a conical gilt paper hat on her head and runs to the foot of the stairs with the paper horn. She blows the horn over and over, grotesquely mounting the stairs, as* VAL *tries to stop her. She breaks away from him and runs up to the landing, blowing the paper horn and crying out*] I've won, I've won, Mr Death, I'm going to bear! [*Then suddenly she falters, catches her breath in a shocked gasp and awkwardly retreats to the stairs. Then turns screaming and runs back down them, her cries dying out as she arrives at the floor level. She retreats haltingly as a blind person, a hand stretched out to* VAL, *as slow, clumping footsteps and hoarse breathing are heard on the stairs. She moans:*] – Oh, God! oh – God! . . .

[JABE *appears on the landing, by the artificial palm tree in its dully lustrous green jardinière, a stained purple robe hangs loosely about his wasted yellowed frame. He is death's self, and malignancy, as he peers, crouching, down into the store's dimness to discover his quarry.*]

JABE: Buzzards! Buzzards! [*Clutching the trunk of the false palm tree, he raises the other hand holding a revolver and fires down into the store.* LADY *screams and rushes to cover Val's motionless figure with hers.* JABE *scrambles down a few steps and fires again and the bullet strikes her, expelling her breath in a great 'Hah!' He fires again; the great 'Hah!' is repeated. She turns to face him, still covering Val with her body, her face with all the passions and secrets of life and death in it now, her fierce eyes blazing, knowing, defying, and accepting. But the revolver is empty; it clicks impotently and* JABE *hurls it toward them; he descends and passes them shouting out hoarsely:*] *I'll have you burned! I burned her father and I'll have you burned!* [*He opens the door and rushes out on to the road, shouting hoarsely*] The clerk is robbing the store, he shot my wife, the clerk is robbing the store, he killed my wife!

VAL: – Did it – ?

LADY: – Yes! – it did. . . .

[*A curious, almost formal, dignity appears in them both. She turns to him with the sort of smile that people offer in apology for an awkward speech, and he looks back at her gravely, raising one hand as if to stay her. But she shakes her head slightly and points to the ghostly radiance of her make-believe orchard and she begins to move a little unsteadily toward it. Music.* LADY *enters the confectionery and looks about it as people look for the last time at a loved place they are deserting.*]

The show is over. The monkey is dead. . . .

[*Music rises to cover whatever sound Death makes in the confectionery. It halts abruptly. Figures appear through the great front window of the store, pocket-lamps stare through the glass, and someone begins to force the front door open.* VAL *cries out.*]

VAL: Which way!

[*He turns and runs through the dim radiance of the confectionery, out of our sight. Something slams. Something cracks open. Men are in the store and the dark is full of hoarse, shouting voices.*]

VOICES OF MEN [*shouting*]: – Keep to the walls. He's armed!
– Upstairs, Dog!
– Jack, the confectionery!

[*Wild cry back of store.*]

Got him. GOT HIM!
– They got him!

345

- Rope, git rope!
- Git rope from th' hardware section!
- I got something better than rope!
- What've you got?
- What's that, what's he got?
- A BLOWTORCH!
- Christ. . . .

[A momentary hush.]

- Come on, what in hell are we waiting for?
- Hold on a minute, I wanta see if it works!
- Wait, Wait!
- Look here!

[A jet of blue flame stabs the dark. It flickers on CAROL's *figure in the confectionery. The men cry out together in hoarse passion crouching towards the fierce blue jet of fire, their faces lit by it like the faces of demons.]*

- Christ!
- It works!

[They rush out. Confused shouting behind. Motors start. Fade quickly. There is almost silence, a dog bays in the distance. Then – the CONJURE MAN *appears with a bundle of garments which he examines, dropping them all except the snakeskin jacket, which he holds up with a toothless mumble of excitement.]*

CAROL *[quietly, gently]*: What have you got there, Uncle? Come here and let me see.

[He crosses to her.]

Oh yes, his snakeskin jacket. I'll give you a gold ring for it.

[She slowly twists ring off her finger. Somewhere there is a cry of anguish. She listens attentively till it fades out, then nods with understanding.]

– Wild things leave skins behind them, they leave clean skins and teeth and white bones behind them, and these are tokens passed from one to another, so that the fugitive kind can always follow their kind. . . .

[*The cry is repeated more terribly than before. It expires again. She draws the jacket about her as if she were cold, nods to the old* NEGRO, *handing him the ring. Then she crosses towards the door, pausing halfway as* SHERIFF TALBOTT *enters with his pocket-lamp.*]

SHERIFF: Don't no one move, don't move!

[*She crosses directly past him as if she no longer saw him, and out the door. He shouts furiously.*]

Stay here!

[*Her laughter rings outside. He follows the girl, shouting.*]

Stop! Stop!

[*Silence. The* NEGRO *looks up with a secret smile as the curtain falls slowly.*]

FOR THE BEST IN PAPERBACKS, LOOK FOR THE

In every corner of the world, on every subject under the sun, Penguin represents quality and variety – the very best in publishing today.

For complete information about books available from Penguin – including Puffins, Penguin Classics and Arkana – and how to order them, write to us at the appropriate address below. Please note that for copyright reasons the selection of books varies from country to country.

In the United Kingdom: Please write to *Dept E.P., Penguin Books Ltd, Harmondsworth, Middlesex, UB7 0DA.*

If you have any difficulty in obtaining a title, please send your order with the correct money, plus ten per cent for postage and packaging, to *PO Box No 11, West Drayton, Middlesex*

In the United States: Please write to *Dept BA, Penguin, 299 Murray Hill Parkway, East Rutherford, New Jersey 07073*

In Canada: Please write to *Penguin Books Canada Ltd, 2801 John Street, Markham, Ontario L3R 1B4*

In Australia: Please write to the *Marketing Department, Penguin Books Australia Ltd, P.O. Box 257, Ringwood, Victoria 3134*

In New Zealand: Please write to the *Marketing Department, Penguin Books (NZ) Ltd, Private Bag, Takapuna, Auckland 9*

In India: Please write to *Penguin Overseas Ltd, 706 Eros Apartments, 56 Nehru Place, New Delhi, 110019*

In the Netherlands: Please write to *Penguin Books Netherlands B.V., Postbus 195, NL–1380AD Weesp*

In West Germany: Please write to *Penguin Books Ltd, Friedrichstrasse 10–12, D–6000 Frankfurt/Main 1*

In Spain: Please write to *Alhambra Longman S.A., Fernandez de la Hoz 9, E–28010 Madrid*

In Italy: Please write to *Penguin Italia s.r.l., Via Como 4, I-20096 Pioltello (Milano)*

In France: Please write to *Penguin Books Ltd, 39 Rue de Montmorency, F-75003 Paris*

In Japan: Please write to *Longman Penguin Japan Co Ltd, Yamaguchi Building, 2–12–9 Kanda Jimbocho, Chiyoda-Ku, Tokyo 101*

CLASSICS OF THE TWENTIETH CENTURY

The Outsider   Albert Camus

Meursault leads an apparently unremarkable bachelor life in Algiers, until his involvement in a violent incident calls into question the fundamental values of society. 'The protagonist of *The Outsider* is undoubtedly the best achieved of all the central figures of the existential novel' – *Listener*

Another Country   James Baldwin

'Let our novelists read Mr Baldwin and tremble. There is a whirlwind loose in the land' – *Sunday Times*. *Another Country* draws us deep into New York's Bohemian underworld of writers and artists as they betray, love and test each other – men and women, men and men, black and white – to the limit

I'm Dying Laughing   Christina Stead

A dazzling novel set in the 1930s and 1940s when fashionable Hollywood Marxism was under threat from the savage repression of McCarthyism. 'The Cassandra of the modern novel in English' – Angela Carter

Christ Stopped at Eboli   Carlo Levi

Exiled to a barren corner of southern Italy for his opposition to Mussolini, Carlo Levi entered a world cut off from history, hedged in by custom and sorrow, without comfort or solace, where, eternally patient, the peasants lived in an age-old stillness, and in the presence of death – for Christ did stop at Eboli.

The Expelled and Other Novellas   Samuel Beckett

Rich in verbal and situational humour, these four stories offer the reader a fascinating insight into Beckett's preoccupation with the helpless individual consciousness.

Chance Acquaintances and Julie de Carneilhan   Colette

Two contrasting works in one volume. Colette's last full-length novel, *Julie de Carneilhan* was 'as close a reckoning with the elements of her second marriage as she ever allowed herself'. In *Chance Acquaintances*, Colette visits a health resort, accompanied only by her cat.

Sweet Bird of Youth
A Streetcar Named Desire
The Glass Menagerie

'If there is any truth in the Aristotelian idea that violence is purged by its poetic representation on a stage, then it may be that my cycle of violent plays have had a moral justification after all' – Tennessee Williams

Sweet Bird of Youth: His first phenomenal Broadway success, set on the Gulf Coast.

A Streetcar Named Desire: In New Orleans a woman's fantasies of primness and respectability are violently stripped away and exposed.

The Glass Menagerie: Falling outside William's cycle of violent plays, this drama is set in a St Louis slum, where a crippled girl lives with her family, her collection of glass animals and her memories.

also published:

Baby Doll and Other Plays

Baby Doll
Something Unspoken
Suddenly Last Summer

Cat on a Hot Tin Roof and Other Plays

Cat on a Hot Tin Roof
The Milk Train Doesn't Stop Here Anymore
The Night of the Iguana

Period of Adjustment and Other Plays

Period of Adjustment
Summer and Smoke
Small Craft Warnings